THEY CALLED HIM A RADICAL

01 02 03 04 05 28 27 26 25 24

Caitlin Press Inc.
3375 Ponderosa Way
Qualicum Beach, BC V9K 2J8
www.caitlinpress.com

Text and cover design by Vici Johnstone
Edited by Anne DeGrace
All photos from the family collection unless otherwise noted.

Printed in Canada

Caitlin Press Inc. acknowledges financial support from the Government of Canada and the Canada Council for the Arts, and the Province of British Columbia through the British Columbia Arts Council and the Book Publisher's Tax Credit.

Library and Archives Canada Cataloguing in Publication

They called him a radical : the memoirs of Pete Maloff and the making of a Doukhobor pacifist / by Pete Maloff ; with Vera Maloff.
Maloff, Pete, 1900–1971, author. | Maloff, Vera, 1951– author.
Canadiana 20230522602 | ISBN 9781773861340 (softcover)
LCSH: LCSH: Maloff, Pete, 1900-1971. | LCSH: Pacifists—Saskatchewan—Biography. | LCSH: Pacifists—British Columbia—Biography. | LCSH: Dukhobors—Saskatchewan—Biography. | LCSH: Dukhobors—British Columbia—Biography. | LCSH: Saskatchewan—Biography. | LCSH: British Columbia—Biography. | LCGFT: Autobiographies. LCC JZ5540.2.M35 A3 2024 | DDC 327.1/72092—dc23

THEY CALLED HIM A RADICAL

The Memoirs of Pete Maloff and the Making of a Doukhobor Pacifist

BY PETE MALOFF

with Vera Maloff

Caitlin Press, 2024

To all spiritual heroes, known and unknown, champions, heralders and martyrs, who perished on crosses, scaffolds, stakes and in prisons; the participants in the past and present great historical procession-struggle against folly, hypocrisy and the universal evil: militarism; and to all future pulsing hearts of world conscience, the vanguard and builders of universal brotherhood of all human beings in the world—I dedicate my work.

—P.N. Maloff, March 20, 1948
from Pete Maloff, *Doukhobors: Their History, Life and Struggle*

CONTENTS

ACKNOWLEDGEMENTS

To bring a manuscript such as this into a book form took the support of many whose hearts and minds were touched by Pete N. Maloff's life and work.

Pete N. Maloff wrote his comprehensive, over 600-page book, *Doukhobors: Their History, Life and Struggle,* on the fiftieth anniversary of Doukhobor migration to Canada. With the assistance of William N. Koochin as editor, he published it in Russian in 1948. Friends across the globe, Nikolai Aleksandrovich Rubakin of Lausanne, Switzerland, Olga Kaydanova Bervy of Kingston, Ontario, Andrei Karpovich Dubovoy of the Shtundist community of North Dakota and many others encouraged him to translate it into English and with their support he completed the initial translation in 1956. Not having the funds to publish the English version, it lay on the shelves of his library for many years. However, the manuscript had another life.

Pete N. Maloff's son, Peter P. Maloff, had typed and retyped the manuscript several times and shared a copy with anthropology professor Dr. Mark Mealing in 1973. Dr. Mealing recognized the unique and valuable first-hand information on Doukhobors and their historical experience and made it available to the Selkirk College library.

In the 2010s, I approached Peter Perepolkin to digitize the work and my partner Steve Denisoff, due to his devotion to Doukhobor heritage, was interested in helping. They visited and over many evenings copied the 607 pages. Because the fading typing was not transcribable into a word processor, a team retyped the pages. Thank you to Sasha Terry, Alena Charlston, Katya Maloff, Elaine Makortoff, Neva Popenoe, Sharon Hoodicoff and Natasha Jmieff for the hours that they spent deciphering and entering the manuscript into Word. Nell Plotnikoff assisted with the initial editing.

I brought portions of Pete N. Maloff's manuscript to my amazing writing group, Brian Deon, Ross Klatte and Dwayne Minton, who made suggestions on how I could contribute to the book. Editors Anne DeGrace and Sarah Corsie supported the work throughout, and my partner, Steve Denisoff, listened to and gave suggestions for several editions of my commentary.

D.E. (Jim) Popoff provided some invaluable historical references and context, and John Kalmakov digitized the photos in the book. Russian teachers

Wendy Voykin and Katya Maloff corrected the complex Russian, Doukhobor and Molokan names, and my patient and accommodating copy editor, Anne Champagne, made the book look grammatically pleasing.

Thank you to Vici Johnstone of Caitlin Press for publishing this memoir, Part II of Pete N. Maloff's history book. Thank you to the Columbia Kootenay Cultural Alliance and the Columbia Basin Trust for providing financial assistance.

I owe a depth of gratitude to all, and particularly to my grandfather Pete N. Maloff whose memoir I have been honoured to bring to completion.

FOREWORD

by Vera Maloff

I am the granddaughter of Pete Maloff. Living next to and growing up with my grandfather, I became imbued with his passion for the Doukhobor movement. It is my great privilege to implement the English translation of this memoir as he wished. I help bring this book into fruition out of love and respect for my grandfather and the Doukhobors of the past centuries. May their lives be an example to us of the twenty-first century who still struggle with oppression, killing of fellow human beings and desecration of our planet Earth.

Grandfather Pete Maloff was born in 1900 to Doukhobor parents newly immigrated from Russia. He spent his childhood in Christian Community of Universal Brotherhood communal villages in Saskatchewan. Desiring education for his sons, his father made the difficult decision to become an Independent farmer; however, Pete's grandmother, who stayed in the community, instilled in him an ardent belief in the Doukhobor faith and way of life. Pete went to school first in a one-room schoolhouse in Saskatchewan and then in Oregon where his family moved to join the Doukhobor Colony of Freedom in 1913. After graduation, Pete apprenticed at a Russian journal in San Francisco. The editor of the magazine inspired Pete Maloff to become a writer and a Doukhobor historian.

Pete Maloff traces the roots of Doukhobor beliefs to early Christians who clung to their principles despite being thrown into the fiery furnace. Their belief that the spark of God lives in all creation including humanity, thus they will not kill, that conscience is their guide rather than the hierarchy of the Orthodox Church and civil authority, subjected them to severe retaliation, imprisonment and exile to remote corners of Russia. Periods of prosperity and of punishment were tied to retribution, rarely clemency, of various tsars.

In 1804, Doukhobors appealed to Tsar Alexander I (reign 1801–1825) to free them from this barbarous treatment and to give them land where they could practise their Christian religion in peace. In a display of tolerance unusual at the time, the tsar liberated the Doukhobors and bequeathed land to them in the Milky Waters area of Tavria,[1] to protect the Doukhobors from further needless

---

1   Now a disputed area between Ukraine and Russia.

and vain meddling with their religion and their personal beliefs. Doukhobors organized nine communal colonies along the Milky Waters River and about 4,000 people settled there by 1812. The villages prospered.

Under the next tsar's reign (Nicholas I, 1825–1855), Doukhobors were again forced into military conscription and admonished to convert to the Orthodox Church. Those who refused were banished and, in 1841, 4,500 Doukhobors were exiled to the remote Caucasus Mountains in Georgia, a volatile area bordering Turkey with an inhospitable climate. Doukhobors adapted their farming practice and thrived, expanding their herds of livestock on the high grassy plateaus and developing nine colonies throughout this area.

When the Russian-Turkish war broke out in 1877, the Grand Duke Vladimir Alexandrovich Romanov insisted that Doukhobors assist the war effort. Even though it was against their principles, Lukeria Vasilievna Kalmikova, the Doukhobor leader at the time, agreed that Doukhobor men would help transport food and provisions to the front and remove wounded soldiers. Following this, in 1886, Doukhobors were enlisted in compulsory military training.

Under the new Doukhobor leader Peter Vasilievich Verigin,[2] in 1895 those who had been in military battalions laid down their guns and, as a result, were arrested, cruelly disciplined and marched in chains to Siberian gulags. The Doukhobor villagers continued in their declaration of pacifism. They gathered their weapons and burned them in huge bonfires in three areas of Georgia. These flames of peace spread throughout Russia and Europe. Tsar Nicholas II responded by giving orders to punish the Doukhobors, drive them from their homes and disperse them amongst indigenous villages where they had no means of subsistence. Many perished.

On hearing of their plight, Russian author Lev (Leo) Tolstoy sent out a plea to his followers to help the beleaguered Doukhobors. Quaker groups in England and the United States responded and, together with the author, contributed money for Doukhobors to emigrate as this seemed to be the only way they could survive. Canada at the time was searching for settlers to cultivate the prairies and with their reputation as excellent farmers, Doukhobors were looked on as desirable immigrants.

Following the country's handling of Quaker and Mennonite pacifists,

---

2   After the passing of Lukeria Vasilievna Kalmikova in December 1886, Peter Vasilievich Verigin became the leader of the Large Party of Doukhobors. He was immediately exiled to the province of Archangel, then Obdorsk, Siberia. He guided Doukhobors through secret couriers who carried letters to his followers. The Large Party of Doukhobors eventually immigrated to Canada.

Canada gave the Doukhobors conscientious objector status and, in 1898, over 7,000 Doukhobors boarded four ships, at Batum on the Black Sea, bound for Canada. This was one of the largest immigrations to Canada at the time. They were settled under the Homestead Act in several regions of what is now Saskatchewan. They formed the Christian Community of Universal Brotherhood (CCUB) and, working communally, were able to fairly quickly develop fifty-seven villages.

I knew my tall, strong, charismatic grandfather in his fifties and sixties, after his incarcerations, his lengthy illness due to ill-treatment in jails, and his forced withdrawal from public life. My family lived next door, and my grandparents' home was our home. Until my grandfather's passing in 1971, I worked beside him in the gardens, and sold produce at local markets where he would be surrounded by people wanting to talk to him. I heard fervent conversations with his friends, Grandfather often punctuating his words with gesturing hands. I knew my grandfather as a kind, caring man interested in his family and his correspondents throughout the world. He was also an avid reader. His passion ignited my spirit. His personal experiences and literary knowledge, and his awareness of the many different aspects of life, opened my eyes to the diversity of people and cultures and fed my eagerness to learn.

Pete Maloff wrote this memoir about the experiences that shaped his character and made him a pacifist. The years from his birth in 1900 to 1927 take us from his family's involvement in the Doukhobor pioneer life in Saskatchewan to a co-operative freedom village in Oregon. In his youth, he apprenticed with a renowned Russian/Ukrainian journalist, Anton Sherbak, and lived with a Russian Molokan family in San Francisco. Later, in a kind of rebellion, he joined some Russian adventurers to travel as a hobo, riding the rails in California. In the 1910s and 1920s he met many in the pacifist movement in California. A Protestant missionary, Mr. Greenfield, who had written the banned book *Ethics of Killing*, gifted him one of the two books that survived. The anti-war activist and writer Fanny Bixby Spencer welcomed him. He befriended those in the early beatnik movement and corresponded with pacifists Scott Nearing and Ammon Hennacy. His memoir chronicles these lives, from the wealthy and well-known to folk who were experimenting with alternative lifestyles.

Through my grandfather's memoir, I have been able to discover the experiences that made him the complex, fascinating character he was. My research into the people he knew and corresponded with, and whose books were left on his bookshelves, led me on a search for information about their lives. Some were the radicals of the early twentieth century and I have been astounded to read of the similarities of their beliefs to those of Pete Maloff.

This book will add personal experience and understanding to the history of migration and the pacifist movement in western Canada and the United States. Anthropologist and folklorist Dr. Mark Mealing of Selkirk College said of this memoir: "A unique, valuable addition to Canadian Immigrant literature, especially strong for research in Canadian and Sectarian History. One must remember the great purpose to which Pete Maloff devoted his time and his labours—indeed his whole life: the spread of pacifism, of fuller understanding of Doukhobor ideas, and the betterment of the human spirit. May the preservation of this manuscript bring his goals a little closer."[3]

Pete Maloff was a Doukhobor pacifist who, despite severe repercussions to him and the family, stood up for his beliefs in the sanctity of human life during World War I and World War II.

---

3   Rev. F.M. Mealing, Ph.D., Prefatory Notes (Castlegar, BC: Selkirk College, 1973, 1974).

Chapter 1

Childhood

I was born in the province of Saskatchewan[4] a year after the Doukhobors immigrated to Canada; that is in the year 1900. My childhood was spent under the influence of that period when the valiant achievements of Doukhobors—the burning of their firearms and their transition into a higher moral standard of life—were still fresh in the memory of many who participated in this amazing enterprise.

I do not know and do not remember what happened in the first few years. My parents moved north from Buchanan to Preeceville, and then, two or three years later, returned and settled in the new settlement then called Khristianovka.

The village of Khristianovka was about four miles from Buchanan, Saskatchewan. It was situated on a plain, and not far off a tree-shrouded river shouted joyfully, almost splashing against some of the outlying houses. On all sides stretched groves of poplars, with various northern conifers amongst them.

We lived communally, two families to a house. The rest was built up later. The field work was done communally. The community house for prayer and meetings was distinguished from the other buildings and we had a communal granary, a bakery, barn and sheep shed. In our village, we had men of initiative with ideas on how to better community life; prominent amongst them was Anton Savelievich Popoff. He took upon himself the responsibility of planting trees around the homes and through his efforts and insistence, rows of trees were planted on each side of the avenue.

Sundays were spent happily; there were choirs whose singing blended and mingled with the twilight and faded into the distant reaches of the night. On Sundays, many of the villagers gathered in the boulevard of trees. Here were the older people, some in their latter years; greybeards who had seen much of life. In our village there were several who distinctly remembered the Molochna Vodi (Milky Waters) and the villages of Tavria.[5] Especially prominent were

---

4   Prior to 1905 this area was part of the Northwest Territories. In 1905 it became a province, Saskatchewan.

5   Wikipedia: Tavria is primarily a geographic toponym for a subregion of Southern Ukraine that encompasses steppe territories between Dnieper and Molochna rivers and Crimean peninsula.

Vakulyushka Strelieff and Alyosha Fedosoff. They came from Tavria when they were between ten and twelve years old. Alyosha was perhaps the older.

Often the youths and even the adults would gather round saying, "Vakulyushka, tell us about Tavria."

Grandfather Vakul was a fascinating storyteller. He would stroke his long grey beard and begin: "So, you want to know something about Tavria. Life was not easy there either. In the Caucasus life was better." Then he would add, "Yes, children, we started out from Tavria by caravan early in spring, and long did we ride; some by oxen, some by horse, and some marched along on foot. How difficult was the migration to the Caucasus? At first it wasn't too bad, but when we came to the Kazbek mountains,[6] how different! There we met with cold, wind, snow. There was no grass and hay had to be hauled from a distance. But with the help of God, we finally gained our destination."

Here someone interrupted, "But did you see the long bridge?"

"What do you mean, did we see it? How else would you be able to cross the mighty Don? What do you take us for, birds? Yes, the bridge was there, boys, I tell you it was there! In all my life, I never saw anything like it. You walk and walk and the end is not in sight and then you take a glance at the river, so wide and so deep that your heart fails within you. How wealthy Russia is! What breadth, what spaciousness, what rivers and forests, but there is no place for her children to live in her; just look where she drives us."

We children were attracted to him by these tales and crowded closer around him. Order was kept by Zakhar Nazaroff. He was a cripple, injured by lightning while still a child. His head seemed loose on his shoulders and wobbled in all directions. He had nowhere to go and he usually spent his time with the old men of whom he was a fiery defender from any attack made upon them. And why shouldn't he defend them, when they held him by the hand and let no harm come to him? Some boys, as you know, like to pester old men and just for the sake of a little fun would ask them endless questions.

Then Zakhar would jump up and his wobbly head and body would writhe grotesquely. "Aha, me give you goot; God too," pointing his hand skywards. He was half mute.

In defence of such outbreaks old Vakul would twitch his whiskers, stroke his long grey beard and resume his story.

"You boys, of course, know nothing about it, and maybe you think that the Emperor Alexander I himself used to visit the Doukhobors in Tavria and

---

6   Kazbek Mountain is on the border of Russia and Georgia. An extinct volcano, it is one of the highest peaks in the Caucasus Mountains.

talk with Kapustin, and that if it hadn't been for his mercy that there would be only bones left of us. Well, I say: Thanks to our guides. They were pretty wise; they knew how to guard their flock, and that's why they were so friendly with kings and princes. Do you think there was any other reason? No. Why do you think Lushechka sent messengers to Petersburg? She knew even before that there would be a war with Turkey, and because of these messengers, Michael, the king's nephew, came to visit her in her home."

All this time, Alyosha would remain silent. From time to time he would tap his cane and gently cough, as though well content with his companion's story. Alyosha had a thin, long nose and reddish hair. His moustache dropped downward like a seal's and bristled so that looking at him, one would imagine that at any moment he might snort.

Sometimes the boys would say: "How about you, Alyosha. Why don't you tell us anything about Tavria?"

"And what do you want to know?" he would ask fiercely.

"Well, how did our ancestors live?"

For a long time, he would make no reply. You could see the feeling of longing in his eyes, and then he would speak.

"How did they live? In suffering and persecution. And now I see very little faith left: they are chasing after farms, selling their souls to the devil. Why do they break up and break away and break apart? That's no good." And spitting profusely, he would add: "What can we do about it? This looks like our fate. Our beloved Lushechka once told us, 'The Doukhobors will ride away on a grey horse to the River Swan and there will be few left. They will scatter in every direction; some will go to the cities to run after the glitter of wealth; and some will be lost for no reason at all. Very few Doukhobors will be left. Very few, indeed.'"

And thinking a little, as though he had just remembered something, Alyosha continued:

"Lushechka said that the Doukhobors would ride away on a grey stallion far across the sea, would live there their appointed time, and then would return on a white duck. This is plain to us now. You see, it took four or five ships to bring the Doukhobors here, but from here there will only be one."

To the villages also came various Doukhobor eccentrics who by their stupid escapades threw everybody off balance. Mitya Swetlikoff, tall and stately, more than once came to our village.

He would pass through the village several times with his coat turned inside out, and repeat these words again and again: "Cows shouldn't be milked, calves shouldn't be starved, eggs shouldn't be eaten, chickens shouldn't be killed, sheep shouldn't be raised, and their wool shouldn't be clipped," and so on and on.

Children crowded after him, some repeating his words, others laughing and teasing him.

One day he went through the village and no one would give him a place to sleep. Our neighbour, that is, the mother of the family with whom we shared the house, Grandmother Kolesnikoff, brought him to her place to sleep. We had a common kitchen and we could see what went on in their quarters. They almost always kept their door open, so that they could make use of the warmth, and not have to keep their own stove going.

Whenever I would stand a long time staring into their room the old man, Vanya, would call out: "Peter, will you have some sugar?" and he would give me a piece so that I would go away.

This time Markhunya led Mitya into the room and asked her husband: "Vanya, I brought Mitya here to spend the night. How about you, have you anything against this?"

"No, no, you shouldn't have done that. He with his foolish ravings will cause trouble amongst the people. Everybody will say that Vanya Kolesnikoff is supporting agitators."

"Well, what shall we do? He is walking around and no one will give him a place to spend the night. And in our psalms it says: Welcome the traveller, feed the hungry."

"What kind of traveller is he? A babbler! He should stay at home. What good is he doing going around hollering, 'Cows shouldn't be milked, calves shouldn't be starved'? If he likes them so much, let him to the barn and sleep with them."

"Very well, let him sleep in the barn. But if I had my way, you would lie down with him and I would sleep on the bench."

"No, no! Heaven forbid! I do not even want him to stay with us."

Markhunya submitted to her husband. Turning to her guest she said to him, "Mitya, dear, please go into the barn. You see the kind of Christians we are. We have no room for a stranger to sleep overnight."

Next morning, alarm! The cows and calves were not there, the sheep fled, and the chickens were out of their coops. Mitya Swetlikoff had let out all the animals.

Vanya scolded his wife Markhunya: "And you wanted to leave him here for the night. I will not let him into this yard again, the scoundrel!"

"You would not let him in? How could you say that?" cried Markhunya. "But how do you know whom you would be turning away? The son of God, descendant of the King of Israel. In the embodiment of Mitya Swetlikoff. God's truth walks throughout the land and if we do not accept it, we do not accept God himself."

"Silence, you fool. Some God you found!"

"Oh, Vanya, Vanya, you do not yet know. Truth is not kind; it is always prickly, and that is why nobody likes it. And you think that our singers will show it to us? No, it will not come from them. They only like to show off and boast about their voices, and to ogle at the women's eyes and breasts, but no good has come from them yet."

One Sunday, a rumour spread that Anatole Konshin from Russia was coming to our village. Our people didn't know exactly who he was. They welcomed all such visitors as messengers from Grandfather Tolstoy. And soon, Konshin appeared. A large crowd gathered and he began, saying that he came from faraway Russia just to visit us, and brought with him warmest greetings to the Doukhobors from all their Russian friends. "Though you left them, there are many who think of you and are lonesome without you."

These cordial words moved our hearts and many wept. Grandfather Vakul couldn't keep quiet; he kept asking Konshin: "How are they all there? Were you at the Caucasus? And how are the Doukhobors who were left behind? Did they let those who were exiled to Siberia return to their homes?" Thinking a little, he added, "Did you perhaps hear anything definite, whether or not Tsar Nicholas is yet begging the Doukhobors to return to Russia? Oh, my brother, to tell you the truth, we grieved the first few years. Here we are strangers, we lived our whole life there, and we are longing to go back—home."

"Couldn't you get used to it?"

"How can you get used to it? Their tongue is strange, just as if it were wooden, you couldn't understand a word. And even these English people themselves, they're so proud and so selfish. Not long ago one of them, a Mr. Schmitt, who lives near a lake and is considered in our locality to be quite rich, came to pay us a visit. Just imagine; we have been living here for five or six years and he did not come here once! A week ago, he bought himself a machine that the boys call an automobile, and he came down here on it. We were all on the boulevard, the whole village, and he didn't even get out and take off his cap. He just sat there as if he were saying: 'Look how rich I am; I came here on a car!'"

At the end of the discussion, our people sang psalms and spiritual songs, and so the day passed in solemn celebration. I remember that Konshin even sang a solo, and our people praised him.

In 1905 the Doukhobors from Siberia, whom we called Yakuts because they were exiled in the Yakutsk region, arrived from banishment. My family were by that time living in a different house, and Vasya and Vasyunya Chutskoff and their children moved in with us. Vasyunya Chutskoff was the daughter of Markhunya and Vanya Kolesnikoff. They lived with us all winter and spring; it was crowded but we bore it. Life was far from quiet, but in a way very happy. We gathered to sing, to talk and to discuss. At that time the Japanese War was at its height and the Yakutsk people brought with them a new song: "The battle of Port Arthur brought us horror, shame and pain. For we say without question that the bloodshed was in vain." This song was sung by everybody and it spun a sort of spiritual thread among us.

On the other hand, many already had left the villages to individual farms and this was tempting others also, among them my parents. They too were preparing to acquire a farm. From time to time the four families that had left used to gather at our house. Others also attended. I remember once, quite a sizable group gathered; among those present was Anton Savelievich Popoff and his educated daughters. My brother had also gone to school for several years, and here Anton Savelievich, apparently wanting to show how useful a school education was, took up a certain journal and said:

"See, here is the battleship Varyaha. The Japanese sunk it." He turned over several pages and said: "And see here—Vasily Vasilyevich Vereshchagin,[7] the artist, who painted the war; he also perished."

He turned to my brother and said: "Well, Nikolka, read to them what is written here."

Nikolai took the journal; he did not yet know how to translate into the Russian language very well. Anton Savelievich took it from him and gave it to his daughter Vasyunya, and asked her to translate it. She did this so clearly and distinctly that it seemed as if she was reading Russian.

Many were astonished: "My God! So that's an English school for you!"

Grandfather Grisha Sherstobitoff was sitting on the bed near me. He said: "And to think of it; we lived our whole life and yet like stupid fools we can't read a word and don't know a thing about anything! Now look for yourself, if we need schools or not! There's no question about it! Vasyunya went through it as easily and as beautifully as a nightingale through her song. What joy it brings to the heart just to hear her, and how pleasant to look upon her—a mere child and yet being able to do that!"

Several other voices took it up. "Yes, Vasyunya, you read it beautifully."

Still another episode occurred in our home at that time. There came from

---

7   Wikipedia: Vasily Vasilyevich Vereshchagin was one of the most famous Russian war artists and one of the first Russian artists to be widely recognized abroad. He visited the Doukhobors in the Caucasus and painted their portraits.

Prince Albert several Sons of Freedom with Ivan Perepolkin at the head. They lived with us for three days. One evening some people from the village gathered at our house, and there were the Sons of Freedom also. I even remembered that they stripped naked and talked earnestly with my family. It almost ended in a fist fight. What they were talking about and quarrelling, I could not clearly understand. This gathering was incomprehensible to me, but it left a sharp impression.

Many years later, I met this Ivan Perepolkin when he was an old man. He told me in detail what had taken place that might, and my parents confirmed his account. His explanation appears in the chapter on "The Sons of Freedom" [in *Doukhobors: Their History, Life and Struggle*].

Thus, I spent my earliest years in the rural customs brought over from far-away Russia. Communally we ploughed, mowed hay, made bricks and prepared food. Everywhere there was the turbulent large-scale productivity of community effort. Music, that is, choir singing, spread out to the very horizon wherever people lived. Civilization was far away and we grew up and developed in these primitive, idyllic surroundings.

On Chapter 1

Childhood in a Doukhobor Communal Village

[Vera] I first began to read my grandfather's book in the original Russian with my mother, Elizabeth. On winter nights we sat by her crackling wood stove and shared memories evoked by his writing. I had not at the time visited his birthplace, Buchanan, but I was able to picture the surrounding nature and the village, and the discussions and arguments of his neighbours rang in my ears.

In 2017, my partner Steve and I participated in a choir that travelled to Verigin, Saskatchewan, to commemorate the hundredth anniversary of the Doukhobor prayer home. Buchanan was a forty-five-minute drive away and we set out to find where Pete Maloff went to school, where the communal village of Khristianovka was, and where his family farmed.

The village of Buchanan today has attractive tree-lined streets laid out in a block system. The 2021 census records show that 237 people live in 121 private dwellings but the village has three churches—Ukrainian Orthodox, Lutheran and Catholic—a municipal office, a curling rink and a community centre, services one would expect in a larger centre and definitely not in 1907 when Pete and his brother Nikolai went to school there. On first glance there didn't appear to be a Doukhobor presence; however, investigating the history of Buchanan, I learned that in 1915 Doukhobors started the Independent Doukhobor Elevator Company, creating an elevator and milling business that continued to be Buchanan's largest industry for thirty years. Strolling through the village cemetery we found six different Doukhobor surnames and learned of private Doukhobor cemeteries in the area.

A rolling prairie landscape surrounded the town, and I felt the freedom of the wind, the limitless sky and the smallness of human life in the vast space. It was so different from the mountains and the narrow river valley in Thrums, British Columbia, where Pete Maloff spent the last forty years of his life and where I grew up. We could not locate Khristianovka or Maloff's farm; these had melded into the landscape of the prairie. But with Grandfather's descriptions, my imagination illuminated the past.

In this memoir Pete Maloff wrote about Khristianovka through the eyes of a young boy immersed in the beauty and activities of the village and the land. In his history book he described more fully the harshness of life for the early settlers. Despite the financial assistance of Leo Tolstoy and the Tolstoyans, the Quaker and Canadian societies, Doukhobors at the time were forced to make unbelievable efforts to cope with austerity. They had no animals, tools or implements, and scarce provisions.

Many men left to work on the railroad to earn cash. The elderly men, women and children left in the villages set about as best they could to build homes and prepare the earth for gardens. Lacking livestock, they harnessed themselves to ploughs. Looking at the photos of the more than a dozen women hitched in tandem with a partner, straining to turn the prairie sod, I think about the strength and determination they needed to survive.

Great-grandmother Malanya shared many stories of the time with her granddaughter, Elizabeth. She said that when Pete was born in 1900, his mother gave birth to him in the barn, as their home was crowded. This was of great significance to Elizabeth, who adored her father; after all, wasn't Christ born in a barn? Before the gardens were thriving, food was in short supply and people were hungry. As a toddler, there were times that Pete wouldn't stop crying. The villagers had planted all the potatoes in the field, but his grandmother Malanya carefully dug around the growing potato plants and collected enough potato cuttings to feed him.

Recently a Doukhobor dugout house was excavated in the Blaine Lake Valley where there were several villages. In the first years of settlement when houses were not yet built, up to three hundred people lived in *zemlankee*, underground homes dug into the hillsides. Several families cooked and ate in a space of under five hundred square feet.[8] This is about the size of a tiny home, but several families shared this space, through a harsh Saskatchewan winter! Surviving those crowded conditions took tenacity, fortitude and co-operation. I put myself in those families' shoes; would I be able to endure?

L.A. Sulerzhitsky in *To America with the Doukhobors* included letters from an accompanying nurse, E. Markova, one of which stated: "I went around all the villages under my care and wept—anemia, undernourishment, signs of scurvy, and so on. They eat bread, only bread, some kind of pickled grass and now the menu is varied by strawberries."[9] Even flour was often in short supply. Doukhobors are great foragers and the pickled grass could have been ferns, dandelions or *suziki* that my family continues to gather each spring and steam or pickle. We

---

8   www.doukhobordugouthouse.com/archeological-activity.

9   L.A. Sulerzhitsky, *To America with the Doukhobors* (Regina: Canadian Plains Research Center, 1982), p. 182.

consider these a delicacy that herald the coming of spring.

Significantly, Maloff does not mention the First Nations in the area. Sergej Tolstoy, in his book *Sergej Tolstoy and the Doukhobors: A Journey to Canada*, writes about his conversation with a local Indian Affairs official who confirmed that the Indigenous people were unhappy with colonists settling in their area. In other areas of Saskatchewan, family stories are still shared about the First Nations people introducing Doukhobors to edible medicinal plants and berries that helped them survive.

Pete Maloff wrote that this extreme need was only for a time. With their readiness to work communally and their knowledge of living on the land, they soon developed many of the necessities for a largely self-sufficient village. Maloff's description of a lively, thriving village is corroborated by Katherine Louise Smith, a Minneapolis journalist who visited the Doukhobors in 1906. In *The Craftsman* (1907), she wrote, "The Universal Community of Christian Brotherhood, now has 44 [Tarasoff, 57][10] villages with 100 to 200 people living in a village and represent a prosperous form of community life. When they came to America, they had nothing. Today they have land, houses, food laid up for emergencies, twenty threshing outfits, six flour mills and five lumber mills. They also have a blacksmith and carpenter shop in every village and a large brickyard. Five years ago, these people came to this country with strong hands and willing hearts. Today they are one of the most interesting communities…. Without priests they have a religion, with no police they have little crime, without lawyers they settle disputes, without financiers they have thriven as regards this world's goods."

Sadly, it was shortly after Smith published her article that the Doukhobor community lost much of their land. Koozma Tarasoff in *Plakun Trava: The Doukhobors* wrote that in June 1907 "75% of improved land reverted to the Crown"[11] as a result of their refusal to comply with the Homestead Act. One of the most onerous orders was that to retain their homesteads they were required to swear an oath of allegiance to defend the king.

---

10   Koozma J. Tarasoff, *Plakun Trava: The Doukhobors* (Grand Forks, BC: Mir Publication Society, 1982), p. 259.

11   Tarasoff, *Plakun Trava*, ibid., p. 260.

On Chapter 2

Babushka Malanya
Semyonovna Androsoff

[Vera] My mother Elizabeth often talked about her great-grandmother, Malanya Semyonovna Androsoff, about how after Malanya's first husband died in the flu epidemic, she was remarried to a man she despised. He was a well-off landowner in the Kars area (at that time under Russian rule, now in the country of Turkey) with a prosperous farm and livestock. They had two children, a half-brother and a half-sister to my great-grandfather Nikolai.

I am astounded by Malanya's courage and determination to escape from her husband and follow the Doukhobors to Canada. Doukhobor marriages at the time were arranged by the parents; however, if the couples were unhappy—though it was not often done—they could separate. During the time of the division of the Doukhobors, before their migration to Canada, many families were torn apart by religious differences.

Sulerzhitsky's account of Doukhobors leaving Russia strikes me with the finality of their move. The Russian government agreed to their departure on the condition that they were never to return. Their Russian passports, their homeland where for generations their ancestors lived and died, where their beloved leader Lushechka was buried, and where current leader Peter Vasilievich Verigin was in exile, were all left behind. Sulerzhitsky's description of Doukhobors saying farewell to Russia made me weep. "The Doukhobors sang a psalm; the mournful drawn-out sounds, full of hopeless sorrow, flowed out to the receding shore. Thousands of voices now joined in a single cry of despair, sorrow, injury. Not only people, but it seemed all nature was stilled, shaken by the soul-searing sobbing of a crowd of thousands mourning their parting from their motherland.... The psalm flowed farther and farther out on an irresistible current, a psalm asking for forgiveness of the land for its sons leaving it."[12]

It was December 23, 1898, when over 2,100 passengers and ten stowaways—as it was discovered later—boarded the three-masted ship, the *Lake Huron*, to take them to Canada. The *Lake Huron* and the second ship, the *Lake Superior*, had been cargo ships Doukhobor carpenters adapted, building two-tiered

---

12   Sulerzhitsky, *To America with the Doukhobors*, ibid., p. 52.

bunks in the hold. Recently, when we visited Halifax where these ships landed, I searched the Canadian Museum of Immigration at Pier 21 immigrant lists for Malanya's family. The *Lake Huron* was carrying those who had been exiled to unhealthy climates where they had no means of support. Many were ill with yellow fever and because of the lack of food, they developed scurvy, trachoma and other diseases.[13] This possibly included my great-grandfather Maloff's family who had been banished to Tatar villages.

The *Lake Superior* carried many Doukhobors from the Kars region where Malanya was from, but I was not able to find her name nor that of her children. They were the stowaways on one of those ships. My mother was told that Malanya hid the children in the coal bins. Darkness, dust and claustrophobia surrounded them.

Malanya needed all of her perseverance, fortitude and stubbornness for this journey. Even in her village, she and her children stayed with relatives, hiding from her husband. From Kars, there was a five-day journey[14] to the Akstafa station where they caught the train to Batum. As they waited in Batum for the ship to arrive and be adapted for the immigrant passengers, shelter from the rain and snow for over two thousand people was in barn-like rooms and under lean-tos in an unused kerosene factory. For all of this, Malanya relied on the communal sharing of resources and the willingness of others to help her and the children.

On board the ship they were to discover the hold was crowded; during stormy weather, practically everyone was seasick. They shared the *syharee* dried bread, kasha, butter, some fresh baked bread, given as a treat, potatoes and onions that over the month-long trip got wet and started to rot. The ventilation was poor. On the first ship, ten people died; on the second, three, some young and some elderly. The bodies were buried at sea, and many became despondent, wondering if they would arrive in Canada after all.

Still, Malanya was supported by the community, which carried on in a calm and orderly manner. During good weather, she would have managed without soap or ashes to wash their clothing. The whole deck became covered with shirts, skirts and pants. The children would have been excited to see schools of dolphins following the ship and strange phosphorescence in the water. In the new year, the *Lake Superior* passed the coast of Gibraltar, and everyone looked forward to a new life in Canada.

---

13   Andrew Donskov, ed., *Sergej Tolstoy and the Doukhobors: A Journey to Canada* (Ottawa: Slavic Research Group at the University of Ottawa, 1998), p. 235.

14   Donskov, *Sergej Tolstoy*, ibid., p. 257.

Many years later, the family was to discover that when the majority of Doukhobors left the Kars area, the Androsoff farm was taken over by local tribes and Malanya's husband lost everything, land, livestock and family. I am thankful that my courageous ancestors, Nikolai and Elizaveta Maloff, and Malanya Androsoff, whom friends called Malasha, brought their family safely to Canada.

Chapter 2

Babushka

My grandmother played a significant role in my upbringing. It was she who instilled into my soul the beginning from which there later developed my spiritual tendencies. Her name was Malanya Semyonovna, formerly Semenoff, but by marriage Maloff and later by a second marriage Androsoff. She was an ardent believer in the Doukhobor faith and philosophy and because of this she always followed the dictates of her conscience. From the very earliest days of my life, she tried to imprint her convictions on my soul, and this to a great degree she achieved. Though illiterate, she had a keen, observing mind and a good memory.

In her youth she had endured many difficulties because of her Doukhobor convictions. Her first husband, Peter I. Maloff, died early leaving her alone with her son, my father. She had lived with her husband for only five years. Her second husband, S. Androsoff, remained behind in Russia. The great spiritual reforms amongst the Doukhobors at that time made no impression upon him and he held to his early convictions. He did not in the least want to part with my grandmother and their two children, Aksinya and Ivan, and tried in every way he could to stop them from leaving Russia. Grandmother and her children had to run away at a time when he was away from home, and only with the help of others of the same convictions were they able to reach Batum. There it was arranged for her to proceed under the passport of a woman who had died en route, and the children were hidden beforehand in the ship's hold. When the people were boarding the ship, special gendarmes and friends of Androsoff stood at the gates with the intention of detaining my grandmother and her children. But she had prepared for this, and with a little acting and disguise, she boarded the ship under their very noses. The gendarmes even searched the ship's hold and several times almost stepped on the children without discovering them.

These events influenced her later life. Perhaps that is why from that time on she chose to remain unmarried.

Doukhobor movements always agitated her, and she followed them no matter where the Doukhobors were headed. Even though my parents left the community, Grandmother remained.

This withdrawal of my parents from the Doukhobor faith hurt her intensely. She could not bear the thought that they had pledged allegiance to the

British Crown. This to her was the greatest betrayal of Doukhobor principles and she could not quite forgive them for it. That is why she tried so hard to instill in her grandchildren the ideal by which she was moved so intensely, and by which she lived. Apparently, she foresaw in little children the opportunity to sow and nurture noble seeds.

Babushka often took me with her to the village and there she instilled her convictions. To go with her to the village was especially pleasant for me as we had to walk several miles through virgin forests and untilled plains. Babushka also liked to be alone; maybe because the presence of people reminded her of her bitter past. She liked berry picking and would often take me with her. I remember once for company she invited Markhunya Kolesnikoff to come with us. We came to the Bourroughs' farm, which my father was at the time renting. It was a hot day and by the time we had gone the three miles or so, we were soaked with perspiration. We soon found raspberries and toward evening had all the pails filled. We were just getting ready to return home when we noticed that dark clouds were gathering. Thunder and lightning followed and a heavy rain with a touch of hail came pouring down upon us. What were we to do? Grandmother advised that we take shelter in the Bourroughs' cottage, which stood nearby. We entered. It was a two-roomed house, with a bed, stove and everything necessary. The Bourrough family lived here only in the winter. In summer, Mr. Bourrough went somewhere else to work.

Grandmother began to light a fire in the stove and Mrs. Kolesnikoff, seeing that she was preparing for the night, protested, "Stay overnight? But I have to bake bread early tomorrow, and my Vanya will go crazy worrying, 'What has become of her?'"

"Never mind, we'll stay," insisted Babushka. "Don't worry, your Vanya will be all right. How could we go in this storm?"

Mrs. Kolesnikoff stayed. The stove was soon hot; we drank some tea and went to bed. Both grandmothers lay down on the bed and I curled myself up behind the stove. Outside, the rain settled in for the night, but only far off could we see the lightning flashing.

"Are you sleeping, Markhusha?" asked Grandmother.

"No, I can't sleep," returned Markhunya. "I was just thinking that if we were in the Caucasus, we wouldn't have decided to spend the night like this."

Suddenly Grandmother seemed to think of something. She sat up and muttered as if to herself, "Why didn't we lock the door?"

She opened the door just slightly and was met by a sheet of wind and rain. She soon slammed it shut again, bolted it and was going to lie down when she sensed something flying about in the room. She lit the lamp and we saw that it was a bat. The grandmothers seized their skirts and, chasing the uninvited guest around the room, they soon drove it out and went back to bed, but not one of us could sleep. They wanted to talk, so I listened. It was interesting to me to wonder what they were going to talk about. My grandmother began to describe her own life going into the more intimate side of her past, paying no attention to me, as if she thought, what can a mere child understand?

"In Slavyanka," she said, "my life was good. I married into a good home, the Maloffs. They were rich. Their horses were famous; they kept a reception house. My father-in-law was friendly with many traders and officials. Engineers going to the copper mines would stop over at our house. My Peter sometimes went with them as a coachman, but more often his father went. Peter loved me and was kind to me and his son was the joy of his life. For five years I lived there like a queen, then my Peter fell sick and died. I was left a widow. I soon married again, this time to Sam Androsoff. This was different. For all the years I lived with him I cannot think of a single good thing to say about him. He became an object of hatred to me for the rest of my life; that's why I never intend to marry again. All men have become distasteful to me and I never want to look at one again."

Markhunya became excited and sat up in bed. She was tall and thin and her face was long and narrow. Grandmother's conclusion touched her and she began enthusiastically, "What foolishness you have in your head, Malasha. My, but you're crazy! If one husband is no good, does that mean that all men are worthless? My Vanya is also not of the best and yet we are living together. He is jealous and scolds me sometimes, but I tell him, 'You can't stop me from being free. I'll go where I like and you can't blindfold me, I'll look where I like too!' And I advise you, Malasha, get married. To live alone like this is unnecessary grief. God created man and woman so they could live close to each other."

For a long time, Grandmother was silent and then she replied seriously, "You do not understand either me or the bitterness of my experience."

"Yes, I do, indeed! You have put up a wall in front of yourself and you cannot climb over it. Forget this foolishness, Malasha. We live in this world for so short a time. And must we live like a worm; without light, without happiness?"

I fell asleep and did not hear how the conversation ended, but this, my grandmother's story, was imprinted on my memory for the rest of my life, perhaps because this was the only time that I ever heard her speak of her past. Usually, she did not like to talk of her past life.

In the morning, we went home. After the rain and storm, the sun sparkled and in one direction only did we see dark clouds, while somewhere far off could be heard the roll of thunder, like the distant rumbling of a wagon passing over a bridge. Birds called merrily to each other in the woods, as though thankful for the rain.

In 1912, my grandmother left for British Columbia with other Doukhobors, but in my soul she left the roots of her convictions and the roots quickly began to grow. Even in my earliest days, I felt an extreme aversion to all cruelty, licentiousness and other moral decadence into which those who had left the community began to fall. In this category were my own parents. Of course, because of my youth little attention was paid to my scruples. This I had to bear whether I liked it or not, but sometimes my indignation would break out in protest or rebellion. These outbreaks were the result of my grandmother's influence.

I remember one mystical experience when Peter Vasilievich Verigin came to our village, that is, when he came after his visit to Siberia. Grandmother was very sick, even on the verge of death. My parents invited Peter Vasilievich to come to our home and visit the sick woman, but for some reason, he categorically, and even harshly, refused. However, the next day, early in the morning, he came and performed some sort of enigmatic rite. He placed both of us boys, my brother and me, side by side. Then he kissed one of us and the other he would not kiss. To my parents this was a riddle. My grandmother attached an important significance to it.

Many years later, a little before her death, I was reading her a booklet by a well-known writer, W.W. Vereschagin, under the title of "Doukhobors and Molokans." As she listened, she suddenly became transported with delight, as though she recalled something from the distant past. "My God!" she exclaimed. "This happened at our home, in Slavyanka. Right after the Turkish war, my father-in-law brought him from Gondji; a clean, attractive gentleman he was. He stayed with us for several days. He heard some Doukhobors singing at our neighbours' at a funeral and said, 'I would like to hear some more of your singing.' Then the melodious Agafonoffs took him to their home and, gathering the Slavyanka choir together, sang to him for several days. We had real singers there: Mavrunya and Masha Strelieff, the Nichvolodoffs, the Konkins and many others. Heavens! Who ever thought that he was going to write a book about us."

My grandmother died in 1943 at the age of ninety-six.

ON CHAPTER 3

DOUKHOBORS AND EDUCATION

[Vera] When Pete became of school age, his father, Nikolai Maloff, arranged for him to attend school in a neighbouring town. Since at the time, going to a public school was against the community rules, their ban from the community was harsh and decisive. He was to regret this break with Doukhobor faith for the rest of his life.

Education became a very contentious issue within the Doukhobor community and in particular between the Sons of Freedom faction and the government of British Columbia. Without a solution for many years, it led to the incendiarism of schools perpetrated by the Sons of Freedom and the seizure and placement of Doukhobor children in the 1930s and 1950s in government institutions. In 2024, the government of British Columbia finally apologized for their disastrous policy of taking children from loving homes.

I have wondered why Doukhobors held out so stoutly against public education. My grandparents had both attended English schools, Lusha to Grade 8 in a Thrums one-room schoolhouse and Pete completed high school in Peoria, Oregon. My mother Elizabeth and her siblings were taught at home, but with many disruptions in their lives, she completed her Grade 10 in adult education courses years later. When I attended the University of British Columbia, Grandfather introduced me to a librarian there who he was friends with. It was not education they were against. As I came to understand, we Doukhobors wanted to teach our children in our own schools, including Russian and English language instruction.

According to Maloff, Doukhobors believe patriotism is the mainspring of many wars, and patriotism is implanted in government schools. Furthermore, he said that though Doukhobor leader Peter Vasilievich Verigin saw the usefulness of elementary literacy and eventually accepted public schooling for children to the age of twelve, he valued inborn wisdom above all. In his early period, in a letter he wrote, "Literacy is not helpful in the process of seeking truth or the meaning of life. When seeking truth, one must not trust books. Every book is imperfect. And though books give much help in the solution of many problems, they sometimes prevent or hinder the solution. But our inward voice never deceives if our wishes are really sincere."[15]

In 1927, when Doukhobor leader Peter Petrovich Verigin arrived, Pete and Lusha Maloff were glad to hear that he endorsed education and acceptance of public schooling became a prerequisite to membership in the CCUB.[16] However, the Sons of Freedom continued to resist public school education for many years, culminating with the forced removal of their children to a residential school in New Denver in the 1950s. The trauma this caused not only reverberated in their families but created fear throughout the community. As a young student, I could not understand why some of my classmates who had been sitting at a desk next to me were now held in a walled compound and only allowed to be visited by their parents every two weeks through a wire fence. In several instances, children had been scooped up and taken to the residential school through mistaken identities.

Even in the early years, Doukhobors saw it as essential to keep their native language and many villages established Russian schools. Where there were no schools, home education was developed. Books in Russian were sent from the Soviet Union. I remember looking through the beautifully illustrated children's books that my grandparents had and being excited to learn the phonetic alphabet so I could begin to read simple stories.

The community set up a system to educate Russian-language teachers and in the 1960s, I along with several friends attended. Though at the time, I resented the loss of my evenings and weekends, those classes enabled me to read my grandfather's book in the original Russian. When we travelled to Russia, I was delighted that my partner Steve and I passed as Russians with a southern dialect. There, especially among the villages, I noticed that our accents were still the same, though the Russians laughed at our old expressions and language.

Eventually, through lobbying of the local school boards by parents and the Russian community, Russian instruction was included in the school systems in the Kootenay and Grand Forks areas of British Columbia. I contacted a friend, Nell Plotnikoff, who had been a Russian teacher and a librarian. She found a paper she had written on Russian-language instruction in public schools. Her excitement about developing a Russian program, when in our past speaking Russian in school was punishable by the dreadful "strap," shines in her letter:

---

15   This letter to Anna Chertkova was printed in *Svobodnoe Slovo* (*The Free Word*), no. 11 (May and June 1904). The letter is also in Pete Maloff's *Doukhobors: Their History, Life and Struggle*, Part II, Doukhobors in Canada, chapter on Peter V. Verigin's Philosophy and Letters.

16   Tarasoff, *Plakun Trava*, ibid., p. 262.

I jumped into my librarian mode, which I still love to do, and started searching in my several boxes filled with information file folders. Way back in the '70s when I was completing requirements for a B.Ed., I wrote a paper in one of the courses about Russian-language instruction in public schools. Lo and behold, I still had that paper in a file folder. The secondary schools in Grand Forks, Castlegar and Nelson offered Russian in Grades 9–12 as an elective since about 1963 or 1964. So, there was work to be done at the elementary level!! Teachers Steve Malloff, Peter Samoyloff and Alex Pereverzoff were instrumental in getting Russian-language instruction established in elementary schools in the three districts. During 1973–1974 they met with the three school boards, lobbied Eileen Dailly, Minister of Education, and developed strategies to establish Russian-language programs in the school districts where the Russian ethnic population was nucleated. This fell into step with the federal government's multicultural department's promotion of heritage languages. By 1977, all three school districts had established Russian-language programs in schools. We Russian-language teachers from the three districts worked together on the curriculum—what great achievements—and fun! Peter Evdokimoff was a good participant, too. I started teaching Russian at Brent Kennedy Elementary and never looked back.[17]

In 1985 my daughter, Sasha, attended a Russian immersion kindergarten class in Castlegar, the first of its kind in Canada, and a bilingual program was developed at the elementary level. I wholeheartedly congratulate this group who brought Russian-language instruction from banned to celebrated!

---

17   Nell Plotnikoff, email, August 30, 2023.

Chapter 3

School Days

While still in the community, my parents, through the influence of a certain progressive element, began to desire education for their children. At first, they took my older brother to Yorkton and settled him in the home of Anton Savelievich Popoff, who had enthusiastically begun to bring up his children under the English school system. My brother was cordially accepted by the Popoffs.

The community then, and for many years after, rejected state education. On the whole, to be associated with any government institution was considered a violation of basic Doukhobor principles. The action of my parents was a direct renunciation of the established order and for this they were soon rejected by the community. This break sent them still further on the downward trend. They felt themselves completely outcast and soon took a homestead and moved away to live on it.

Our farm was situated four miles from Buchanan. There was no school nearby so we attended the town school. Father built us a little house in town and there we lived during the school season for a year or more without any exceptional incident. Then a school was built near our farm, on vacant land in the woods. At first our teachers were two brothers in succession, Jack and Cecil Bradley from Virden, Manitoba. They stayed a session apiece and never returned. Their place was taken by Harold Martin from Belmont, Manitoba. We became intimately acquainted with him through the following occurrence: One day in the spring, having gathered in school before school-time, a group of us wandered to a nearby pond. Suddenly, I heard the shrill cries of a small animal, and rushing to it saw a weasel caught by her legs in a trap. I did not hesitate, but threw open the trap, and the animal, limping away, was soon lost in the bushes.

My companions jumped at me and said, "You have no right to do that!"

I replied that I had a right to save a life. They, unsatisfied with my explanation, hurried to put the matter before our teacher.

Meanwhile, a little further on, I found more traps set. I took a stick and snapped them all shut; I even threw one of them into the bushes. I had not yet finished my work with the traps when I was surrounded by a mob of boys, with the teacher at their head.

"Peter, you must not do that," began the teacher excitedly. "Don't you know that you can't do things like that on someone else's property? The owner can register a complaint and I shall get into trouble; they'll say that the teacher is ruining the children, making rascals of them."

"But I didn't do anything wrong," I replied. "I just saved a poor animal from dying a horrible death."

I was going to go on with my explanation, when a Norwegian, Carlson, just a little older than I, interrupted me: "Pete not only let the weasel go, but even threw a trap into that thicket. I saw him do it."

This especially enraged the teacher. I saw him start toward me. Sizing up the situation, I decided to run home. I started then and there, right through the bushes. The teacher soon realized what was happening and shouted, "Catch him!"

The death of Maloff's teacher and friend Harold Martin in World War I strengthened his resolve to work toward peaceful resolution of conflicts.

I went through the underbrush as fast as I could go but I could hear two of them, Carlson and MacIntosh, catching up with me. They caught me by the arms and took me back. The teacher seized me by the collar so tightly that I could scarcely breathe, and all the children surrounding their criminal escorted me into the school and opened the trial.

"Pete, you are guilty of causing a neighbourhood scandal," was the charge against me. The teacher took the strap and heartily administered five lashes on my quivering palms. I felt hot all over, stars danced about my head. I could scarcely wait till evening came. Everybody was staring at me and the teacher would turn and look at me once in a while as if he were afraid that I would commit some offence. On the way home I thought, "I'm not going to school anymore."

At home I did not say anything of what happened. And why should I say anything when my brother was also running around with traps. In the morning, I told the family that I wasn't going to school anymore. My father was alarmed and shocked.

"What is going on here—you won't go, you say? Oh, yes, you will! Ill drag you there on a rope if I have to, but you'll go to school, all right!"

We quarrelled and quarrelled, but I stood my ground and did not go.

Father became enraged and said, "You are only staying home until tomorrow, but you are not going to have a holiday. You'll have to take the cow over to the bull."

I was only eleven or twelve years old at the time. I could do nothing but obey, so I obeyed. I had to take the cow to the village, quite a distance away. We had a black cow and I led her away, planning how best I could get away from school.

We reached the school land, an unoccupied farm. Here was spaciousness. Spring was in the air, and as if in a dream, I walked free from the dreaded school ties, I whistled and danced with joy. The cow at first refused to go and balked and sometimes would pause to nibble at the grass that was just breaking through. Whoever would have expected danger was threatening. We just got past a thicket, when I noticed a moving mass that had no reason to be where it was. The farther we went, the closer it came upon us. I could not make out what it was, but looking more closely, I saw that it was a herd of steers. I seized a stick, intending to defend the cow, but this was something fearful to behold. They came upon me in a whirl of dust. Huge steers milled around the cow; some were jumping on her, others fought amongst themselves. I was scared to death. I dropped the halter rope, and that's the last that I remembered. I only became conscious of what had occurred when I looked around me and there was no sign of either steers or my cow. I followed the tracks; they were easy enough. They left a trail like that of a huge machine right through the Demoskoffs' yard and through all the fences. In some places wheat was sprouting, but they ploughed it under in their stampede. I came home, but the cow was not there either.

Mother rushed out gasping, pointed to the nearby slough and asked me, "What in the world is that?"

"I don't know either," I replied.

Coming nearer the slough, we saw that the whole herd was in it. "Aha," I thought, "so they got thirsty." But looking closer we saw that was not the case; the poor cow was so spent that she just dropped in the middle of the slough and her pursuers, more than forty of them, stood around on alert, just in case she should get up, so that they could again press their suit.

My brother ran up to help, but there was nothing he could do.

We sent for Father. He came, took one look and exclaimed, "What goes on here?"

We each took a stick and began to chase them, but again with no success. Then at last we managed to get the cow up. We led her into the barn and, with difficulty, we returned the bulls to the school farm.

Father was furious with me, as he had good reason to be. This herd trampled most of the crop, which was only getting a good start, and broke down our fences.

"You useless greenhorn!" began my father. "No matter where I send you, there is sure to be nothing but trouble from it. Who was it that upset the load of seeding wheat into the ditch? You! Who was it that got stuck in the slough with the oxen when ploughing? You!"

Father cited several other escapades and failures, and then, raising the stick which he had in his hand, he proclaimed in a threatening voice: "Tomorrow you will either go to school without one word out of you, or this thing will dance all over you!"

Where did these steers come from? Later I found out that the Doukhobors who left for British Columbia had brought their working beasts to this vacant land until they could be sold. Long after this, I often wondered how I ever got out of this incident alive.

In the morning, with great misgivings, I went back to school. My path led through Grandfather Kolesnikoff's yard. He was a huge man, strong and confident. We were great friends with him. He used to come to our bathhouse and I used to bathe with him and keep the steam up; that is, I poured water on the hot stones while he was sitting on the top shelf. They did not have a bathhouse of their own. He bought my aunty Aksinya's land and she, being extremely civilized, instead of a bathhouse, used a bathtub.

When he came to our place the first time he explained, "My Nikolasha, but your sister is some Englishwoman! She built herself such a small bathtub that even my Okaya can't get into it as comfortably as she should, and what do you think I'll have to do, bathe sitting down? I wanted to smash it to pieces but Okaya wouldn't let me, saying, 'You make a bathhouse first and then you can do as you like.'"

We had a real Russian steam bathhouse, so he used to come to ours on Saturdays. And did he love that steam! At times I could scarcely bear it on the floor and he from the top shelf near the ceiling would call out: "Hey, Peter, would you splash a little more water on? If I don't have a good steaming, I can't even eat or sleep as I should." He lived to the age of 101.

This morning I, as usual, was walking through their yard when he walked out and waved to me. "Hey, Peter, come over here. I was very displeased with you. The whole school reported on you yesterday that you ruined all my traps. I set the trap to catch the weasel that has just about killed all my chickens, and what did you do?"

"Grandfather," I said, "I did all that myself and you have nobody to blame but me. Now you can do what you like with me. The teacher gave me a licking and if my folks ever find out they also wouldn't exactly praise me. I know all that, but I can't stand for such savage cruelty, that's all."

"Hmm, what are you thinking of! But do you know that you have no right to do things like that on somebody else's property? On your own land you are master and you can do whatever you like, but you have no business going on another man's; that's the Canadian law. If I had caught you there, Peter, there would have been trouble!" On saying this he grabbed me and shook me a couple of times.

Here Okaya saw us and, running out, barged into our conversation: "But I sure praised you, Peter. That's the only way to teach these old fools because they have forgotten their own faith and religion. Just think of it; they used to live in a community! How God-fearing they were then! And here you see nothing but traps, guns, meat, whisky and tobacco. What rank, dastardly disgrace! You should be ashamed to torture the boy for your own sins."

"Shut up, Okaya, or I'll smash you to pieces. You said yourself that either we catch the weasel or all our chickens are lost."

While they were quarrelling with each other I disappeared unnoticed.

At school the teacher met me with an entirely different attitude. This instilled in me a new interest in education.

After school he approached me. "I am very sorry that we had a disagreement with you. Tell me, who taught you such love toward animals?"

"My grandmother," I replied. Then I told him that I had never even so much as tasted any meat.

He was still more amazed and exclaimed, "I have never in my whole life met anybody like that before!"

After that we became friends. He ceased to become angry at me, no matter what I did, even though I was at times quite mischievous. He went away to the United States but he continued to teach and write me the warmest and most friendly letters. In 1915 he volunteered for the army and even then, he wrote to me from the different places where he was stationed. What a pity that I have lost my early archives. Among them were his letters from England, France and even from the front.

Harold was very fond of my father and often used to say to him, "What a genuine person your son is. There's no farce about him. If all your people were like that, then your ideals would be very good indeed."

Once I wrote to him in effect, "You have made a sad mistake, my dear, dear friend. You should have been convincing others, not to kill anybody or anything, but you, you have cheated your own self!"

To this he replied briefly and somewhat dryly: "Perhaps you are right, but now it is too late." Several years passed and I heard no word from him. In 1918 I wrote to his father to find out what happened to Harold. In reply I received the following letter:

Belmont, Manitoba,
Nov. 13, 1918
My Dear Mr. Maloff:

I received your letter yesterday evening in which you ask for Harold's address. I am very sorry to have to inform you that he was killed on the 9th of April, 1917 on the day when the Canadians captured Vimy Ridge. I was informed by his sergeant of his death at the hands of a machine gun, on the third line of German trenches. He was buried on Vimy Ridge with thousands of other Canadians fallen on that day. His sergeant was wounded at the time also and wrote me that every soldier of that platoon was either killed or wounded. Out of eleven hundred soldiers of the 78th Battalion who advanced that morning, only a hundred and forty returned on the third day. I am sending you this last photograph, as you were his friend, and his friends, we consider our friends. If you should ever happen to be in this vicinity you must most certainly pay us a visit. The war is over. Eric, Harold's kid brother, is overseas for two years now, and we sure would be glad to see him home again.

Sincerely yours,
Charles Martin

The incident of the forty steers was not so easily forgotten or passed over. After that I began to sleep very poorly, jumping up and screaming at nights.

When Grandmother found out, she came over and said, "We'll have to heal Peter or we'll lose him. I'll take him to a healer, Babushka Strelieff. She'll pour the 'fright' [cure] on his head and he'll get well soon enough."

All the way there, Grandmother was assuring me that all this happened because of our renunciation of the true faith, because of our withdrawal from the community. When we came to Babushka Strelieff's, she already had a patient. From behind the door, we could hear how something was sputtering and falling into water. It would give off a strange sound.

I asked my grandmother, "What is that? Are you sure they wouldn't burn me with some kind of an iron?"

"No, my child, don't be afraid," said Babushka. "Babushka Strelieff knows everything. She'll just pour the 'fright' over your head. She'll hold a bowl of water over your head and into it will drop some molten lead. She'll see what will form; if a dragon, then the sickness is from a spell, and if something else, then she will know what kind of a prayer to read and what to fortify the water against. That's what it is all about, my child."

Soon the patient left. He was quite an aged man. I thought, "How could he have been scared by anything?"

The healer waved her hand in the direction of the patient, and as though divining my perplexity, volunteered, "Ghosts are torturing him. Every night they come to him and won't let him sleep."

We entered the healer's room. Babushka Strelieff was very old and talked very slowly. She patted my head and assured me: "Don't be afraid, Peter, I'll heal you and you'll be well again."

She put some lead on the stove, then took a dipper of cold water and held it over my head whispering something all the while. As soon as the lead began to sizzle on the pan, she poured it into the dipper over my head, then she charmed the water and as an added protection, she grafted me; that is, she placed me against the lintel of the door, bored a hole in it and pounded a stick into the hole saying, "That is where we have driven your illness."

Babushka Strelieff's son sat nearby on a bench. Evidently, he was used to such scenes; it made no difference to him who she was healing, the old, the young or the stupid. To him it seemed amusing to watch these healings and it was evident that he had very little faith in them.

He finally appealed to my grandmother: "I'd advise you, Malasha, to take Peter to the doctor. They say that cattle-frights can't be cured by whispering."

This sarcasm was aimed at the old belief of the grandmothers.

Mine answered first: "May they all perish, your doctors. Did you hear what they did north of here? A doctor prescribed some medicine for one woman, and the druggist gave her poison instead. She died. They had an inquest and a trial. They agreed that the druggist made a mistake. A mistake is a mistake, all right, but that person is no more. That's how it goes. Believe in them if you like."

Here Babushka Strelieff joined the argument, and, as though striving to convince her son of the correctness of her method of healing, she said, "With these Englishmen, you scarcely have time to die, when they take out your insides and wallow in your stomach. This is not good. A doctor should know when a man is dying, but still he keeps on stuffing pills and medicine into him. Death is nothing to play around with. We should be preparing for it so that the soul can easily leave the body. But what is this? Is it right to torture a person? How will the soul appear before the throne of the Righteous Judge when his body is being cut up by knives and not given any peace. That's what your doctors are like!"

However fantastic it may seem, I remember that this healing actually reacted on me very favourably and the illness gradually began to leave me.

Doukhobor Healers

[**Vera**] Grandfather's terror of the incident with the forty (forty!) steers sent shivers down my back. As a child, investigating our neighbourhood, I had climbed over a fence into the neighbour's field and was immediately spotted by a bull who did not take kindly to an invader in his territory. He lowered his massive head and charged at me. My heart pumping, adrenalin kicked in, I dashed to the fence and clambered over just before that bull rammed the boards. I never discussed the incident with anyone.

Curious about Doukhobor cures for trauma, I asked friends if they had any experience with Doukhobor healers. I learned that a few elderly women continue to practise shamanic remedies, but it is kept within the family.

I was especially struck by Babushka Strelieff's comments on the effort taken by modern medicine to keep a person alive. At the end of her long life, my mother Elizabeth did not wish for any extraordinary care to prolong her life and was ready to make her peace with death. At that stage, even antibiotics may just prolong a life that is prepared to pass away.

When Doukhobor villages were built in British Columbia, a hospital was established in Ootischenia and a Russian doctor was invited to take care of it. However, Doukhobors looked with suspicion at doctors and their medicines and I was surprised that eventually they threw all the medicines into the river, discharged the doctor, closed the hospital and declared that they could do without them very well.[18] Throughout the centuries, Doukhobor healers such as Babushka Strelieff established natural home remedies that worked for many common illnesses and Doukhobor bone-setters were known for their excellent work.[19]

---

18   Peter Maloff, Part II, Chapter 13: "The Inner Life of the Community," in *Doukhobors: Their History, Life and Struggle* (Thrums, BC: self-published, 1948).

19   Svetlana A. Inikova has collected prayers and incantations against sickness in *Doukhobor Incantations through the Centuries* (Ottawa: Legas, 1999).

The March to Meet Christ, 1902–1903

[Vera] The March to Meet Christ that occurred in 1902 in Canada had a profound effect on the community and began to divide the Doukhobors. Even former friends of the Doukhobors started to question their support. Although as a youngster, Maloff was not aware of this event, in later years, he was able to speak to leaders and participants of the march and record the incident. Pete Maloff wrote in detail about this march in his book on Doukhobor history.

In the early 1900s, with a change of government, officials began to pressure Doukhobors to take land individually rather than working the land communally and living in villages as they previously agreed to under the "hamlet clause." With the fear of losing their land, some Doukhobors, including Maloff's parents, began to accept homesteads and become assimilated in the Canadian way of life. A small group, staunch in spirit and decision, consisting of the most passionate and restless characters in the community, protested against what they saw as an abandonment of Doukhobor principles. When they saw that many Doukhobors, particularly the Independents, were leaving the basic tenets of their faith, they started a protest march, a *pahod*.

First, they let their animals go free. Then, leaving their property behind, they went through the villages preaching that if it was not right to slaughter animals for meat, it was also wrong to exploit the "lesser brothers," the horses and oxen, for personal welfare. It was wrong to steal milk from calves for our gluttony. They said that the time had come for Doukhobors to leave all the cares of the world and their material worries and go out to the world preaching the second coming of Christ. This group received the name "Sons of Freedom" because they gave freedom to their livestock.

The Sons of Freedom went from village to village and at first, they were met with hearty welcome and hospitality. From almost every village, new adherents joined them and their numbers rapidly increased. Many declared their willingness to join, but said that they were unable to do so for one reason or another: one had a large family to support, another had small children, and so on. Where adherents were found, the Sons of Freedom remained for several days, waiting until these recruits could free their livestock and get ready to march. In some villages, they were treated indifferently and even with ill will. Many looked upon this campaign as a crazy superfluity and said that there was no need to go anywhere but to stay at home and live peacefully.

As the *pahod* continued, Maloff wrote that the Sons of Freedom became more and more radical. They threw off their leather shoes and belts as these were obtained from dead animals. Metal was procured through heavy labour in the mines, so everything made of metal was put in a pile and left behind. Money had Caesar's stamp on it and they gave it back to the government agent.

I found Maloff's description of the motivation of the marchers especially poignant:

> They were of various dispositions: the simpler and more passionate were actually prepared to march on and on until they came to some other country which would be glad to accept them for good. Others knew that they could not get very far on foot, but hoped that perhaps some country would sympathize with them and take them right off the road. Others did not stop to think about what would happen to them: they just marched, urged by some kind of invisible inner power. They gave themselves to it unconditionally, regardless of where this power might lead them. However, all agreed that they were doing something great, although they were not fully able to understand it. They believed that the campaign itself irrespective of its conclusion or outcome carried enormous significance.[20]

The authorities tried to convince the Doukhobors to return to their homes, but without result, and in the end, the police rounded up the marchers and escorted them back under duress. Shortly afterward Peter Vasilievich was allowed to leave his exile in Siberia to come to Canada. He praised the marchers for their efforts, saying that when they had started their march, the authorities in Russia and Canada agreed to his prompt release, whereas before there had been many delays. He thanked them and advised them to return to their villages.

A similar inner motivational force drove many of the Sons of Freedom in 1962, when many of the men were incarcerated in Agassiz Mountain Prison. Their Sons of Freedom families began a trek from the Kootenays to the coast of British Columbia, a distance of over six hundred kilometres. As a child of eleven, I watched this procession from the side of the road as marchers—men,

---

20   Maloff, Part II, Chapter 4: "The March to Meet Christ," in *Doukhobors: Their History, Life and Struggle*, ibid.

The March to Meet Christ in 1902. Government pressure on Doukhobors to take land individually rather than working communally and living in villages resulted in a small group marching in protest. They changed their name to Sons of Freedom when they freed all their livestock.

women and children—followed by cars and trucks overflowing with blankets and household goods slowly passed by our house in Thrums. My parents did not explain what was happening. Was it explicable? An upwelling of an inner drive, an urge that must be followed. I felt an unease, uncertainty and then fear at what seemed to be an irrational event.

Pete Maloff's chapter "Life on the Farm" describes the extent of the change in the values of the Independent farmers, whom the Maloffs were part of. Their life confirms the deep division among Doukhobors and is a stark contrast to the Sons of Freedom and Community Doukhobor austerity and striving to fulfill fundamental Doukhobor beliefs.

CHAPTER 4

LIFE ON THE FARM

During my childhood Doukhobors lived through many changes and upheavals. First there were the marches of 1902–1903, which shook them profoundly.[21] These movements did not pass without aftereffects. It was at this time that the more ardent element definitely broke away from the main party and began to lead a more or less independent existence under the name of Sons of Freedom.

Before Doukhobors had a chance to forget these upheavals, new ones began to develop. The mode of life of the Doukhobor community was not acceptable to the Canadian government, and it decided to take a hand in the matter. The government announced to the Doukhobors that they would be compelled to swear allegiance to the king. In case of non-compliance, their land would be liable to confiscation. Since this demand contradicted the basic Doukhobor principles, they replied with a flat refusal. They remained true to their ideal, regardless of the fact that doing so led to complete material ruin.

Because I was so young, these events passed almost unnoticed by me. I heard very little about it at the time. Years later, when life again associated me closely with Doukhobor movements, I began gradually to understand the underlying significance of these incidents.

As a result of these events, another splinter from the Doukhobor centre began to emerge, enlarge and lead an independent life. The sober, secluded community life was too much for some Doukhobors, and little by little they began to give it up. The wide expanse of the Canadian prairie and the unlimited individual freedom tempted these industrious people. Land was almost given away (ten dollars per homestead, plus the pledge of allegiance), and people, one tempting another, raced after these spoils. From that time on these Doukhobors were called *farmalyee* (farmers).

While the communal members submitted to a decrease in material gain and increasing want, the Farmers prospered. Many began to eat meat, drink liquor, smoke tobacco and fall into other bad habits. They owned guns and traps, and some Doukhobors even joined the army at the time of the First World War.

The withdrawal of my parents from the community made no impression

---

21   Maloff writes about this trek in detail in Part II, "The March to Meet Christ," in *Doukhobors: Their History, Life and Struggle*, ibid.

on me. The surrounding mode of life taught me neither the moral principles nor the convictions and philosophy of the Doukhobors. These I had from my grandmother. It was she who brought me to the realization that we were cut off from something, though exactly from what I did not definitely understand.

In our village four families were rejected from the community. We were excluded because my father sent my brother Nick to English school, and in addition he took Grandmother to the doctor, which was strictly forbidden.

Gregory G. Sherstobitoff, my aunt's husband, was excluded because he had carelessly said these words, which at the time were considered blasphemous: "If I had had the money Peter Vasilievich had, I could have run the community as well as he."

Aresha Demoskoff was excluded for a similar offence. At the meetings where dues were collected, he usually raised an argument and once he stated that his earnings weren't used for the community, but for Tiunechka's skirts.[22] For these words he was immediately excluded. Anton Savelievich Popoff was the first in our village to send his children to the English schools and was the first to be rejected.

Once my grandmother began to admonish my father to re-enter the community, but he told her how deeply hurt he had been.

"Peter Vasilievich himself," said he, "wants us to live on the farm. Once the four of us appeared at a service where Peter Vasilievich was present to request readmission into the community. While waiting our turn, Peter Vasilievich, seeing us standing together, looked toward us and demanded of those around him, 'Why did you let them come here to the service? They have their pockets full of stones.'

"After this we were told to withdraw from the meeting. This made us especially uneasy. Aresha and I were seriously agitated. We went to Horeloe village following Peter Vasilievich. We reached there toward nightfall. Peter Vasilievich was already asleep. The members of the community allowed us to put up our horses in the common stable, but would not let us stay overnight. With difficulty we found where a farmer, Alex Kalmikoff, lived. We spent the night with him intending to call on Peter Vasilievich in the morning. The morning brought us a still greater shock; someone had let our horses out of the barn and by the time we found them, we had lost all inclination to re-enter the community."

On hearing this, Grandmother became lost in thought. What she thought, I have no idea, but never again did she ask Father to re-enter the community.

---

22   Reference to Anastasia Holoboff, companion to Peter V. Verigin for twenty years in Canada.

Life on the farm in those early years was excessively busy. As a matter of course, we had left the community with nothing, and at first our parents had to live through many hardships. My father had grown up an orphan under the care of other people, and the independent ownership of property invigorated him. He was a sincere enthusiast, easily swayed by stronger natures, and he gave himself ardently, in any matter, private or public, that tempted him. Though not an educated man, he had learned to read during the time of his incarceration in the Tiflis prison with the rest of the Doukhobors. During exile in Baku, he took advantage of the Baku newspapers and developed the ability to read comparatively well. I remember, on the farm, on long winter nights he read us several books. I especially recall *Uncle Tom's Cabin*. He read it aloud and wept, and I in bed would muffle myself under the blanket and weep irrepressibly. He subscribed to Russian newspapers, first Lomakin's *Svet*, from Pittsburgh, and then the *Russkii Golos* (*Russian Voice*) edited by Ivan Kuzmich Okuntsov.

My parents began to adopt the new habits: meat-eating, drinking alcoholic beverages and attending dancing parties. In this unwholesome atmosphere I spent my boyhood. I will not dwell in detail on this phase of my life, but I would like to relate a few characteristic episodes which have been vividly retained in my memory.

One spring, the surrounding rivers and lakes were exceptionally full of fish. Seeing my brother hitching up the horses, I asked, "Where to?"

"For some fish, to the Krilovka River," he replied.

I had been there once and liked the place. I decided to go along with him. The fishing was at its height; hundreds of men were shouting, waving their hands and rushing about. They had waded in from various directions and were driving the fish into a compact mass from which they simply threw them ashore with pitchforks. My father and brother ran up and down till they were covered with sweat, and had a wagonload of fish.

Not until later did the injustice of my enthusiasm for fishing dawn upon my conscience. My parents were busy with their spring work and could not use all the fish. They began to rot and had to be thrown away. This awakened in me a repulsion toward meat-eating and I began to use every means of persuasion to convince my parents to return to vegetarianism.

In the fall of that same year at threshing time, while waiting for the threshing machine, my mother was preparing supper. When the teamsters came, she asked them to kill several chickens, as she could not yet bring herself to kill them. I guessed what she wanted to do, so I boarded up the door of the chicken house as well as I could, and hid all the axes and knives. When the workers reached the chicken coop, they were surprised to find the doors and windows completely boarded up. Mother soon grasped the situation and told them that this was the work of our vegetarian.

Not finding an axe, the men began to tear the chickens' heads off with their bare hands. To me this seemed the ultimate measure of brutality.

I ran to them trying to stop them in whatever way I could, but they caught and held me. I thrashed about to free myself, wept in my helplessness and bit their hands crying out at the top of my voice: "You savages!"

My brother, though he did not eat meat, was strongly attracted toward hunting and shot at anything he caught sight of.

One day he was not to be found at home. Toward evening he appeared, hitched up the team of racers and away he went. Afterwards I learned that he had killed a young deer and had taken it to Aunt Aksinya for safekeeping. From there he planned to bring meat home a little at a time for his parents.

Many were my conflicts with the rest of the family. Sometimes they developed into quite serious quarrels. Often when my parents had just prepared some meat, I would seize it and throw it out to the dogs or into the slops. Finally, they began to take me seriously and served meat only in my absence.

At my aunt Aksinya Sherstobitoff's, festive parties often gathered. I was present many times and witnessed the drunken revelry. Guests even came from Kamsack: the Konkins, grey Bill and our brother-in-law Gregory were especially comical—both could dance well, they would spin around like so many windmills.

At one such party Gregory commanded, "To the hunt!"

About ten men gathered. They had four guns, and off they went into the bushes. Attracted by their joviality and carefree spirit I went along with them. We walked through the woods; the trees bowed down with icy snow. Suddenly we heard a bang. Vasil Konkin had fired. Snow flew up in a cloud and from under it a flock of prairie chickens sputtered into the air. Two of them began to thrash around. Everyone rushed to them and began to investigate with as much delight as if they had just fallen upon priceless treasure. I looked. From one chicken flowed bright-red blood; on the snow it looked almost translucent. The chicken quivered and died. My heart shrank within me, my good humour vanished, and I decided to go no farther. I returned to my aunt and told her I was going home.

Aresha Demoskoff was one of our neighbours. His son, Ivan, was a close companion of mine. Aresha himself liked to have a good time and several times they had large gatherings of people, some of whom came from as far away as Canora. Among them were Nikolasha Hoodicoff with his violin, Mitya Gritchin the dancer, Larrion I. Verigin the singer and caller, and Sakatoff who always carried some kind of a book in his pocket.

We had ample opportunity to watch their celebrations. Nikola Hoodikoff was a "Siberian" but soon after his arrival in Canada he went to live on a farm. He was well along in years but played well. It is said that he became disillusioned with the Doukhobor way while he was in Siberia. He understood that when money was sent from Canada to those who were in Siberia, it did not reach them, but much of it fell into the hands of Peter Vasilievich Verigin, Vasily Vasilievich Verigin and some others of the Verigins, and that they used it for their personal expenditures.

And so, people gathered at the Demoskoffs' and without any qualms partook of every kind of revelry known to them. At first Gritchin would step out alone and exhibit his remarkable grace and agility: his feet seemed to float noiselessly.

One of the ladies would call, "How about the Kamarinsky, Mitya."

At this he would dance and spring up and down, as though he were descending out of the blue. Everyone would clap their hands in applause. "Well done, Mitya!"

Mitya was not only a good dancer, but could sing, too. In outer appearance he seemed gentle, almost ladylike.

In justice, I must state that not all the farmers gave way to revelry and debauchery. The close fellowship of community life perpetuated in some Doukhobors their higher and nobler characteristics. Under other circumstances different traits developed. Because of this, amongst the Doukhobors appeared many original personalities—men and women of high moral standards and outstanding talents. Some were idealists and colonizers not content with the form of life of the farmers at that time. They dreamed of better things, such as the foundation of a colony where their life could be spent in more congenial circumstances. They even envisaged a form of life intrinsically better than the community. To realize this, some thought of emigrating to the United States, to settle in the state of Oregon.

My parents were attracted by this idea. There was great uneasiness and indecision: to go or not to go; to go finally conquered and in 1913 we found ourselves in the United States of America.

ON CHAPTER 5

A COLONY OF FREEDOM IN OREGON

[Vera] In 1913, the Maloffs joined forty Independent Doukhobor families to establish a Svoboda Colony of Freedom in the Willamette Valley of Oregon. Among our family, this is remembered as a bountiful land of "milk and honey" where one could grow food year-round. And this is true, the valley has been a destination of choice for immigrants since the 1800s with its variation of a Mediterranean climate, a long growing season, moderate temperatures and fertile soil. It is now known for its wineries, acres of colourful gardens where numerous varieties of fruit, vegetables, nuts and flowers grow.

Besides a climate more fitting for vegetarians, the move was to create a democratic colony. Members of this group included the Bloodoff, Popoff, Vereschagin, Reibin, Lapshinoff, Vanin, Davidoff, Nikishin, Drazdoff, Sherstobitoff and Maloff families, among others. They purchased one thousand acres of land in the wide valley close to the city of Corvallis and hoped to establish an ideal Doukhobor lifestyle. In the coming chapter, Pete Maloff describes the life of the community, their effort to maintain Doukhobor principles and the unfortunate loss.

In 2016, almost a century after the colony had dissolved, my partner Steve and I drove along the rugged Oregon seaside enjoying wild ocean views and windswept scenery. At Umpqua River, we turned inland to search for the land where the Freedom Colony had been situated, following directions from friends—the Kooznetsoffs, whose family had also lived in the colony—close to the village of Peoria, across from a blueberry farm and a Doukhobor-style house.

We located the most likely spot for the settlement, and though we saw no remains of the colony, standing on the land I felt connected to my *predkee* who had searched for freedom to live and speak as they wished, in harmony and co-operation with their fellow man. The land they had built houses on, gardened, where Grandfather walked daily to school, perhaps carrying his homework in a rucksack, was expansive and enticing, with acres of tilled farmland visible to the south and east. That fall, the Willamette River flowed gently, the same river that in the spring flooded forty-five acres of the colony land, where Pete and his friends enjoyed paddling, and where colonist Anton Popoff was devising a plan to drain.

In 1923 Doukhobor leader Peter V. Verigin purchased eight hundred acres in Oregon to create a "Friend-Loving" Druzhelyubaya Dolina colony for Doukhobor and Molokans to live in a united community. After his death in 1924 this scheme was abandoned. The sign Dukhobor Road remains.

The colony was in existence for five years. The families lost their land through what sounded like a fraudulent contract. We investigated the information available at the library in the closest town, Corvallis, and with the help of an obliging librarian, and newspaper files, learned that there had been similar crooked land schemes a decade earlier. This was a reason that many neighbouring farmers and journalist Mrs. Osborne were interested and supportive of the colonists. However, in 1918, after losing an appeal through the courts, the colony was dissolved and the families were told to vacate the land.

In 1923, there was an attempt by leader Peter V. Verigin to move Doukhobors to Oregon to create a united community of Doukhobors and Molokans. There was precedent for this unification. In Russia in the seventeenth century, when these two groups rejected the Orthodox religion with its priests and icon worship, they were known as Spiritual Christians. Their split came in the 1730s when the leader Ilarion Pobirokhin rejected the Bible as the infallible word of God, calling it the "Troublemaker." Pobirokhin said that "man should broaden his outlook and worship God in spirit and in truth." His son-in-law, Semyon Uklein, maintained that the Bible was the sacred word of God and should be considered the only reliable authority in matters of faith. A large section of people followed Uklein and they became known as the Molokans.[23] However, Molokans and Doukhobors lived in close proximity in the Milky Waters area of Russia and under Tsar Nicholas I, the sects were both exiled to the Caucasus Mountains. Doukhobors immigrated to Canada in 1899 and many Molokans arrived in the United States in 1906.

Verigin purchased eight hundred acres of land close to the capital of Eugene and sent a vanguard of families to build and prepare for a larger group. With his death in 1924, this scheme was abandoned, the families returned to Canada and in 1928 his son Peter Petrovich Verigin sold the property.

On that day in 2016, we drove the hills west of Eugene and, on a narrow dead-end road, found the only remnant, a sign that read, "Dukhobor Road." Looking around at the hilly landscape beginning to be clothed in fall colours, and the vineyard next door, we felt the heavy sadness of a worthwhile project terminated with the murder of Peter V. Verigin, Lordly.

The peaceful passing of Savushka Popoff that Pete Maloff wrote about in this chapter was often remarked on by my mother Elizabeth. As she neared her life's end, she wished for a tranquil transition tuned in to the cycle of nature. The way Savushka took leave of his family, and his time on this earth, was her guide. She died just short of her 103rd birthday, with prayers of family around her.

---

23   Maloff, Section I, Chapter 1: "The Spiritual Origin of Doukhobor Beliefs and the Russian Sectarian Movement," in *Doukhobors: Their History, Life and Struggle*, ibid.

CHAPTER 5

LIFE IN OREGON

We reached Oregon in the winter. In comparison with Saskatchewan this was a heaven on earth. It was warm and green and the rivers shouted merrily. We were met by a delegation that had already settled. From the station we went by horse and wagon. Vasily V. Vereschagin fluently set forth the advantage of this land over cold Canada.

We settled and entered the new circumstances in a smooth and orderly way. We brought with us money so we suffered no undue hardship. Thanks to the help of the colonization carpenter, Alyosha Bloodoff, our home was soon ready for occupancy.

Life passed so pleasantly here that for several years, I lost sight of the Doukhobor horizon. Our colonists bought one thousand acres of land, which they subdivided. We were not far from the town of Peoria, in the valley of the Willamette River, an area stretching several hundred miles in length and from fifty to sixty miles in width. Majestic mountain ranges rose on each side of this valley. A Caucasian from Portland who visited us told us that the place reminded him very much of the Kuban River range.

The Willamette, what a rapid billowy twister it was! In winter, when it overflowed, we boys used to like to ride upon it, whole days at a time, on boats, sometimes to catch a supply of wood and sometimes just to watch the river. In Oregon nature itself uplifts and strengthens toward a better life. The whole atmosphere seems tireless, fresh and always alive. The trees are enormous, the air invigorating, and the rustle of the leaves of oak, maple and ash, as well as of other varieties of southern trees, gave intimations of inexplicable mystery.

Here I attended school and helped my parents in the work at home. My brother, Nikolai, was usually working and my sister Tanya was still a child. I passed Grade 10 and decided to leave school. I took a job with a surveyor, Mr. Eaton from Albany, and dragged the tapes, noted data and sometimes felled trees. Mr. Eaton became attached to me and insisted that I continue my schooling saying, "If you haven't the resources, I'll lend you enough to see you through university."

But fate willed it otherwise. I returned to high school and also took a course in wireless telegraphy, but further than this I did not go. From the farm I visited Portland several times a year. There, I especially enjoyed the river, the

Nikolai and Elizaveta Maloff's family joined a democratic Svoboda Colony of Freedom in Oregon in 1914. Their sons finished their high school education there and if not for American conscription in World War I they may have become part of the American "melting pot."

parks with their roses, and the theatres where talented artists made their appearances, and I lost no opportunity to visit such persons. I was fortunate enough to see Anna Pavlova, Caruso, Kreisler and others.

The initiators of our migration to Oregon were prominent men: Anton Savelievich Popoff, Vasily V. Vereschagin, M.F. Reibin, V. Lapshinoff and others. These men of character and intellect formed as select a group of Doukhobors as could be found anywhere. They had come to the conclusion that the community founded by Peter Vasilievich Verigin was not completely satisfactory in that it curtailed individual freedom and resorted to boycotting. So, these secessionists with reckless confidence sought a new abode as far as possible from the Doukhobor leaders.

Anton Savelievich Popoff was one of the main initiators of this migration. He was an indefatigable man, forever in search of the ideal place, and never finding it. More than once he travelled to various parts of the world with this end in view. He was in Florida, Cuba, Paraguay and in 1927 visited the Soviet Union. I remember how several times he vanished without a trace, and then would unexpectedly reappear in our midst. He had a sector of land in Oregon to which he intended to bring his family.

Every time he appeared, he aroused the interest of the colonists. He was sure to have some new idea. At our evening gatherings he would present his scheme for a future colony. He even drew plans and sketches of how the settlement would look and where the community home should stand. He especially liked to work out theories of how best to dry out the land and get rid of excess moisture and what varieties of fruit should be planted. In his outer appearance he reminded me of Vladimir Ilyich Lenin, and I suppose that his businesslike nature could also compare to his.

Another outstanding founder of our colony was Vasily Vasilyevich Vereschagin. Here was a man with the gentle character of a child and a constant aspiration toward Christian excellence. His zeal for more decency might almost have been called esthetic; a strict vegetarian himself, he strongly encouraged vegetarianism. He also abstained from alcohol. He was a man who brought cheer and goodwill wherever he went. All his life he upheld the Doukhobor principles, and never accepted allegiance, but his search for something better made him a wanderer throughout the earth. Before settling in our colony, he visited the Quakers in Philadelphia, but living there a whole year he did not find what he was looking for. He also went to California, Mexico and other places. Being with him filled my soul with happiness and eagerness to see him again. From his whole being there emanated an inexplicable attraction.

"We should prize Doukhobor attainments," he always said. Vegetarianism, abstinence from alcohol, and anti-militarism were his slogans. But to one opinion he strongly held to the day of his death: he refused to recognize the Doukhobor leaders. He partially infected me with his independent spirit, so that I was obliged to go through many winding trails before I gained the right road. He died in 1931. My recollections of him are of the noblest.

Alexei Vasilyevich Vereschagin, brother of Vasily Vasilyevich, was strongly built, severe and sober-faced. He was a talented speaker and a subtle critic. A veteran of the Siberian forests for his Doukhobor convictions, he held considerable sway in the affairs of our life. Whether he was at home or at work, even though only away for a day, you would be sure to see him with a newspaper or magazine sticking out of his pocket. If anyone wanted to know anything of what was going on in the world, Alexei Vasilyevich was the man to ask. He was up to date with all the news, including that which concerned Doukhobors. At times he would express his views on the Doukhobor communities, although he usually spoke of them in negative terms. He was especially pained that Doukhobors rejected education. On this basis he criticized the whole Doukhobor structure. Later in life he changed his views and, in many respects, began to defend what he formerly criticized.

A fourth was Gregory Fyodorovich Vanin. In character and appearance, he resembled Alexei Vasilyevich though they were not related by blood. Vanin, too, had gone through the Siberian exile for his Doukhobor ideals and he had passed through the trials of the disciplinary battalions where he had been subjected to thirty briar lashes. He was unquestionably a man of superior hardihood. Soon after his arrival from Siberia he decided to return to Russia. After living there several years he came back to Canada and soon migrated with his family to Oregon. His journey to Russia was not entirely fruitless. There he met Leo N. Tolstoy, Chertkov, P. Berukoff, V.D. Bonch-Bruevich and others. His free nature could not endure spiritual restrictions and though neutral in his feelings toward the Doukhobor community, he stood for full freedom of thought, and said that a man must rise above the level where someone else is needed to control his thoughts.

My father, Nikolai Petrovitch Maloff, presented a direct contrast to these great men. Naturally, he was under their influence, but from time to time his soul rebelled, and he would break out with the declaration that sooner or later we must return to the Doukhobor midst, or be lost. He and Nikolai Nikolayevich Davidoff would stand out against the Vereschagins' criticism of the Doukhobors for a time, but this opposition could not hold out for long.

Here likewise lived Pavil Yegorovich Popoff, Peter Zharikoff, Chutskoffs, Alyosha Popoff, and his son Ivan (the lame), two families of Davidoffs, Vasili Nikishin, the Drazdoffs whose father was quite a comedian, Vasili Ivanovich Bloodoff and others. They somehow took very little interest in community affairs.

There were many boys in the colony but few girls, twenty-five to two at this time. Under these circumstances, where could we go? In the evenings we would resort to "Ivan the Terrible," whose real name was Sherstobitoff. He had an original, even eccentric character. You could not convince him of anything. Sometimes while we were gathered at his table, if anyone put his elbows on the tablecloth, he would burst out, "Why do you always gather here; you have worn this tablecloth through already with your elbows." Once when my brother Nikolai tried to tease him, he seized his muzzle-loader—in contrast to the other colonists he still had a gun—and ran after Nikolai shouting, "I'm going to kill you!"

The other boys caught him, took his gun away and told him, "If you are going to act like that, we are going to throw your gun into the river."

He often boasted that once when a flock of geese were flying over, he fired, and two of them dropped right at his doorstep.

Near "the Terrible" lived his sister Paraniusha. She was married to Yegotia Popoff. Yegorushka was about twenty years her senior. He maintained that he was of the Tavria stock, and that he took part in the Turkish supply column. He would tell about a Cossack whom no kind of bullet could harm.

Our Colony of Freedom was so named by our leaders because this was the first centre of free Doukhobor life, where each had the full right to tell the truth and fear no one. Truly our life here was interesting. We captured the sympathy of the surrounding people by our industriousness and our rapid adaption to the new circumstances. Word of our success spread in all directions. Our brethren, the Molokans, visited us—Vasil Semyonovich Dobrinin, Kosser, Seapin and others. These two sectarian peoples—the Doukhobors and the Molokans—though they sprang from the same root, had after a century of separation become different in customs and habits.

The first year witnessed interesting debates on the subject of the Molokan and Doukhobor understanding of life. When matters touched upon anything in the past, the Doukhobors defended their own side and rebuffed the Molokans. The Molokan Vasil Semyonovich Dobrinin was a sharp and intelligent critic; from time to time he fired telling blows at our Doukhobors for their deviations from the basis of the Doukhobor faith. Our orators were ill-pleased with Dobrinin's pointed thrusts. My father in such cases would side with Dobrinin, and be glad that he triumphed over our speakers. In view of my youth, I took no part in such debates, but I was always an interested listener.

Vasil Semyonovich Dobrinin was a man of unusual animation and penetrating intelligence. He had served in the army in Russia and had spent three years in Moscow. Evidently his association with all kinds of people gave him an understanding of human nature because of which he could quickly orient himself with anyone. He settled in Peoria and in recent years has become a well-to-do farmer.

Vasil Semyonovich had a son, Andrei, of approximately my age. Andrei and I became close friends, and soon after our acquaintance, he protested against meat-eating, announcing to his family: "I am not going to eat any more meat." From that time on he was a vegetarian. My friendship with Andrei is one of the happiest recollections of my Oregon life.

Doukhobors from Saskatchewan, Molokans from California and many others visited us. Our settlement was also twice visited by one of the Sons of Freedom, Ivan Yefimovich Vlasoff. He would stay weeks at a time and preach complete freedom of man on earth. He even wanted to stay and live with us, but some of our brethren did not approve of him. They said, "He will just be getting on our nerves here, with his ideas."

Personally, I had nothing in common with him, perhaps because he once scolded me for carrying a violin, which I used to play now and then. He stopped me and wanted to smash it, but he returned it to me with the words, "You'd have done better to have learned to play on your own violin strings," said he, pointing to my throat.

Often Vanya Kanigan would come from Hillsboro where he had already lived for several years. By this time, he was an American citizen and tried to get others, among them my father, to accept American naturalization. My father refused even to listen to such advice:

"We have already wandered from the right path," he said, "by taking British citizenship. I wouldn't make another. We should repent our Canadian mistake."

During our five years of life in Oregon, there was not a single funeral. After we moved to California several families remained behind. Among them was the old man Savushka Popoff, Anton Savelievich's father. He lived with Davidoff, his son-in-law. Soon after our departure Savushka died. His last few hours on earth were characteristic of him.

Savushka Popoff was a Tavrian who left Tavria as a boy of twelve. Every time I passed the Davidoffs' I was almost sure to see him. Of medium height with a large black beard, he had a habit of tossing his head back as if he were always looking at the horizon. While he peacefully tended his geese, he would talk to himself.

One morning, as they afterwards told me, he rose early, came to the kitchen and announced, "Come here, everybody. I am going to die today and I want to bid you all farewell."

The family did not take this announcement seriously.

His daughter said, "Father, what are you saying? Are you still sleeping?"

Savushka looked at her and said, "No, I am not sleeping! Today I had a dream: my Tavrian comrades came after me, and took me with them to Tavria. Now you can tell me anything you like, but I know that today I shall die."

About ten o'clock he went outside, walked about, prayed to God and began to take his leave of earth: "Farewell sun, birds, trees and all you wide, wide world." He walked a few minutes longer, then fell. He never rose again. He died before his daughter's eyes.

Life in Oregon passed quietly for about four years, and then was suddenly cut short. There appeared to be serious shortcomings in the documents dealing with buying of the land. There were forty owners for a thousand acres. The documents were drawn up inadequately; if any one of the settlers failed to pay

Oregonian journalist Mrs. Osborne became good friends with Pete Maloff's mother, Elizaveta Maloff, and Masha Bloodoff. She advocated for the colonists when they lost their land due to a fraudulent land scheme.

his share, all the rest must lose their land too. Quite a commotion was created over this matter.[24] Neighbouring farmers and others, hearing of it, came to help us in our misfortune. A local trial was called.

On that occasion a Mrs. Osborne came from Eugene where she kept a luxurious café. Mrs. Osborne was a well-known journalist, who had served many years on the staff of the Portland *Oregonian*. She had travelled widely, crossing the ocean eight times. She was familiar with the Doukhobors from the time of their migration to Canada when the Philadelphia Quakers had sent her to Winnipeg to distribute resources they had collected. All the Doukhobors knew her and called her "our sister."

In our colony Mrs. Osborne became closely acquainted with Alyosha and Masha Bloodoff. My mother often spoke of how she and Masha were at Mrs. Osborne's café several times. She had a museum of Doukhobor handicrafts: even the famous grandsire Makortoff gave her an elegant piece of woodwork. Babushka Verigin had given her a Doukhobor skirt and an apron.

Mrs. Osborne took an active role in the defence of the colonists against the claims of the landlords. She procured a lawyer and invited a Russian interpreter from Portland. The trial was held in the nearby town of Albany. What an event this was. All the surrounding farmers gathered for the trial and became deeply interested in our fate. The interpreter, Vladimir Vladimirovich Gelvoni, proved to be a Russian in every sense of the word though he had lived in Portland for more than twenty-five years, serving as an engineer for the Southern Pacific

---

24   This land deal was reminiscent of fraudulent land schemes in Oregon a decade earlier, in which many people were indicted. *The Oregon Encyclopedia*, s.v. "Oregon Land Fraud Trials (1904–1910)."

Railways. He was amazed to find a Russian society so far removed from Russia. At that time, he was already well along in years, but showed himself to be in every respect a well-informed and intelligent man. His energetic, almost vehement efforts amazed many, and some people asked if this was one of the Doukhobor leaders from Canada come to defend them.

The trial lasted several days and the decision was most agreeably in our favour. But the owners soon appealed to a higher court and a few months later we were informed differently: this time the landlords had won and we were told to vacate the land. The decision shook the colony, and for a long time it could not recover. Little by little, the colonists began to leave. But this failure did not ruin everything: the Russian is not afraid to venture. Someone brought a rumour to our colony that the State of Colorado had virgin land for settlement. A meeting was gathered and a decision reached to send a delegate. My father was chosen to go.

It was the year 1915 on his way to Colorado that my father stopped in San Francisco and made the acquaintance of several Molokan brethren, especially the Sisoev family. There he also met Anton Petrovich Sherbak, editor of the *Tikhii Okean*, the *Pacific Ocean*. In conversation with Anton Petrovich, he mentioned that he had a son who was very eager to learn Russian grammar: would there be a place for him in the shop? Anton Petrovich gladly accepted this proposal.[25]

When my father returned from Colorado, he immediately sent me off to San Francisco to Anton Petrovich Sherbak. I was fifteen. Since then, I have never attended Russian school and only by additional study at home did I learn what little I know of reading and writing in the Russian language.

---

25   Anton Petrovich Sherbak published the Russian-language newspaper *Pacific Ocean* (*Tikhii Okean*) three times a week, first in Los Angeles from 1909 to 1915, then in San Francisco from 1915 to 1917. Subscriptions were $2.50 a year. Molokane.org/people/Sherbak_Anton/.

ON CHAPTER 6

SAN FRANCISCO AND
ANTON PETROVICH SHERBAK

[Vera] I never heard Grandfather Pete speak of Anton Petrovich Sherbak, but his influence shines in much of what he accomplished. Pete, as a lad of fifteen, was Sherbak's apprentice for nine months in San Fransisco. It was through working at his *Tikhii Okean* Russian-language journal that Pete began to learn the trade of publishing and his desire to write was kindled. In those short months, Sherbak's passion for justice, fairness and freedom was imprinted on Maloff for the rest of his life. It was Sherbak's achievement of starting a magazine and writing a book with little or no funding that boosted Maloff's belief that he too, with little money, could write and publish his history book, in the 1950s start the Russian *Literary Journal of Free Thought* and in the 1960s his *Anti-militarism and Vegetarian Idealism Magazine*.

As I search for information about Anton Sherbak, I realize that Doukhobor leader Peter Vasilievich Verigin and Sherbak must have met. Verigin arrived in Canada from his exile in Siberia in December of 1902 and Sherbak visited the Doukhobors in Saskatchewan in 1907, subsequently writing *The Kingdom of Russian Peasant Doukhobors*.

By 1907, the Canadian government had been demanding individual ownership of homesteads and an oath of allegiance from members of the Doukhobor community. A *New York Times* article of November of 1910 declared that Anton Sherbak was promoting the unification of all Spiritual Christians in a big Russian colony close to Santa Barbara. A meeting was convened in Los Angeles, on November 2, 1910, to discuss this possibility and Spiritual Russians from California, Mexico and Canada were invited.[26] Sherbak returned to Russia sometime at the end of the Russian Civil War, and it was in the 1920s that Verigin purchased the Oregon land; however, I like to think the vision may have had its origins at their first meeting when these two leaders sat down to chai in a pioneer Doukhobor village in Saskatchewan and discussed the idea of a united Molokan-Doukhobor community.

Pete Maloff lived with a Molokan family in San Francisco and developed

---

Molokane.org/people/Sherbak_Anton/.

a close friendship with the Molokan brethren. He kept this connection for years through trips to California and reciprocal Molokan visits to British Columbia. As a child, I remember these strong proud men and women at the Maloff farm, the men with full beards and women with their heads covered in *platkee* similar to those of the Doukhobor women. When I heard them sing at Doukhobor festivals, I was entranced by their beautiful rich voices and joyous movement, unlike the more sedate demeanour of singers in Doukhobor choirs.

Realizing this connection, in 1929, Doukhobor leader Peter Petrovich Verigin asked Pete Maloff to lead a Doukhobor choir to visit the Molokans. The Maloff family album has photos of these two groups with their arms clasped around each other's shoulders. Parked behind the posed photo of the choirs is a 1920s bus. A note underneath states that the Molokans hired the bus for the Doukhobor choir to travel to California.

Grandfather Pete wrote about his life as a teenager in San Francisco in 1915. Thousands of unemployed,

Петр Н. Малов
время пребывания у А. П. Щербаı

Pete Maloff apprenticed with Anton Petrovich Sherbak at his Russian-language journal in San Francisco.

hungry people gathered in the streets and parks. He attended worker meetings for a time, but became disheartened when he saw that he could do little to help. It was at these meetings where many spoke against American participation in the war. Scott Nearing and Ammon Hennacy were two such lecturers who, banned from the academic lecture circuit because of their pacifist beliefs, spoke to people in the streets. In Grandfather Maloff's library, I was to find several books gifted to him by these so-called radicals.

Chapter 6

San Francisco, 1915–1916

In the summer of 1915, I was approaching San Francisco, the metropolis of the west. It was a bright sunny day and our ferry slowly idled from Oakland. Most of the passengers were on deck straining their eyes toward the silhouette of man's miraculous works. Many of them who had never been to the west before were coming to see the World's Fair. They were perhaps as full of excitement and expectation as I; my soul was wild with anticipation of new experiences.

I reached Russian Hill and was soon at the home of Fyodor Timofeyevich Sisoev. He lived on Carolina Street. His was an ardent Molokan family; the father, a veritable giant, Timofey Lukyanovich, had three sons here and three who were left behind in Russia. They greeted me as warmly as if I was one of their own and showed me to a room the window of which overlooked the whole city.

In the evening the city was lit up by thousands and thousands of lights, especially in the direction of the fair. Hundreds of beams of artificial lights streaked high into the air and danced about in multicoloured radiance. Fyodor Timofeyevich explained that those wonder-lights were a memorial to the great Edison, who captured the power of electricity for us. That very evening Fyodor Timofeyevich took me through the whole of San Francisco; we even looked in on the fair.

After seeing all this my head began to spin and I felt like a frightened animal: "Just think what miracles men had performed, while we sat in the woods of Oregon and didn't know a thing about it."

Meeting Anton Petrovich Sherbak and Working at *Tikhii Okean*

Next day the old man, Timofey Lukyanovich, bustled me off to the office of Anton Petrovich Sherbak. He worked there, putting addresses on newspapers and hauling the sacks to the post office. This man of unusually massive bulk, with a beard that reached to his belt, often amazed me as he stood at the machines slapping on the prepared labels. His huge figure was completely out of harmony with the narrow dusty chambers of the printing shop.

This morning we came to Sansome Street, took an elevator to the third storey of the building and entered a large room where the office was and where all kinds of machines and presses were situated. Anton Petrovich was not there yet. At a writing desk sat a neatly dressed young man. Timofey Lukyanovich introduced him as the translator and compositor.

The young man rose, gave me his hand saying, "They call me Vasil Lukach."

Then they showed me the printing press and said, "You will work with us."

The old man Timofey Lukyanovich added, "You will work with him," pointing to Lukach. "He's a good man."

At this moment Anton Petrovich Sherbak walked in with rapid strides. He made a strong impression on me at first sight. He was of middle height, well-built, sober-faced, and his hair fell like a mane over his shoulders.

Timofey Lukyanovich said to him, indicating me, "Here is that worker from Oregon that Nikolai Petrovich Maloff promised to send." On saying this he smiled encouragingly.

Anton Petrovich came up, looked fixedly at me for a moment, then slapped me on the back and said, "Good! Now we shall have a Doukhobor on the staff, too."

Then he turned to me and said, "See that you learn well, and there is a lot to learn here. Look, there are the machines, linotype and presses in the cellar, translations, books and everything else. The first week you will have a holiday, help Dedushka Timofey Lukyanovich and make yourself acquainted with our printing works. Then we shall give you a steady job."

I began to paste on the addresses with the grandfather.

Vasil Lukach sat at the table translating. I could see that he wanted to start a conversation with me. He turned to me and asked, "And how are the Doukhobors?"

Before I had a chance to open my mouth Anton Petrovich in measured tones began to reply in my stead, "Vasil, what an inappropriate question—how are the Doukhobors? The Doukhobors are also people, clean, honest and good. I think perhaps a little better than you and I."

After this Vasil did not ask me about the Doukhobors.

A week later Anton Petrovich showed me what my responsibilities would be. The first thing in the morning I must run up to Market Street and buy three different morning papers for the office, then take the mail to Anton Petrovich's rooms. He lived about six houses from the office further up on California Street, in the Pacific Hotel. In the morning I came up with the mail and without knocking opened the door and walked in.

He took the mail saying, "The next time you come—knock at the door; that will be better."

Anton Petrovich occupied two or three rooms in the hotel. One room contained books and books and books and his work desk. Often, I would stare at all those books and wonder: Why have so many books? Anton Petrovich evidently guessed my perplexity and often asked me to rearrange the books in their proper order.

"Many make use of them, and they are often left in disorder."

Once I brought him the mail as usual and was going to go when Anton Petrovich stopped me and spoke to me kindly: "Trust yourself to me in everything. I myself am a father, and have brought up a big family—six sons and two daughters. You will be like my very own."

And truly, he kept this promise. When he had to go somewhere on business, he would often take me along. Several times he took me to the fair, explaining the significance of the various buildings and the remarkable exhibits. Indeed, he treated me as his own, clothed me, gave me spending money and was like another father to me. Gradually I became friendly with him and began to feel completely at ease in his presence.

Once he and I were left at the office when everyone else was gone.

He proposed to me that I should take the responsibility of setting the forms into the presses. "This is a very important part of the printing," said he. "If the forms of type are not set properly, they can fly out and do a lot of damage, perhaps even kill someone. That's the first thing to learn in printing."

I told him that I was afraid that I would not be able to manage it.

He rose to his feet and sternly asked, "What do you mean you can't? Do you think people are born with knowledge? Don't you ever talk such nonsense to me again!"

I put in the forms for the first time, tested them with a little hammer and took them down to the cellar for printing.

A couple of hours later when I brought the papers up to him, he chuckled, "Now, then, look! And you said that you couldn't manage!"

When Anton Petrovich finally became convinced that I understood the full significance of this responsibility, he quickly composed himself and began to ask about the Doukhobors and their life. He asked a whole series of questions: Who was Ivan Evseevich Konkin and what kind of a position did he hold in the community? Was it true that Peter Vasilievich ruled the Doukhobors like a monarch? Why do the Doukhobors refuse schooling? Why did most of the Siberian martyrs leave the community? What kind of a man was Semyon Vereschagin? Why did the Doukhobors take their clothes off? But what could I tell him? I was a poor Doukhobor; I grew up far from the Doukhobor centre and knew next to nothing. For that matter I was still too young to have interested myself in such matters. I knew nothing of what he asked and gave him confused indefinite answers.

Anton Petrovich was intensely interested in the Doukhobors. He never missed an opportunity of contact with them. He personally met several of the more prominent members and carried on an active correspondence with them. He eagerly questioned all of them, but this did not satisfy him, and he could not fully understand this puzzling subject that troubled him so acutely. Perhaps by taking me into his employ he thought that I might be able to enlighten him. Once I saw he was visibly disappointed by my vague replies and this worried me.

"Look," he said, "I am not a Doukhobor, but I have written a booklet about you." He pointed to a stack of books on which I could see the title *The Kingdom of Russian Peasant Doukhobors.* There were many of them, perhaps several hundred. They lay in a stack on his desk; evidently, they were recently off the press.

"I visited you in Saskatchewan: in Blaine Lake, in Yorkton," he continued. "I even tried to get your people freed from prison."

These insistent questions about the Doukhobors swept me off my feet, and I often tried to avoid talking with him. I was very much ashamed that I knew so little about my own people and their life.

In the years 1915–16, the United States had not yet entered the World War but apparently Europe's confusion could not leave them in peace, and in San Francisco the army that was in preparation began its parades. There were days of celebration when they marched through the main streets in full regalia, swinging to the tune of their ceremonial marches and accompanied by the terror-inspiring thunder of the huge bass drum. They exhibited a proud scorn for everything not military. On watching the parade, the question arose: "Is all this necessary? These are supposed to be intelligent people, educated, but yet, there they go, banging at their drum and strutting about like so many bantams, and, to top it off, they even drag a cannon behind them. I doubt if the wildest savages could have made greater fools of themselves."

The World's Fair continued and I often went there, though even the fair soon became boring. There were times when I felt extremely lonely. Then I'd ride all over the city so as not to have to stay in any one place. My soul was restless and I wanted something new, something different, but what—I did not know. No end of questions arose in my mind, but the answers I could not find. I did not quite dare to ask Anton Petrovich, and besides, he was always so busy.

Sometimes I would attend workers' meetings, where gifted orators tried to stir up the working man to think for himself, instead of having someone else always leading him by the nose. But all this was just talk; reality presented an entirely different picture. There were thousands of unemployed, many were suffering from hunger, begging, ragged and uncared for. I gave all I could but soon I saw that I could not help them all, and I gave up going there, so as not to witness their misery.

Best of all I liked to visit Golden Gate Park. There I walked along the trails, sat under practically every tree and hedge and at last got up and went elsewhere. Or else I would walk south along the seashore for a mile or more. At that time, it was all uninhabited; there was not a single house in sight. I used to sit down under a tree and listen to the rumble of the ocean waves; now they would stealthily crouch, whispering among themselves, deciding how to make their strong attack upon the shore. Then a wave would rush at a rock lying in its path and shower me with salt spray.

It seemed to me that God himself breathed here: the ocean was his lungs, the sun his eye, and the stars, they were his children or perhaps his grandchildren; and so I sat there, whole hours at a time, and under the spray of the ocean waves forgot myself in my fantasies and dreams. Sometimes I would stay there till nightfall, and the moon would roll out, and the stars, so clear and close that I could almost reach them by stretching out my hand. "What a big family God has!" I thought, "and he never quarrels with them, and neither do they quarrel among themselves; they don't need any parades with cannons and bass drums. How they all shine with the light of kindness, and warmth, extending their friendship to everybody on earth. They say, 'Look up at us. We sparkle with thousands of fires of life, we rejoice and are happy.'" In such enraptured moments I would exclaim, "Oh you, great and mighty Creator of all worlds and kingdoms, when will man at last understand and truly prize the vastness of your creation?"

Then, as if under a spell, I would rise and walk back and forth. Unconsciously my gaze would wander toward the city and this scene would produce contradictory thoughts and feelings. From a distance the town was a vast collection of yellowish lights, intermingling in one huge ball of radiance, now brilliantly clear, now a dull smoky glimmer. Gazing at this intermittent ball of light, the city appeared to me as some sort of enormous beast. I even imagined that I heard the crunching of insatiable, gluttonous jaws hungry for more drink, more excitement, more pleasure, debauchery, robbery, murder. Here, in that death-hole, I thought, lie the germs of the irrepressible urges of human flesh, of the body and of the blood. Here is waged the ceaseless struggle of people, of friends, of foes trampled under every kind of artificially created, conflicting conditions of pleasure, pain, rapture, terror, of safety and of peril. Here, and nowhere else, lies the tragic, fatal root of man's self-deception.

Every Monday morning my friend Anton Petrovich would ask me, "Peter, where were you yesterday?"

"At the seashore."

"Whom did you go there with?"

"Alone!"

"And you'd just sit there alone? You should at least have taken some book along. You would have enjoyed yourself more."

"I enjoyed it very much without a book."

"Next Sunday," said Anton Petrovich, "I'll take you with me to Berkeley."

We went. Anton Petrovich was unusually kind to me this time and we joked all the way. We visited a Russian family, and then dropped in on a newly arrived Professor Kahn on the Slavonic faculty at the university.

Anton Petrovich praised me profusely wherever we went, saying, "This is an heir of those famous Russian peasants who performed such miraculous feats in Russia in their struggle against militarism."

The Molokans and Anton Petrovich Sherbak

Anton Petrovich often visited the Sisoevs, where I lived. I recall one memorable night he was invited for tea by one of the Sisoev brothers, I think it was Vasili. The Molokans have a custom that when a stranger is invited, they also invite for their guests some of the more honourable members of their brotherhood. And so it happened this time: there gathered, besides Anton Petrovich, several elderly Molokans. Timofey Lukyanovich, the father of the Sisoev brothers, and their uncle Nikolai Lukyanovich, Grandfather Slivkov and also two middle-aged men of wealth from Los Angeles, both Jumpers as the Molokans call themselves. One of them had a beard as red as blood.

A very serious discussion got under way. Anton Petrovich as usual began to express his strong convictions.

"My friends, Molokans, watch this America closely; it is extremely dangerous. On the surface it glitters, hums and seems friendly enough, but it gulps down human souls at every breath. You are strong in character; that is good! But I'm afraid, my friends, that after living a while in this America, you will become wealthy, own a lot of machines and the Messiah whom you await will never be able to lead you out from here."

Anton Petrovich stopped, glanced at them and continued: "Now this Bible before us: it is a huge volume, interesting, and much of everything is written in it. You say that it is deep and that much good is contained there. I agree with you, but with one stipulation: only for one who knows how to get at it. To me, the Bible is like the ocean bottom; only a good swimmer or a good diver can bring up a pearl from its depths, another can easily drown in the attempt, as most people have done in the world today. Don't you think that they read the Bible, too? Look how many and what luxurious churches there are in San Francisco alone. And Bibles are everywhere in thousands and are being read by millions of people every day.

"Why shouldn't you, my friends, Molokans, simplify your search, and make it more easily attainable for your youth? Why not sometimes accept some treasures from others, for example, from Leo Tolstoy. He has brought to the surface many jewels from the ocean bottom. Why don't I ever see his books in your homes? Instill his ideas in your children and you will gain much yourselves. But the Bible, as I have said, is good only for him who understands it, but another will lose himself in it. What is this Bible? A book in which is recorded the history of man, both the good and the bad."

The bearded Molokans sat as if they were frozen to their places, sober and silent. You could see that they did not like such ideas as Anton Petrovich put forward.

Only one Molokan, Fyodor Timofeyevich, answered: "I also, my dear Anton Petrovich, advised my brethren to start a library, where we would be able to read not only Tolstoy, but I think we should also read Maxim Gorky, Nekrasov, Akunsov, Sherbak and others, and also include magazines and newspapers. We could have lectures in it too."

It was evident that Anton Petrovich was very pleased with this statement. "Very good! Now you're talking some sense, Fedya. Man needs the full light and we need not be afraid of it, no matter from where it breaks through. And why are you so silent, brother Molokans? Or have Fyodor and I been reasoning incorrectly?"

Nikolai Lukyanovich was a well-built man, with a wide forehead. His long nose and beard gave him an imposing appearance, suggesting one of the ancient prophets.

He cleared his throat impressively, and turning to Anton Petrovich began in measured tones, "You were not reasoning correctly. Perhaps I may not be able to express it all in words, but my heart tells me that you, Anton Petrovich, and my nephew here are gravely mistaken! You see, the difference is, Anton Petrovich, that we have different religions: learned men cannot understand our spiritual matters. I know only this: if our youth began to read worldly books instead of studying the sacred scriptures, that you might just as well throw them into the ocean, for all the good they will be. When we read worldly books, we

Molokans and Doukhobors share a love of singing and have exchanged visits with choirs such as this Molokan brotherhood choir. Many of their common hymns originated in Russia. Pete lived at the home of Fyodor Timofeyevich Sisoev, seated on the right.

lose the Holy Spirit. That is why we do not want worldly books for our youth."

To Anton Petrovich this reply seemed absurd. "Oh brother Molokans," he said, "is this some kind of a new joke you are trying to play on men? Either I can't understand what you mean or you can't understand it yourselves and don't know what you are talking about."

Anton Petrovich laughed and repeated the words several times: "They'll lose the Holy Spirit; they'll lose the Holy Spirit! Nikolai Lukyanovich, please explain, I can't understand you. Let's reason this out: We have the Spirit of Life in its magnificent scope and elusiveness and supposing that you should read some kind of worldly book, what then—does the Holy Spirit vanish into the air? I again repeat, I can't understand this at all."

Nikolai Lukyanovich rose and said, "I can't tell you anything more, except more of the same. There is a great difference between wisdoms of the world and wisdom of God. And they can never mix together and will never agree."

Here the Los Angeles brother with the red beard arose and, raising his hand, began imposingly, "Believe me, Anton Petrovich, the Holy Spirit is not found in the wisdom of man, but its might is manifested in the living spirit. Man's teaching blinds the mind of simple people. Christ told us, 'I am the light of the world,' and also Christ has proclaimed: 'I am the door, and whoever enter not by my gate, the same is a thief and a robber.'"

Anton Petrovich, seeing their persistence, said, "Well, I am not going to quarrel with you, have it your way. Only I tell you that you shouldn't shut yourself up in a narrow spiritual cage, as if to say 'Don't anyone look at our affairs. We already have everything that is good.' Hold your door wide open, and look in on others more often and I am certain that you will not lose your spirit, but will refreshen it."

Truly, my life in San Francisco was on the whole diverse and interesting. During the day I worked in the printing shop and in the evenings, I walked or rode wherever I liked. Sometimes Fyodor Timofeyevich would take me to the Molokans' singing parties. He had a surprisingly soft baritone and many people used to flatter him: "What a voice, in Russia there is Shalyapin, and here we have Fyodor Sisoev." And truly he sang beautifully.

Sometimes he would come to my room and insist, "Let's sing some kind of song together." But what could I do, I had no voice at all for singing!

Then he would sing along till his brothers would pound on the floor above us, calling out, "Enough or you'll wake the children."

Fyodor Timofeyevich would often jest with me saying, "Well, so Sherbak is going to make a writer out of you. And why not? Anton Petrovich is quite a man. I'd give him every one of my children to bring up, if he'd take them. Well, Peter, you'll rattle off newspapers and I'll sing. And so together we will go out into the world. How will that be, good?"

"Not bad," I replied.

PHILOSOPHY AND NUDITY OF THE SONS OF FREEDOM

[Vera] Anton Petrovich Sherbak was fascinated with the Doukhobor Sons of Freedom and arranged a meeting with them and his Molokan and Russian friends in San Fransisco. Pete Maloff recorded Ivan Vlasoff explaining the Sons of Freedom Doukhobor philosophy. Sherbak became sympathetic to their point of view, until, after the discussion, the Sons of Freedom stripped off their clothing. Upon learning this Sherbak threw out his idealist vision of these Doukhobors.

In 1928, when Pete Maloff and his family returned to Canada, he formed a close association with the Sons of Freedom and wrote extensively about their philosophy. He believed the Sons of Freedom stayed true to their Doukhobor principles and he wholeheartedly joined them in peace demonstrations. In 1929, nine Doukhobor organizers, including Maloff, led a walk on Baker Street in Nelson, BC, protesting against land taxes being diverted toward military purposes. City firemen responded by dispersing the seventy marchers with blasts of water from fire hoses. The organizers, including Maloff, were arrested and charged for obstructing a police officer and spent six months doing hard time in Oakalla Prison.

Despite his involvement with the Sons of Freedom, Pete Maloff was not a proponent of their use of nudity. He said, "I have often told them that I do not share their ideas about nudity. Of course, I see nothing especially terrifying or criminal about it. I consider it to be unjust to put men into prison for several years for publicly appearing nude. But at the same time, I consider it to be more decent, especially in our environment, to wear clothes. If men are so afraid of others' nudity, they must not be forced to observe it. I have said to the Sons of Freedom, 'If someday I should accept your point of view completely, even then I would insist that you have applied this weapon too often and its use could in many cases have been avoided. You weaken this weapon of yours through too much use, and it will soon lose its power.' But all my words and arguments brought no results."[27]

---

27   Maloff, Part II, "Sons of Freedom" chapter, in *Doukhobors: Their History, Life and Struggle*, ibid.

Protesting stark naked had shock value, but many—even supporters of the Sons of Freedom—called it stark madness. In 1932, the government responded to nude protests by introducing a law that public nudity be punished by three years in a federal jail. In the spring of that year, 570 Doukhobor men and women were arrested for protesting in the nude against the loss of their land and the incarceration of their Doukhobor leader, saying, "You have taken our outer garments, you may as well take our underwear too." They received a three-year sentence in a prison on Piers Island that was specially built for the peaceful protestors. The children of those imprisoned, 365 youngsters, including my mother Elizabeth and her four siblings, were taken into government institutions.

How did the Maloff family become involved in this tragic circumstance? I was to find out that while Pete was in the Oakalla Prison, his father, Nikolai, was arrested for being at a nude protest. With their breadwinners in jail and the five Maloff children between six months and twelve years old, Elizaveta and Lusha had no financial support. Not realizing the drastic consequences, they decided to join the protestors. Lusha and Elizaveta were both sentenced to three years' imprisonment on Piers Island. My mother Leeza was taken to the British Columbia Industrial School for Girls,[28] her siblings held in an orphanage and the youngest, Nadya, was in foster care. I was not aware of the extent of this incarceration until years later when my mother told me about her confinement. She always felt she had done something wrong to have her family jailed.

Visiting One of the First Russian-Ukrainian Settlers in California

Anton Sherbak introduced Pete to a Ukrainian American publisher, Agapiy Goncherenko, whose residence has now become a historic park in California. Pete was to regret his childish response to this visit; instead of a famous person he could have learned much from, he saw an ill old man.

I went on a search of the history of Agapiy Goncherenko. *Bibliography: The Russian Press in the United States* by David Shub states that in 1864, Priest Agapiy Goncherenko was one of the first Ukrainian-Russian refugees in the United States. In 1860 in Russia, he had been arrested for contributing to the anti-tsarist magazine *Kolokol*, but escaped from prison and fled to England, then to the United States. Following the purchase of Alaska in 1867, the American government offered to subsidize a Russian American newspaper to introduce the former Russians to the "American way of life." Supported financially by the

---

28   A reform school for wayward girls.

United States government, Goncherenko published the *Alaska Herald* from his base in San Francisco and also ministered to the Russian-Ukrainian residents. Goncherenko continued to be persecuted by the Russian Orthodox Church—even in the United States—for his opposition to the church's use of serf labour. To escape the harassment, he moved to a remote area in the hills of California, now the site of the park Ukraina.

CHAPTER 7

ANTON PETROVICH SHERBAK

Anton Petrovich was an exceptional man. The features of his face were sympathetic and he charmed everyone with his general appearance. He spoke in a resounding bass voice, and his head of hair was indeed a magnet. Often, as I accompanied him on the streetcar, I would notice curious glances cast his way.

He sometimes stayed at the editorial office whole days at a time, interviewing visitors. And who did not come to visit him? They all came—intelligentsias, workers, the poor, the idealists and the fools, of every nationality.

Whenever anyone asked him of what nationality he was he had a characteristic reply:

"I am a Kharkov Hohol [Ukrainian]!"

One day two Doukhobors walked into his office: Ivan Yefimovich Vlasoff and Fyodor Petrovich Rezansoff. They were part of the group who, beset by an indomitable spiritual urge to serve God, were going to the Hawaiian Islands in search of the Promised Land, where they could establish an ideal life.

Anton Petrovich, inviting these distinctive Doukhobors in, sent me for Fyodor Ivanovich Melikov, a prominent resident of San Francisco. Melikov was also interested in such raw material. Anton Petrovich telephoned Dolgei and in a short time quite a company assembled. On the one side were the Russian intelligentsias; on the other, simple peasants, the Doukhobors. Anton Petrovich was obviously very much interested in these men and was noticeably excited.

A serious dispute was soon raging on the subject of civilization; whether it was beneficial or actually harmful.

Ivan Yefimovich Vlasoff Explains
Doukhobor Sons of Freedom Philosophy

Anton Petrovich suggested, "Here they are, genuine specimens of the Russian peasant. If their kind does not bring truth and freedom to the world, then I do not know where we can find it. Well, Vlasoff, tell us about your Doukhobor truth."

Vlasoff was an original, a resourceful character, who could speak logically. "We, Sons of Freedom," he began, "never dreamed, but always understood life simply, just as it is. We live by faith and believe that we can be free. But your life, the life of the learned men, is not good at all. The last war in Europe proves it. You see, in your civilization everything is sacrificed to mannerly habits, everything is shallow polish: neckties, red lips, bathtubs, dances and the like, but the conscience and the soul are left out. And so, we call your education banditry and false in every respect. Your learning is supposed to ease the life of man, but what is it doing? It is inventing cannons that can shoot farther."

Here Dolgei impatiently protested, "Why do you mix everything together, Vlasoff? You should separate the good from the bad. Use science for beneficial purposes and the cannons will be left useless. Your thoughts are suffering from conceit. You are clouding the issue, Mr. Vlasoff."

"Well, you certainly are," angrily retorted Vlasoff, "sitting around in the city with all kinds of cannons and defences around you. Nikolai Lukyanovich took us last night to see your naval fleet. And if that's what you call clear, then we have nothing to talk about here, and might as well go."

Vlasoff and his friend rose to leave. Anton Petrovich grasped Vlasoff by the shoulder and said, "No, no, you're not going anywhere; we are going to talk. You, Dolgei, be still."

Vlasoff thought for a moment, glanced at them all and said, "Last night we saw your battleships, took one look at those long cannons and said to ourselves, 'Wise men they are, ordering and storing up hate and death for the future. Look what cannons they have, those muzzles sticking out in both directions.' We counted twenty-five ships, and, taking a closer look at them, we saw that on every one, thousands of sailors were strutting about. What clothes and food they must need to go on making such asses of themselves! And besides they tell us that every ship costs over $25 million to build, and it's you who pay the taxes, Mr. Working Man, so that they can make those cannons. And that's your proletariat for you, your everlasting toiler! I ask you: Whose hands built these colossal forms of evil? His; and whose hands could have as suddenly turned the fate of man in an entirely opposite direction?

"No matter how much he shouts, the working man himself has not yet groped close enough to the right door to be able to open it. The savage goal of these twenty-five battleships is witness to that. Man doesn't want to live naturally and die peacefully; he has to have these long cannons to smoulder in their fire so that he can weep at the mock laughter of their explosions. What a horrible price man will pay for such blunders! Yes, believe me, man will pay and pay dearly for all this. How pitiful is poor man. How skilfully and cleverly he is appeased by his various overlords. All they need to do is to shout, and wave a few slogans of such ineptitude as courage, heroism and patriotism over their heads and these slaves will come by the thousands and prostrate themselves: Come on, we are ready to die.

"But just think: If this energy were directed toward a better, more righteous cause, what good it will bring to all the people. I will also say this: for this fraud, this masquerade of shrewd clowns, man will one day suffer in poisonous horror, because of his contradictions to the law of life. Man is an intelligent being and shouldn't be dancing about to the music of these bloodthirsty fools. The world thinks that it is good to have private possessions, lots of wealth, land, money and so on, but we Sons of Freedom say: this is evil, this is an illusion. No one has the right to keep to himself what God gave to all.

"Personally, I may even say this." Here Vlasoff got up, his black hair and beard quivering and his black eyes glittering like buttons. "As soon as you get a hundred dollars and put them somewhere in the bank or in a can, you hang a devil around your neck; two hundred, two devils, and once you get a thousand—you've got a whole devil's colony sitting on top of you."

At this point an Armenian, a storekeeper, walked into the office. He often dropped in for a paper, and knew Anton Petrovich very well. His head was high and, it seemed, almost precariously set on his shoulders.

Anton Petrovich introduced the guests. "Doukhobors," he said. "Get acquainted with them."

"What? Doukhobors?" He turned wide-eyed to the guests. "Bayrock and my father were friends. He used to say, 'How wise and good is a Doukhobor, there is none on earth to compare with him.' The Doukhobors of the Caucasus burned their guns. What are you doing now? Tell me your program," the Armenian asked the Doukhobors.

"I do not know what you mean by a program," said Vlasoff, "but our understanding I can explain," and here Vlasoff said a few words to him in Armenian.

The Armenian laughed heartily. "There's a Doukhobor for you; he has not forgotten Armenian. But do you mean really, Doukhobor, tell me the truth, do you mean it seriously when you say money is a devil or maybe you are joking?"

"Money is not only a devil," said Vlasoff, "but it is one of the devil's temptations, poisoning the whole race. But we should make our life so that we could live without it."

Here the Armenian jumped up, protesting passionately: "Doukhobor, your head has gone crazy. How my store run without money? How me buy at the bazaar and how without money my store sell?" He appealed to Anton Petrovich: "Tell me, does Doukhobor say we can be without these?" He took a wad of paper banknotes out of his pocket.

Anton Petrovich calmed him. "Well, Artes, let's hear their program and then we shall see if we can, or cannot."

"Good, I agree," said Artes, "but I have no time. I go but you will after tell me how Doukhobor know to run my store without money."

The Armenian left, and Vlasoff continued on the same theme.

"We, Sons of Freedom, invite man to complete freedom, not somewhere in the air, but here, on earth, and such that man, even though without wings, could fly. And we see now after many years of experience that it is possible to reach. Only we must understand one most important thing: We should neither own, nor hoard, nor be greedy for anything. Nothing in this earth is mine; everything is God's and belongs to us all together. And it is given to me only for a time, and only as much of it as I need to live my life honestly, and not one bit more. Everything above this is theft and robbery against my own brother—man. Our ownership should be limited to the pack on our shoulders and that's all. Then life would be happy for all on earth. Because, what kind of a system is this?

"Here Fedya"—he pointed to his friend—"and I stopped at Chico to earn a little money for the road. We are going to Hawaii, you see, we want to live more on fruit. We believe that way man can get rid of his sin more easily. Well, we hired out to a Mr. Kaiser, to weed corn, and he turned out to have a hundred thousand acres of land. Just to think of it makes your hair stand on end. We began to talk with him: 'Why do you have such a large acreage, when others are in need of land?' But he shouted at us that it was none of our business. 'A hundred thousand acres,' says he, 'that's rubbish; near San Francisco one rich man owns a million and a half, and one in Texas owns three million; that's something. I'm boss here and I have the right to either keep it or sell it, just as I like.' But we told him that there is just one boss, God, and that all the rest of the bosses were just devils. For this he chased us away. 'If you don't like it,' he said, 'then go on.'"

"Then what do you think we should do, Vlasoff, so that there would be happiness for everybody on earth?" asked Melikov.

"Happiness, my friend, is not easily found. We cannot gain it unless by struggling toward a righteous end. But what kind of happiness and what kind of end are we striving for?" continued Vlasoff. "Why this suffocation in the licentiousness and debauchery? There is a healthier standard for a life philosophy: we call it love and brotherly regard for each other. But what kind of regard can we have here in town? Truth is one, there aren't ten of it.

"For example, take your San Francisco. Why did these people all crowd in? I ask you, what is the sense of these fifteen-storey buildings? To us, they're prisons. And what's more, I tell you: you city people are hanging on the neck of the land workers. Just imagine how much work on the land is needed to feed all of you, and to bring the food here to you. And, most important, life in such congestion isn't healthy. People sit in their prison houses, and because of their unnatural manner of life, invent every kind of fable, stupidity and rubbish, or, to say it more correctly, still more chains for their own selves.

"Yes, and who is it that thinks up these wars? It's the town people who have nothing else to do. Here the soul dries up and shrivels, and man, no matter how much he tries to build himself up and better his life, cannot, because around him are all kinds of pitfalls. We know and say: man cannot attain his real growth there, because here we have a wolfish life, the survival of the fittest. But all people should be living on the land and, as has been said, 'by the sweat of their brow earn their bread and their living.' And then we'd see what all the lords who rule the earth would do, how many wars and other plots they would be able to think up. And I also say man can survive and become a living stronghold only on the land. If the working man wasn't a fool, and didn't push into the cities, then there wouldn't have been a place for bankers, the rich, and their servants, the preachers, to nestle. But he, the poor worker, himself hung them on his neck and now hauls them around, and futilely curses, that they are such bloodsuckers. We say—away with this rotten civilization," concluded Vlasoff.

"What do you mean? How is it rotten?" asked Melikov.

Anton Petrovich quickly caught Vlasoff's meaning and explained to Melikov, "He meant to say that our civilization has turned into toilet accessories; that is, enamelled sinks, bathtubs, coiffures, but man himself is forgotten."

The whole gathering livened up. Old Timofey Lukyanovich also became interested in Vlasoff's speech.

Someone even said, "That's telling them, Vlas!"

All were silent for a time, as though that question was settled.

Then Dolgei began to search for a question to pin Vlasoff's ears back with. He apparently thought of one, smiled to himself, turned to Vlasoff and asked, "Tell me, Vlasoff, the honest truth: Do you believe in God, and what does he look like to you?"

"Oho, the recognition of God—that's another matter altogether. That's no question to fool around with here, brothers. I would like to ask you: Why is it that you walk on the earth and don't fall through? Why do you breathe air in all the time and never choke? A question about God is not a common question. You can't describe him in words. Last night, for instance, Fedya and I were riding on a streetcar, still on this Hawaiian business, and so we sat there, it was cozy. The streetcar went swiftly and we were beginning to think it quite a handy thing, this streetcar, when you need it. When would we be able to get all the way here, to your place, if we were to walk? We came to a crossing and, looking, we saw an automobile shoving along—slam right into the streetcar. Lights and fenders flew every which way. Good thing the streetcar just started or there would have been pudding, and I guess we may be a part of it too. They got after us—you're witnesses; to court; who's right and who's wrong? We only got away by saying we're leaving on the boat tomorrow. Well seeing this mix-up, we thought to ourselves: My, man, but you're a stupid creation; you can't even see a wide-open road ahead of you, and yet you try to stick your nose into something else. But our God, he does everything without knocking and slamming, and he does it wonderfully well. Every day the sun rises and shines and never forgets and is never late either. And the stars in the sky and the moon all spin round, shuffle around and never crash into another. The oceans, the rivers, the forests all have their order and their beauty, not like this San Francisco, just dust and noise."

Timofey Lukyanovich here could no longer contain himself and in simple sincerity appealed to Vlasoff. "And you believe that God is the centre of all life, of the universe? Tell me, what should be done, then, for instance, what should the Molokans do? We did not come to live here in this town forever. We went away, but had to come back again."

"Even if you have to come back ten more times, you still have to get out of this Babylon," Vlasoff replied. "Away from these towns; that's the first step toward a righteous life, and the second step, of course, is true honesty, and not only in words but also in notions, deeds, well, simply, in all our life. Right now, everybody is trying to better our lives by words. Listen to the different preachers and priests—they chirp like nightingales, but what's the good? It's just talk! No, here we need effort, and how! Without effort you cannot gain the freedom of the spirit. If you just start to live as truth demands, you'll be dragged to prison before you know it, and thrown in so hard that you might be able to get up and you might not.

"Just think of it: a war in Europe, and why? Because people follow worthless leaders; worthless because they are all rogues and scoundrels, thinking only of their own individual interests. Do you think men like that can bring the people to any good? Never! It is men like that who cause life to run in zigs and zags; not ahead, but backwards. That is why man has become backward to the issue of real life," finished Vlasoff.

Dolgei was silent for a moment and then said, "You just said that all we need is a pack on our shoulders. But how are you going to support your family? Perhaps you could get along that way yourself but you can't carry your wife and children on your back."

"You do not understand us," said Vlasoff. "We were talking of our aspirations, of our aims, what we should strive for. Man could have paradise, and not somewhere else, but right here on earth, but instead he builds himself a madhouse and tries to drive everyone into it. I ask all of you smart ones: Do they build a highway without markers? I guess not. First, they look the path over, plant the markers and only then do they begin to build the road and walk and ride along it. So it is in spiritual life; it also requires its pioneers, engineers and builders. And how else did you think?

"You referred to the family and the children, as though we did not think about this important problem. But is the question about the family and its needs, the children, correctly answered in our present time? There's still the question of whether we should give birth to so many children as are being brought forth into this world of suffering and madness today. Is marriage only to enslave the female to serve the lust of the male? Just yesterday our Molokan brother Nikolai Lukyanovich Sisoev brought to our attention something that you clever ones haven't said a word about. Nikolai Lukyanovich said that you have here, in San Francisco, in the Chinese sector up to ten thousand women, with permission of the law to live there, whose only occupation is to satiate the lusts of men. Give her a dollar and kiss her and do anything else you like with her. Ten thousand licensed, and, I suppose, about ten thousand unlicensed. And is this what you call life?

"And it is the same in every town. Just think of how we are living and how these masses live, wallowing in debauchery, crazed by opiates and liquor and infected by every kind of disease. No one should live like this; it's absurd and sinful. Man has become worse than any living animal. Animals recognize the natural order of sexual life, but man has lost every sense of order. And we, Sons of Freedom, have just about revealed the secret why man has become entangled and is tumbling into such a pitfall. It is because man has wandered away from the law of nature, lives improperly and, especially, feeds improperly, overheating his blood with meat-eating, liquor and tobacco and every kind of stimulant. And so, it turns out that man has no other alternative but to have in readiness hundreds of thousands of mothers to satisfy their animal cravings. Here our brother Nikolai Lukyanovich was right when he said that if it weren't for these ten thousand prostitutes, the soldiers and sailors would be dragging decent respectable girls and women out of their homes to satisfy their lust. There's the answer to our question. The city cannot live otherwise. It is the greatest stronghold of the god of war.

"But according to us, the mother is the door of the human race. We must respect her as the more sacred body, that is, to recognize the father only as the seed, and the mother as the body in which the seed grows. But we have invented all kinds of fables such as wives, lovers, mistresses and so forth, and are only spending our time thinking about how we are going to get that mother under us. But civilization with its wars goes still further and further into licentiousness. That's where the trouble lies, my learned friends. We talk of this so that we can find a more righteous way of life, so as to overpower the beast within us and give the better nature a chance to answer. But you are afraid that you might lose that beast. We do not say that we have attained all this; far from it. I am not even satisfied with my own self and my animal cravings, and I am waging a struggle with myself to better myself," triumphantly concluded Vlasoff.

"The ideas that you preach may be possible to a few Progressivists, but to the majority they are not acceptable. But, nevertheless, your thoughts are interesting," said Dolgei.

Anton Petrovich jumped up enthusiastically: "This, Doukhobors, I understand. This, is the honest to goodness truth! Man should watch his step and see where it's leading him. A man like that is worth a king's ransom. Thanks a lot, Vlasoff."

But Melikov interrupted him. "Wait Anton Petrovich. We haven't yet finished talking with your peasants. We like to know from Vlasoff how to live without money."

"How? Here's how!" said Vlasoff. "You see this shirt on me, and these pants, and these shoes? We made them ourselves from flax. I grew it and spun it with Akayula, my companion. Now tell me: What do we need from your townspeople? And soon we'll get to the bananas, and just sing all day long, and here you will be in the dust and noise if you don't listen to reason."

Anton Petrovich again rose and said, "All your thoughts I sincerely welcome, but I think you are making a mistake by going to Hawaii. What good will come of it if you will be sitting in a bush somewhere eating bananas? That is also its own form of egoism and selfishness. You should set up your way of life here, and practise it, but you, I see, seem to be afraid of something. I am sorry to see such power wasted in some dark forest, when such a field of endeavour lies open in all directions before us."

"No, my friend Sherbak, we are not going in vain. You all, I see, are thinking of the political line, but we do not even dream about that. We have higher aims than this—the soul, the conscience. It is the voice of our conscience that calls us there, to a distance, because there is no place here for such as we are. But to tell you more definitely the real reason of why we are going: the sacrifices of our brethren fallen in Canadian prisons, scalded to death by having hot meat soup forcibly poured into them, twelve men already in the grave from these tortures, force us to look for something different."

"Right here is where you begin to tell on yourselves," replied Dolgei. "Your struggle is fruitless sacrifice. You should organize a force, then they would not dare to scald you to death with hot soup. Here's what you need." He clenched his fist and shook it in the air. "But you just stick your backs up and say, 'Kill me, I love you.'"

"No, my friend, you are still young in questions like these," said Vlasoff. "Force, compulsion—these are the guns of the devil, but Love, the sword of the indestructible Christ. If we would only stop and reason it out, who would consciously decide to kill another man? You go if you like, it is allowed, and how! It is glamorized not only by the law of man, but by the very church, this pseudo proclaimer of eternal truth. Of course, we are not worried about the safety of our hides, that is to say, our physical bodies, whether we live or not. But we are seriously concerned only that there should live and appear through us everything that is wise, human, so that we would have a meaning to our life. We do not know what we will meet in Hawaii, we are only going to try it and then we shall see," concluded Vlasoff.

"In that case, good luck to you!" said Anton Petrovich.

All went away in good spirits, uplifted and refreshed by Vlasoff's thoughts. You could see that in that office there were never such visitors as they, and this meeting brought with it a sort of freshness of the fields and woods to our monotonous city life.

Hearing Vlasoff, it seemed to me that he was expressing a part of my own private thoughts, only these thoughts in me were in their original, raw, uncultivated state, just misty wanderings of the mind, but Vlasoff spoke with assurances and inspiration, as about questions to which he had given serious thought and apparently, he had experienced some of them in his own life.

Next morning Timofey Lukyanovich came to the office fearfully upset.

As soon as Anton Petrovich walked in, he said to him, "Well, Anton Petrovich, here you were praising this Vlasoff up and down, but do you know what they did last night? At our spiritual service they stripped off their clothes, and even the wife of Nikolai Lukyanovich, a Molokan, accompanied them."

This news hit Anton Petrovich like a hammer. Evidently, he was writing his impressions of yesterday's interview for his paper, but as soon as he heard this, he swept the papers off his desk and pushed them all into the wastepaper basket, saying in a cutting tone, "Virtue and open-mindedness without a brain is like a wagon without a tongue."

For about three days Anton Petrovich was upset and disappointed by the whole episode, and looked upon me as though I was responsible for all of this.

The Sons of Freedom left and in our editorial room everything gradually returned to normal again. But this meeting and the incident connected with them left on me an indelible impression. I often thought about them, but could not understand them at all, and the more I thought about them, the more interested I became in them. From that time, in the years following, I tried to follow up on these eccentrics—the Sons of Freedom—as closely as I could.

Visiting One of the First Russian Settlers in California

One morning when I brought the mail to Anton Petrovich's quarters, he announced that today he and I would go to Hayward. "There," he said, "lives an old man, A. Goncherenko, and even though he and I have not the same view of life, well, he's a Russian, one of the first Russian settlers in California. And as he is one of the pioneers, I must visit him. Here's the letter. He is very sick." Anton Petrovich threw the letter on the table from the bed.

We crossed the ferry to Oakland. The foam-flecked waves of the bay beat against our ferry in good earnest, and the storm seemed to have awakened in Anton Petrovich something long forgotten. He paced back and forth like a trapped animal, but this did not calm him.

Finally, he sat down saying, "What a wind; it feels as if it were whistling right through your soul. Gracious, but that little goat Elena upset me yesterday." This was his daughter. She had come to the office the day before and he gave her some money, but instead of thanking him, she acted rudely to him. "These children! How much trouble they are, and how little they realize or appreciate."

We came to the town and from there we hired a horse and a buggy. Our driver hurried us away, first through the plain, and then we began to climb uphill. Anton Petrovich had been to see Goncherenko before, and the driver knew where to go. We came to the house. A little way off stood several large fir trees, and in the distance spread the wide plain, which was partly a plateau.

At the door we were met by a woman, a neighbour of Goncherenko. She led us into a sparsely furnished room. Goncherenko lay on the bed and did not even attempt to rise in welcome. Anton Petrovich took his hand and sat down beside him.

I looked: the old man was ending his days, and to me there was nothing exceptional in his appearance. Like any old man, he lay on the bed, the beard hid his face. They began to talk, but I was attracted outside. Unnoticed, I walked out and began to look about me. The house stood on a ledge; below tripped a little brooklet. I picked up several stones and threw them into the distance out of sheer joy, and then went down to the valley. Here a large flock of sheep were being driven and behind them walked two huge dogs. I was attracted by this procession and followed after them. I tried to get a good look at the dogs' faces, but the man riding on horseback did not let me come close enough, saying, "They'll fight a stranger."

I dropped behind and, after wandering about a little longer, returned to the house. When I came to Goncherenko's gate, I saw an inscription on an old weather-beaten board saying: "The Ukraine." This inscription I had not noticed before, and thought to myself: "Also a Hohol. Hohol visits Hohol."

When I got back to the house, Anton Petrovich chided me: "Where in the world have you been?"

"I was watching a flock of sheep and the dogs," I replied.

"You're almost like a sheep yourself. Oh, you dreamer, when will you wake up!"

The hostess served us tea. While Anton Petrovich and I drank it Goncherenko drank some sort of medicine. The hostess then brought a suitcase and set it at Anton Petrovich's feet. He began to dig among some documents. Goncherenko quietly told him that he had decided to give all his papers to the safekeeping of a certain professor in the university, who was interested in the Russian settlement in California. Anton Petrovich approved his intentions and advised him to do it as soon as possible. Then Goncherenko permitted Anton Petrovich to take certain papers, perhaps the *Vestnik Alaskey*, the *Alaska Herald*. Anton Petrovich thanked him and wished him health. We rose to go.

Anton Petrovich again turned to Goncherenko who said, "Oh, yes, I know the Doukhobors. I met them in the year 1902 on the ferry at San Francisco, when they came to build the railway." Goncherenko tried to remember several names, but remembered only one—Cheveldayoff.

Many years later I realized how much I had missed at that time. Anton Petrovich was not wrong in calling me a sheep. Perhaps they even talked of how Goncherenko was at Herzen[29] and Cgarov[30] and how he gathered his famous "Kolokol" bell. Or perhaps Goncherenko told of his meeting with the Decem-

---

29   Wikipedia: Herzen State Pedagogical University of Russia, one of the largest universities in Russia, founded in 1797 in St. Petersburg. First developed as foundling house that took in and educated poor children. Developed facilities that specialized in education of children from birth to higher education, established basis for women's pedagogical education across Russia. Over the years it has been a workspace for outstanding scientists, academicians and professors.

30   Wikipedia: Possibly Pirogov Russian national research university—one of the oldest medical higher schools in Russia. First organization in Russia that provided women with the opportunity to get higher medical education and to develop a Faculty of Pediatrics.

brist Prince Troubetskoff,[31] how Vasily Vasilyevich Vereshchagin,[32] the famous Russian painter, visited him and dug a grave for him. Very likely he may have been telling him how he, Goncherenko, worked with the brilliant American socialist Henry George.[33] I suppose he told him all about this, and of when he was in Greece, and of how they were going to kill him in Constantinople; how he struggled for Alaskan independence and how he published his paper, the *Alaska Herald*. All this, however, was lost to me forever. Perhaps Anton Petrovich, in his memoirs, which I know he kept, wrote about these visits of his to the aged Goncherenko. Later I found that Anton Petrovich's archives were in the possession of the university in Kharkov.

---

31   Wikipedia: Sergei Petrovich Trubetskoy, leader of Decembrists who sought improvement of the Russian Empire, desiring constitutional monarchy.

. 32   Wikipedia: Vasily Vereshchagin, famous Russian war artist, 1842–1904, studied art in St. Petersburg Academy 1862 and in Paris 1864, exhibited a drawing of Doukhobors chanting their psalms in the Paris Salon of 1866, travelled widely in Europe and Asia. Paintings often depicted the tragedy of war, some denied showing in Russia on the grounds that they portrayed the military in a poor light.

33   Wikipedia: Political economist and journalist who wrote *Progress and Poverty* (San Francisco: W.M. Hinton & Co., 1879).

CHAPTER 8

RIDING THE RAILS AND
SURVIVING AS A HOBO

I lived with Anton Petrovich about nine months. My life was interesting. Then I happened to become tied up with two Russian adventurers, and they confused me, saying I was wasting my time in this printing office, and what kind of an occupation is it to be a typesetter.

"The pay is trifling, and you are going to ruin yourself for life; all typesetters have tuberculosis. Go with us to Los Angeles," they said. "There's a lot of work there"—they were electricians—"and we'll make some money soon that will give you something to show for your work."

I gave them money. As soon as the money was spent, they said that we'd better be going. Under their influence I decided not to return to the printing office again, but to go with them. I did not say a word of this to Anton Petrovich. We rode into Oakland and there we tried to catch a freight train. Before we could do so we were arrested, but one of my friends managed to slip away and the two of us were left. We were questioned, but we were able to get away by mentioning Sherbak's printing house, saying that we worked there and were just going on our vacations. After this we did not try to risk catching the train in Oakland but decided to head to Richmond, and catch the freight train from there. For our last few pennies, we bought streetcar tickets to Richmond, but we didn't try to catch the train from there either. Instead, we went along on foot, and walked all night.

Passing the station of Crockett, where the long tunnel began, my friend commanded, "We'd better run here or a train might catch us in the tunnel."

It was dark and I was tired, and could not keep up to him, but fear of the dark drove me on, especially when I thought of the train. And, at last, ahead, we could see the outlet. We had just time to run out when a train, breaking from behind us, showered us with a cloud of dust and smoke.

"I can't go any farther," I told my companion. "Let's lie down here and take a rest."

"We can't, the place is full of rattlesnakes. We'd never wake up alive," he replied. "Let's go farther."

What could I do, I went, even though I didn't have any more strength left. Toward morning we somehow got to Martinez station. We walked into the station and went to sleep.

There, we were able to catch a ride to Benicia, the first capital of California, but it was hard to catch the freight train there too; the police were too vigilant. We met a hobo who told us that the only time you can catch a freight train was about four o'clock in the morning when these bulls—he pointed to the policemen—slept. We waited.

At one o'clock the hobo invited us, saying, "Let's go for a walk to town."

We passed a tannery. The work was in full swing, and we were especially interested in the paddles that were beating the hides soft. A man would aim them and they would dance away at the hides spread out before them. We envied him. Here was a man who was well fed and worked with a will. We were so taken up by the scene that we didn't notice an approaching policeman.

"Why are you going around peeping into windows at this time of night? Don't you know that it is already two o'clock in the morning?"

We told him we were just out for a walk. He took us with him and locked us in a cell. My companions were soon asleep, but I went into a corner and cried: "Now look where I've landed!"

In the morning we woke, my companions wanted to smoke. The most depressing and trapped feeling I ever had occurred when it turned out that neither of my friends had a match. They began to think of a way to get a light. The electrician was inventive. He stood on his companions' shoulders and wrapped the light bulb tightly in paper. They waited for the paper to burn. Suddenly it burst into flame. The ceiling was of old boards. I was frightened to death. Now, I thought, the jail will catch fire and we will burn like rats in a trap. But they quickly took the paper down and began to smoke.

I thought to myself: "What filth, this tobacco, and for it they had to risk our lives."

We were let out toward evening. My friends left me and I was alone. Now I decided that I had had enough of bumming; I would try to get a job somewhere. It was a time of extreme depression and thousands wandered unemployed. Here I was forced to witness hunger and cold, and to live through many trying experiences. I slept under an old bridge and in the daytime begged and tried to find work.

At this time a curious incident occurred; something I had never heard of before, and knew nothing about. I was accosted by an unfamiliar Maltese of middle age, and he became very friendly with me. He promised to help me out of my troubles and once even gave me some money to buy food. He invited me to sleep in the stable, where he was bedded very comfortably in the hay. He even had a blanket. We went to bed. In the middle of the night, I awoke and felt as though somebody was on top of me and gripping me in a fierce grasp. True, it was my new-found friend trying to drag my pants off. I soon realized with horror what he was after and quickly freed myself, as I was stronger than he. I was furious with indignation and prepared to leave, but my friend pleaded for forgiveness, saying he was asleep and did not know what he was doing. He begged me to stay. I waited for morning at the other end of the loft. At dawn, I left.

Return to San Francisco

After considerable wandering, I wrote to my brother and he, in reply to my letter, sent me fifteen dollars with which I returned safely to San Francisco.

I did not have the courage to go back to Anton Petrovich as I felt that I was gravely guilty. I found work in a Spanish restaurant, where I was employed as a delivery boy. Everything here went well. My work was comparatively light and I soon earned the trust and the goodwill of the manager, and the sympathy of my fellow workers. What especially interested them was that I neither ate meat, drank alcohol, nor smoked. My master was well disposed to me because of these qualities.

In connection with my work, I met the most heterogeneous collection of people. I worked from four o'clock in the afternoon to two o'clock in the morning. During the day I delivered orders of Spanish pancakes, "enchiladas," to the different Spanish and Italian cafés. At night there were orders for tamales and often I had to deliver them to private homes. It sometimes happened that I was sent with orders to fashionable centres of amusement and licentiousness, where I occasionally witnessed scenes that were almost overpowering. Here I had occasion to see depravity disguised as a sort of aristocratic debauchery. I was shocked on one occasion to see completely naked men and women madly chasing one another. I remember the recent incident of the Sons of Freedom at the Molokan service which so greatly disturbed Anton Petrovich. To me these were similar incidents, but the contradictory outlook of the people in question made this scene still more incomprehensible to me.

These temptations had not the slightest attraction, but became more and more repulsive to me. The more I saw, the stronger grew my moral conscience. I found my pleasure in attending musical recitals, visiting museums, strolling through the park.

Some time after, two Spanish musicians with their stringed instruments appeared in our restaurant. One of them had lived in Moscow for five years and spoke some Russian. I became acquainted with him, and often went to hear them. How beautifully they played! You could listen to them for hours and never tire. Several times they played Russian songs.

I especially remember one occasion when they played some Russian songs exceptionally beautifully while one of them harmonized with vocal intonations. This Russian song in an atmosphere so foreign to it, and the musician's interest in a Russian person, stirred my soul to its depths and made me think of Anton Petrovich and my own guilt. I decided as soon as possible to go and reconcile myself to him.

Anton Petrovich Prepares to Leave for Russia

That evening I went to the second floor of the hotel where Anton Petrovich stayed, and knocked at his door. He opened the door, and, as soon as he saw me, wanted to close it again, but I was quick enough to enter.

"You runaway! I thought that you were gone for good. I reported your running away to your father," said Anton Petrovich.

"Forgive me, Uncle, for my foolishness," I said. "I know I am guilty before your fatherly care."

Anton Petrovich was silent. Then he abruptly shouted: "You have acted very badly, Peter. For such a trick you deserve to be paddled Russian-style. Why did you disgrace the greatness of the Russian character?"

I was stunned by his severity and stood, speechless and beside myself with grief. This touched him. He asked me where I was and what I was now doing, whether I intended to go back home, and so on.

Then he said, "Well, you cannot come back to me. And not just because you ran away and violated your education agreement, but because of another reason entirely. My life is beginning to revolve in a different orbit. I have decided to return to Russia. As soon as the way is open, I will be gone. That is why I am working day and night; setting the papers in order. You understand, I am tired of all this rubbish." He indicated a stack of papers. Then he took some letters and said to me, "Let's go! We'll mail these, have some tea and a good talk together."

Perhaps my simplicity and freshness from the country refreshed him. I suppose that I often expressed myself in a primitive manner and this would make him laugh heartily in spite of himself. He prized my moral cleanliness, but mentally I was extremely absent-minded and he used every method he could think of to awaken my mental powers.

We went down to the main floor and walked out into the street. Anton Petrovich said, "We'll take a walk and drink some tea in an Italian café. There it is quiet, cozy and clean."

The town swarmed with its turbulent life, but above shone the stars.

Anton Petrovich shivered, looked up as though the beauty of the heavens had poured oil on his burning soul, and began to talk of Russia. "This war means the doom of the capitalistic system, and in our Russia it is inevitable. And once the transformation triumphs in Russia, there will be found a basis for a future righteous order of mankind."

We walked into the café and ordered supper. He ate as earnestly as he talked. I could not eat in comfort under the fire of his passion, but like an untiring machine, he continued.

"There will be mistakes; I do not doubt that. The people that will be setting up this new life are still green, inexperienced. They have always been bound hand and foot by the outmoded chains of despotism and fanaticism. Yes, thousand-year-old chains are not easily dropped. But once the youth shall free itself from the cinders of the old world, it will build a new wonder, 'The Home of Life.' I have no doubt of this."

His excited thoughts stirred my soul and broke in upon my mind like bedlam or like a flock of birds. For some reason, for the first time, he spoke of his broken family ties.

"Maybe you think I haven't my troubles? No, my son, your Sherbak, too, is having a hard life of it and he has no one to talk to about it. I have six sons, two daughters and a wife, and yet I have to live alone. Do you think I would have needed this person if it were otherwise?"

He referred to a certain woman, a Russian German with whom he was on friendly terms. She helped him in the editorial work and often remained and worked in the office long into the night when everybody else had gone. She followed him to Russia.

"I am an idealist, a socialist, and cannot betray this great cause. I hate the capitalist system worse than commercialism; sell and buy, buy and sell, and that's the whole aim of this life. This system is poison to the better qualities of man. It gives much to our body, but nothing to our spirit. To satisfy the spirit one must have freedom. You should get to understand this higher freedom. For it, the better Russian people have struggled and are struggling, and for it your Doukhobors have shed their blood in Russia. Freedom, it's a magic word. If properly understood, it gives us everything: the aim, the justification and the law."

I left, hypnotized by the animated thoughts of Anton Petrovich. And even though I did not understand the depth and the meaning of all that he said, my soul responded. I knew that he spoke of a very great truth, which, I thought, some day I also would understand.

Anton Petrovich's personality was dynamic. I often overheard him speaking. He always spoke enthusiastically, briskly and passionately. His affairs went not altogether smoothly and he often experienced material difficulties, he had to borrow money from his friends; from Fyodor Sisoev, from the Armenian storekeeper and some others. But no material difficulties could destroy his energetic, lively spirit. I always felt that he was not an ordinary Russian, but a highly gifted person. He left me a living memory of himself for the rest of my life. Many years later I tried to get some information about him, but few could tell me anything. Most characteristic is the following letter of L. Buristak, which my friend, Molokan Vasili Nikolayevich Dobrinin, was kind enough to send me.

March 20th, 1946,
Alta Loma, California
My much-respected friend Dobrinin:

I.I. Cheremain was over and told me that you asked him not for Tverski's book but Anton Petrovich's under the title *Tsarztvo Russkikh Muzhikov Opyt Russkoy Kommuny v Amerike*. I have no such book, and know not whether there was any such published or not.

I met A.P. Sherbak in 1907 when we first came to Southern California. He had just returned to his family (in Alta Loma) from a trip to Europe. At that time, he visited the Doukhobors in Canada, from there he brought with him the first chapter of the book you asked about. I read this book and even rewrote it for him. This chapter he was supposed to send to one of the great Russian journals of that time, either the *Russkoye Bogatstvo* (*Russian Wealth*) or the *Russkoye Duma* (*Russian Thought*), I am not certain which. Victor Sherbak told me that he would try to find a person more acquainted with the deceased A.P. Sherbak, who might be able to give you more reliable information as to the book and about Sherbak himself.

I can say this, though: that this chapter of the book on the Doukhobors was a wonderful thing. As I understand you, you would like to have more details about A.P. Sherbak himself. This was an unusual man; a man of amazing energy, a passionate struggler for truth, and for the freedom of simple and helpless people. He won the admiration and the remembrance of many prominent writers and social workers of his time. He visited Leo Tolstoy in Yasnaya Polyana and was friendly with Korolenko,[34] and Gorky.[35] The poet, Balmont,[36] gave him a book of his compositions with the inscription: "To my dear and truly living Anton Petrovich Sherbak." This book I had, but unfortunately it was lost.

A.P. Sherbak was born in the year 1867 or 1868 in the town of Sumac, of the Kharkov district, where he grew up and reared a family. In the beginning of the '90s he left with his wife and children for America, where he acquired some land in Alta Loma, fifty-four miles from Los Angeles. After living on the farm for some time and also working for the surrounding farmers, he was drawn back to Russia where at this time the revolution of 1905 broke out.

He joined the famous Peasant's Union and became leader of the peasants of his district, for which he was arrested, but released on bail on a surety of three thousand roubles. After being freed from prison he left the country, settling in Paris, where he became a student in the University of Freedom founded by the famous Russian professor M. Kovalevsky in co-operation with many other prominent Russian emigrants, fugitives from Tsarist rule. He soon became very popular in the Russian colony due to his active and sympathetic nature. He did not live long in Paris, however. Becoming well-known through the great progressive Russian journals by his articles and addresses, he received a commission from one of these journals to study and write a book on the life of the Doukhobors in Canada. It was then that he went there (in 1907) and gathered on the spot, a lot of interesting information on the life and disposition of this glorious and ancient Russian sect. This material he brought to Alta Loma and began to write the above-mentioned book.

However, such an unsettled spirit, living for the good of the people, could not long live in such a quiet rural surrounding as an American village and after a year A.P. again left. He went to Los Angeles where, without a penny in his pocket, he

---

34   Vladimir Korolenko, 1853–1921, Ukrainian-born Russian writer, journalist, human rights activist and humanitarian.

35   Maxim Gorky, 1868–1936, Russian author and political activist.

36   Konstantin Balmont, 1867–1942, Russian poet who was exiled in France in 1920.

started the publication of the militant paper *Tikhii Okean* (*Pacific Ocean*). Several years later the newspaper was transferred to San Francisco, where it continued publication until 1917. The paper carried the energetic and restless character of its editor, reflecting the needs and the misgivings of simple Russian emigrants, the workers.

The Russian Revolution accepted Sherbak with wide-open arms. He eagerly threw himself into the difficult and inspiring task of creating a new world, new to the workers and peasants. But his time was near. His age told upon him. A.P. was a strong man in his time, but the cold and hunger of the revolution proved too much for him. He was placed in a home for aged men of letters, named after Lenin, where he died in 1921. His wife died a few years later in Alta Loma. He left six sons and two daughters. Every single one of them inherited the iron will and the energy of their father, applying their capabilities to farming. They have attained average prosperity and everyone's respect.

L. Buristak

But fate brought me in contact with Anton Petrovich once more. Of this I shall speak in a later chapter.

ON RIDING THE RAILS
AND SURVIVING AS A HOBO

[Vera] I appreciated my grandfather's frankness about his experience as a sixteen-year-old beggar living under a bridge in California. He was accepting and forgiving of others because he had made rash decisions himself.

What was constant throughout Pete Maloff's life was his sobriety and vegetarianism. His experience of working in the San Fransico restaurant has become a family story. Several of his co-workers, not understanding his abstinence, tried to force him to drink and eat meat. The owner of the restaurant, catching them in these shenanigans, swore that if they tried that again, they would be "out the door," this at a time of high unemployment. Grandparents enjoyed many vegetarian delights when they could and it was at their home in Thrums that I discovered the exotic taste of fresh figs, papayas, pomegranates, artichokes and various nuts before they became widely available in our rural area in the Kootenays of British Columbia.

Peter Maloff swallowed his pride and apologized to Anton Sherbak. However, he was not able to resume his apprenticeship at the *Tikhii Okean*. Sherbak was determined to return to Russia and establish "a righteous order of mankind

Антон Петрович Щербак.

Ukrainian idealist and socialist writer Anton Sherbak inspired Pete Maloff to create his literary journal and *Anti-militarism and Vegetarian Idealism Magazine*. Sherbak moved to Russia after the revolution, to help establish a "righteous order of mankind" there. The United States government did not allow him to return to the United States to rejoin his family.

where one would have freedom to satisfy the spirit."[37] He resettled in his home-town of Sumy and published his journal there. I find it heart-rending that so many who saw such possibilities in the socialist republic of USSR were to perish in the aftermath of the civil war through starvation, chaos and disillusionment. Pete Maloff dreamed of following Sherbak; however, in the 1920s he lost contact with his mentor.

There is confusion about the date of Anton Sherbak's death. Contrary to L. Buristak's letter, the Molokane website states that the US government did not allow him to return to the United States and he died in Russia sometime between 1930 and 1940.[38] It is tragic that the peace and new order of life Sherbak hoped for did not transpire. Sumy, in northeastern Ukraine, continues to be a battleground in the Russian-Ukrainian war.

---

37   Molokane.org/molokan/Berokoff/Chapter-5.htm#9.

38   Molokane.org/people/Sherbak_Anton/.

CHAPTER 9

MY YOUTHFUL YEARS

Recalling my youthful years, I now see that my life presents a contrast to that of most young Doukhobors. First, I enjoyed unusual physical energy and a fiery, passionate character. Add to this the fact that my parents allowed me almost unlimited freedom and in most cases I was left to my own devices. My energy gave me no rest and drove me in various directions. I seemed to be always seeking something and I spent much of my time travelling. Circumstances generally favoured me and my plan was rarely impeded. Fate was kind to me and gave me occasion to taste the bitter and the sweet in reasonable proportion.

In my travels, I saw and experienced much that was interesting and amazing. Likewise, I had the good fortune to meet many remarkable people. To describe it all in detail would be impossible but I would like to recount a few of the particularly interesting events and tell of some acquaintances who influenced my life.

On the advice of Anton Petrovich, I returned to Oregon, but I was not destined to remain there long. After the loss of the Doukhobor Colony of Freedom land in Oregon, several settlers had already left. My parents bought land in Orland, California and were preparing to move there.

Russian American Pacifists–Voleen and Panchuk

At that time, America entered the European war and recruiting units were set up throughout the country. Some of our colonists went back to Canada where the Doukhobors had exemption from military obligations. This did not concern me, as I was still too young for conscription. In Oregon an incident occurred which impressed me greatly. There happened to be two young men of Russian origin who had the courage to protest against militarism in their own way. Their names were Gabriel Fomich Voleen and Dimitri Panchuk. These two, having refused to comply with the law of military registration, were arrested and tried in Eugene. They appeared in their own defence and this they presented in an original manner, basing their plea on the principle "Thou shalt not kill." They justified their action by the New Testament, bringing up the point that Christ, on the strength of his convictions, cursed war, therefore no follower of His should take part in it, directly or indirectly, no matter what that particular war might be fought about. They were sentenced to two years' imprisonment.

The stand of these two Russians astounded me. I likewise resolved not to return to Canada, but, in the event of draft, to make the same stand. This event awakened my pacifistic inclination and I began to express decided opinions against war. Once, at the Eugene station, I expressed my thoughts to a few young recruits who listened to me and even agreed with my views. Hearing my speech, the enraged station agent could not contain himself and sharply informed me: "Either you stop blabbering, or I'll call the police!"

The agent's rage aroused the laughter of the bystanders. As an agitator, I was still a greenhorn and the recruits stood up for me, saying that I was very young and didn't know what I was talking about. It sometimes happed that people who heard me condescendingly confirmed my argument and this inspired me to go on.

I followed the fate of Voleen and Panchuk with interest. They were imprisoned in Portland. Their cases caught the interest of that same Vladimir Vladimirovich Gelvoni who was the interpreter in our land dispute. He made a direct appeal to President Wilson who took an interest in their plight and after nine months imprisonment, they were set free.

This V.V. Gelvoni was a riddle to many who could not understand why so intelligent and influential a man could live for twenty-five years completely apart from the Russian society in America. This mystery was somewhat clarified when Voleen went to thank him for his efforts. Gelvoni told him part of his tragedy. In Russia he had been the victim of jealousy in a family affair in which he shot his wife and her lover. After this, he fled to America.

Before long, we left for California. After a short time, my brother Nikolai went back to Canada but the rest of the family decided to continue there.

Orland is as flat as the palm of your hand; endless plains stretch for hundreds of miles without interruption. To the north rises the mighty Mount Shasta clothed in eternal snow, and on sunny days the volcanic Mount Lassen could be seen. At that time, it often belched forth fire, coughing up enormous clouds of smoke. In the face of this remarkable phenomenon of nature, we thought what an insignificant and helpless being is man.

How wonderful it was to feel the spring warmth of the sun after the rainy winter in Oregon. The orchards were already clothed in blossoms and the chatter of birds in the trees was enchanting. It was February, but here the orange groves strained under their load and the black fruit of the olive trees contrasted sharply with the silvery foliage.

Vegetarian Influences

We soon adapted ourselves to this land where the cold of northern frosts was foreign. Even before we arrived, several of our colonists had settled here, the two Vereschagin families, Peter Zharikoff and others. It was an ideal land for lovers of nature, and our Doukhobor vegetarianism and sobriety was favoured by the abundance of every kind of fruit and plant.

My spiritual and mental forces began to revive. I was fascinated by the beauties of nature. Often, I would spend whole nights under the open sky, admiring the heavenly bodies and their miraculous movements. Radiant sunshine and the wonderful surroundings induced a jubilant spirit. The physical toil on the farm weighed upon me not at all, but was in reality a pleasure and my associates envied my superb health.

At this time, I chanced upon Howard Williams's *Ethics of Diet*, which awakened a desire to understand the basis of vegetarianism. This book is a veritable encyclopedia of a murderless subsistence. In our family and in that of V.V. Vereschagin, the book encouraged the adoption of a strict vegetarian diet, excluding eggs and milk products. The conditions under which we then lived made this easy to do.

The sensitivity awakened by Williams's book was strengthened by the following incident. I read in the paper that on March 6, 1917, a famous sculptor and vegetarian, Prince Paul Troubetzkoy, would come to San Francisco and give a lecture on vegetarianism. I made up my mind to hear him and away I went. In San Francisco, I decided to call on Anton Petrovich Sherbak. I had not seen him for almost a year. I swept in on him like a whirlwind, paper in hand, and began to invite him to Prince Troubetzkoy's lecture. I was elated by the thought of this lecture and my enthusiasm infected him.

Anton Petrovich was obviously glad to see me and treated me kindly. He seemed to notice an improvement since the time of our separation and he accepted my invitation, saying:

"Good, we shall go to Troubetzkoy. Even though I haven't much use for princes, I guess we could listen to him."

This was the day before Troubetzkoy's evening lecture. Anton Petrovich said that a meeting with Troubetzkoy could perhaps be arranged sooner. He telephoned the hotel in which the Troubetzkoys were staying, and received an invitation to come there as soon as we liked.

Prince Troubetzkoy and his wife were staying in the most expensive and luxurious hotel in the city, the Saint Francis, but when we called upon them, we understood at once that we had come to sincere vegetarians.

His wife, an Englishwoman, served some fruit salad, saying, "We often eat in our rooms when we travel because in ordinary restaurants there is little for vegetarians to eat. There everything is unnatural."

Prince Troubetzkoy was tall, almost huge. From under his thick black brows his eyes shone with benevolence and gave his whole face a sort of transparency. In the room were various animal exhibits. Troubetzkoy explained that the aim of his lecture was to awaken in man a love for animals. He took from the dresser a model of a young deer, and, turning to us, he said, "Here is my ideal."

Anton Petrovich was baffled and asked, "What do you mean? Do you consider animals to be on a higher plane than man?"

"Yes," Troubetzkoy quietly replied. "Animals are superior to man. They have neither police, nor laws, nor churches, they neither marry nor divorce; they have no money and yet they enjoy life many times more deeply than we do. In the face of this, what right have we to kill them? Men kill each other only because they kill animals and eat them. This is my decided opinion."

I had no time to speak for myself when Anton Petrovich introduced me to Troubetzkoy with the words: "Here, then, is a brother of yours; he never ate meat in all his life."

"That's interesting," said Troubetzkoy, "and who may you be?"

"A Doukhobor," I answered.

"A Doukhobor, Doukhobor," the prince repeated several times, as though trying to recall something. "Oh, yes; do you know that when I was at Tolstoy's at Yasnaya Polyana, this is what he said to me: 'Here's what you should mould or chisel out of a stone: a Doukhobor. The Doukhobors are the real vegetarians.'"

Troubetzkoy asked me where the Doukhobor centre was. I told him that it was in Canada, and he asked his wife to make a note of it.

Anton Petrovich was absorbed with some other thoughts and paid little attention to what Troubetzkoy was saying. It must be stated that in spite of his broad outlook and humanitarian views, Anton Petrovich deliberately ignored vegetarian ethics. Therefore, he reacted indifferently to Troubetskoy's reasoning. He was much more interested in the sculptures. Examining the various works, he softly said to Troubetzkoy: "What beautiful work you do, Paul. Your hands, they are miraculous!"

In the evening at the lecture, Troubetzkoy produced powerful arguments in defence of a bloodless subsistence. He said that the only difference between man and the animal world was that man could speak. "What a crime to make our stomachs the graves of dead animals. Eat pure food: vegetables, fruits, nuts and suitable cereals and you will be purer and healthier, will live longer and better and even get to love one another more."

Returning from the lecture, Anton Petrovich said: "Prince Troubetzkoy is a pretty good preacher of vegetarianism, but I do not agree with him." In exactly what he disagreed, Anton Petrovich did not say.

This meeting with Troubetzkoy made me even more conscious of the fruitfulness of the vegetarian life.

Last Meeting with Anton Petrovich

The next day I again visited Anton Petrovich. This time we spoke in more detail. He asked me where I lived, what I did; I mentioned that I was reading books. Anton Petrovich, on hearing this, said, "That's good. A man without knowledge is like a midnight traveller without a light. And I, I will be going away to Russia, very soon now."

He was full of enthusiasm and of a deep consciousness of beauty. His soul was aflame with what was going on in the motherland. Some of his thoughts to this day ring in my memory.

"The Russian people are great," he continued, "because they are basically strong. In them we have an uncultivated field for the founding of a better society; here we have the raw materials for this. Here we have goodness, breadth and sacrifice in the name of higher ideals. That is the true picture of the Russian, and even though a rebellious spirit at times overrules his better impulses, the silky tenderness and the elastic flexibility of his heart will conquer in the end. The many-sided Russian soul has given us such giants as Tolstoy, Dostoevsky, the Decembrists, the Doukhobors and others; it will indubitably triumph over its shortcomings and the obstacles in its path."

That evening I was again with Anton Petrovich. His friend Dolgei, whom I afterwards met many times, came too. Dolgei was a free-thinking man. He argued long with Anton Petrovich on the subject of his proposed departure for Russia. I remember that he even tried to dissuade him from going.

"People like you, Anton Petrovich, are needed everywhere, and more than anywhere, you are needed right here in California, where the Russian colonists are fairly numerous [he had the Molokans in mind]. Why should you leave, Anton Petrovich? It is the very same as in Russia. You, with your experience and talent, could do no less here than in the motherland. There are enough workers there without you."

But Anton Petrovich was adamant. "Please bear in mind, my dear Dolgei, the conditions and the setting, that's where the root of the matter lies. What use is gold locked in a chest or buried in the ground? So it is with a living spring. It is only good when it is given a free flow and a clear course. But here everything is locked up and barred. May this capitalistic madhouse rot! I will not remain in it. That's my reply to you."

Dolgei made several cutting remarks after which he dramatically left.

A feeling of unbearable pain came over me. I deliberately tried to control myself and said: "Uncle, Anton Petrovich, can it be that we shall never see each other again?"

"No! Soon, now, very soon, my fate will take a new turn. But this is what I say to you, Peter; you proved to be a poor student, you were not able to stand my test, but never mind, I will tell you more things anyhow, and maybe someday you will remember my kindness to you. I esteem your moral purity and sobriety, but that is not enough; life demands more than that from us. If only you knew how many people are dying, having lived in vain. Your failing is that you have not developed your mind. My advice to you is: work on this instrument, and, of course, hold on to and never renounce your Doukhobor ideals, and they will carry you through." He pointed to the stack of his books, *The Kingdom of Russian Peasant Doukhobors*. "I do not want to believe that I have worked for them in vain; I do not want to believe that I was deceived. You, young Doukhobors, should not put out the torch lit by your fathers and grandfathers. It will be to your shame should such a great and sacred flame as the Doukhobor movement ever die out."

This was my last meeting with Anton Petrovich. He went to Kharkov and there several years later he died. His memory remains in my heart indelibly. What a great Russian he was and how generously he gave his all to others. In my youth, I benefited very little from his talents, but I could have gained much. Still, I am thankful for the little that I received from him. I retain it in my memory.

Discussion of the Russian Provisional Government

Once Fyodor Timofeyevich Sisoev from San Francisco came to my home. He was looking for a suitable place to settle. Father telephoned the Vereschagin brothers, Alexei Vasilyevich and Vasily Vasilyevich. They came with their families and we had a neighbourhood gathering. At first, we all sang together and then Fyodor Timofeyevich sang several Russian folk songs in honour of the Russian Revolution, which at that time was taking on a new character under the leadership of the Provisional Government of Georgy Lvov, Alexander Kerensky and others.

Sisoev was a fascinating character: the features of his face expressed a depth of kindness and gentleness. He bore himself without constraint and sang as though he sang about himself. His singing was touching and his voice pierced to the very heart; one would have liked to listen to him forever.

After this began the reading of the papers. They read an article from the Doukhobor community in Canada, which was printed in Okuntsov's *Russian Voice*. I do not remember what article this was, but I do remember that the community had justified its rejection of schools. My father tried to defend the views of the community but the Vereschagin brothers, being the more talented speakers, destroyed his arguments as quickly as he could put them forth.

Fyodor Timofeyevich, seeing his helplessness, came to his rescue. "I think that Nikolasha is partly right in his reasoning," he began. "The Doukhobors are progressing and I firmly hold this to be true. The Doukhobor-communists reject state education on the basis of their convictions. Whether they are right or not, that is their business; they believe they are. And if we stand for complete freedom of speech and freedom of religion, then what right have we to judge and condemn them in this?"

This was said for the benefit of the Vereschagin brothers. They more than anyone else always spoke up for the broader viewpoint. Nevertheless, they listened intently to Fyodor Timofeyevich. After a pause, he began to compare the Doukhobors and the Molokans.

"You are worried, I see, for fear the Doukhobors are on the wrong track and are falling into extremes, but they have something besides extremes. Look how closely they group themselves around the community; they do not go to war and do not fall into evil ways. Isn't this progress? But our Molokans heap a stack of great big Bibles on the table and jump around them, while their children are surrounded by city life, with all its temptations, and are perishing like moths flying into a fire. That's what we should be worrying about."

Vasily Vasilyevich Vereschagin quietly arose and said, "I welcome your words, Fyodor Timofeyevich; it isn't right to try to cover up what's wrong. If there is something wrong with the Doukhobors, say it, and if amongst the Molokans, say it right out too. Only then will we be able to form a correct idea of social order. But like Nikolasha Maloff, I censure him strongly for this; in the Doukhobor community he counts all the stupidity, blunders and foolishness as some kind of sacred decree. On those grounds we always argue with him, but in every other respect, Nikolasha is one of the best of men."

After this they passed on to a reading of Kerensky's proclamation from Petersburg in which he calls on the Russian people for a democratic form of government. Alexei Vasilyevich read this pronouncement with great enthusiasm.

Vasily Vasilyevich was the first to comment: "Kerensky's invitation deserves the fullest consideration. Indeed, that's the only way out for the Russian people after centuries of tsaristic despotism. Let's gather a hundred dollars or so and send them to Kerensky in Petersburg to help the Russian people."

This suggestion stung my father to the quick, and he completely lost his temper and could hardly contain himself: "So you need a government now? And who was it that was just struggling against one and who was just boasting that his father died at the hands of Russian despotism for the Doukhobor ideal, on his way to Siberia: So, you want a democracy now? Very well, Vasya, tell me, just what is a democracy? I'm not exactly sure what it means."

"Sure, I'll tell you, you bet I'll tell you, Nikolasha," said Vereschagin. "The word democracy is a great thing, and everyone should know what it means and signifies."

Vasily Vereschágin took from his pocket a little notebook, dug into it for a little while and continued: "When I was visiting the Quakers in 1908, I was disappointed with them. What big business men they have become—veritable exploiters. Almost nothing remained of their ancestors; they trade everything for dollars. From there I went to New York where an acquaintance of mine took me to a small island, the foot of the Statue of Liberty. There I learned what the word democracy means. To get an idea of this gigantic structure you almost have to see it for yourself; there only lives the essence of the underlying meaning of democracy. But, most important, on this Statue of Liberty is written these words; Nikolasha, I ask you, listen carefully.

"'Give me your tired, your poor, your huddled masses yearning to breathe free, the wretched refuse of your teeming shore. Send these, the homeless, tempest-tossed, to me, I lift my lamp beside the golden door.'

"Yes, that's where the full meaning and aim of democracy is," said Vasily Vasilyevich with unusual pathos in his voice.

These words about the Statue of Liberty silenced my father. It was as though he had been hit by a hammer-blow. For the first time, he could say nothing against Vereschagin's argument, and felt himself completely bested. The Statue of Liberty had defeated him. The Vereschagin brothers on the other hand felt a decided superiority after putting my father in their bag. Afterwards, although they gathered many times, my father never again tried to contradict them.

Pacifism and Democracy

[Vera] Expatriates continued to follow the outcome of the Russian Revolution through Russian-language newspapers. On April 30, 1917, when Kerensky was the prime minister of the Russian Provisional Government, the leaders of the Doukhobor community in Canada congratulated the newly formed government in Petrograd. "Hearty congratulations on the new government of all the Russian people. Glory to God in Heaven and peace on earth." They then appealed: "We beg all those on whom the life of Nicholas, the entire Romanov family, all former ministers, and the obsolete false clergy depends, to be merciful.... Judgment should be left to the will of God."[39] Doukhobor leader Peter V. Verigin sent the Provisional Government suggestions for reforms—among them, the maximal reduction of taxes, transformation of the army into a voluntary one and the proclamation of political neutrality.[40]

Doukhobor and Molokan Discussion on Democracy

Until 1957, Doukhobors in British Columbia were prohibited from voting in federal and provincial elections. This disenfranchisement was similar to that of Indigenous people, Chinese and Japanese Canadians, who were barred from voting until 1948, except for a short time when soldiers who had fought in the world wars were allowed voting privileges. Officially, Doukhobors were denied because conscientious objectors were banned from voting; however, Jehovah's Witnesses and Quakers—also pacifists—were given franchise. Tarasoff speculates that Doukhobors may have been excluded because they could be persuaded to vote as a large bloc and thus influence elections.[41]

Though they were banned from voting, in 1931 a convention of "Named Doukhobors" "turned the tables" and conscientiously rejected their right to vote. This resolution was retained during the formation of the Union of Spiritu-

---

39 Maloff, *Doukhobors: Their History, Life and Struggle*, Russian text, p. 239.

40 A.I. Klibanov, *History of Religious Sectarianism in Russia (1860s–1917)*, (Oxford: Pergamon Press, 1982), p. 146–47.

41 Koozma Tarasoff, "Canadian Doukhobors and Voting," February 3, 2015, updated July 2020, goo.gl/gK7HZO.

al Communities of Christ (USCC) in 1938 when, during a week-long meeting, it was stated that *"they have never given nor will they ever give their votes during elections, thereby are free from any responsibility before God or man for the acts of any government established by men."*[42]

For that reason, my grandparents and parents, together with many Doukhobors, often refused to vote even when they were able to. When I was of age, I began to vote because I wanted to support a local candidate who spoke for peace. But it was only when my mother was in her nineties that she was proud to take part in an election. Doukhobors' vote for school board and municipal elections was never rescinded and it was with the school board support that a Russian-language program was adopted in the local schools.

---

42   Tarasoff, ibid.

PACIFISTS DURING THE WAR

[Vera] As America joined World War I, war fever gripped the country. Grand-father describes an incident where this frenzy was taken out on a railway station unfortunately named Germantown. In this madness it was challenging to be a pacifist. Even speaking out against the draft, as Pete's correspondent Scott Near-ing did, landed him in a prolonged court case. He was branded as a dangerous foe of the American way of life.[43] Freed in the court of law but found guilty by the establishment, publishers who had previously published his books refused to accept his calls. The academic field was closed to him and he was excluded from most speaking engagements.

Years later, Nearing wrote of what he had endured. "From personal expe-rience, I can bear witness that war not only negates truth, decency, and human kindness but brings disaster also to truth-seekers and those who are devoting their energies to social improvement. War is hell. More than that, war drags human beings from their tasks of building and improving, and pushes them en masse into the category of destroyers and killers."[44]

It was fortunate that Pete Maloff was released by the sheriff shortly after be-ing arrested, for avoiding the draft was a serious offence in America during World War I. Conscription was mandatory for all men aged twenty-one to forty-five.

---

43   Scott Nearing, *The Making of a Radical: A Political Autobiography* (New York: Harper & Row, 1972), p. 120.

44   Nearing, *The Making of a Radical*, ibid., p. 121.

Chapter 10

Soldiers Riot at the Germantown Station

In the meantime, the war in Europe blazed fiercer and fiercer and America began to send troops to Europe. I was working with a neighbour, Larson, on his farm about seven miles south of Orland, near a little place called Germantown. The neighbour had cut some alfalfa and we were baling it. About a quarter of a mile from us stood the railway station of Germantown. Troop trains often stopped there to allow the express train, the Shasta Limited, to pass.

One day, as usual, a train loaded with troops stopped there. Suddenly we heard a commotion from that direction.

A boy ran up shouting, "The soldiers are tearing the station to pieces."

Larson and I left our work and ran to the station. We saw that the riot was no joke. The sign Germantown was already smashed, the window was shattered and several soldiers were putting up a ladder to take down the sign from the other side. A little window above the sign was still intact but a soldier from the train shouted: "Watch me finish off that German window." And he let a bottle fly as hard as he could at it, and almost hit the station agent on the head. He was running about not knowing what to do.

Another soldier standing on the platform called back: "Hey, Kelly, I'll finish that window for you," and he hit it so hard that only splinters of glass were left.

More and more soldiers got off the trains and crowded around the station. Larson and I tried to get nearer but the soldiers crowded us back. One tall soldier with a black moustache went around the people gathered at the station and asked almost everyone: "Are you a German? Are you a German?" Then he came to us and asked me: "You are big enough to be in a uniform. Why aren't you?"

Larson spoke up for me: "He is too young; he is not of age."

The soldier got after him: "Why, you old fool." He grabbed him by the shirt front and shook him menacingly, adding: "What business is it of yours to answer for him? Let him speak for himself. Are you a German, or aren't you?"

Larson was terrified and, trembling, blurted out, "No, I'm Swede, a Swede" and tried to get free from the soldier.

The soldier released him saying, "You're lucky you are a Swede or I'd make hash out of you."

Larson ran away but I still stood by and watched; several soldiers brought up a thick plank they had found, battered in the door and started to wreck the door frame. Others ran into the office and began to smash everything within reach, throwing paper around. One of them tore off the telegraphic apparatus, saying, "They shouldn't be sending any telegrams to these Germans anyway."

Just then the through-train flew by. The officers ran out and began to drive the soldiers back to the train, but they resisted, shouting, "We haven't finished yet." Several voices roared in unison: "Burn that damned German pest-house down."

This egged them on all the more. Before they could all get back on, the train started off; two were left behind.

They went back to the station waving their fists and yelling, "That's just what we are going to do to the Kaiser's bunch."

The two were soon caught up and hauled off in pursuit of the train. Clouds of smoke rose from the engine, and the whistle wailed dolefully in the distance as though saying, "I'm taking these young men away; far away—and forever."

The rest of the people began to leave. To me all this was terrifying and incomprehensible. Young, handsome, energetic men from every part of America had turned into madmen, hurrying away, heaven knows where, driven by some unknown power to their death. Why? And for what?

Here I recalled Tolstoy's words that Vasily Vasilyevich Vereschagin had copied for me from a letter. How true they were. "I cannot sympathise with any militaristic movement, not even that of David against Goliath; I sympathise only with those who are destroying the cause of such conflict: the prestige of gold, wealth, military heroism, and the main cause of all evil—patriotism, the false religion which sanctifies the murder of one's own brother."

Larson did not wait for me but went home. When I returned, the baling machine was in full operation. Larson was seriously frightened and asked, "They didn't try to kill you there, did they?"

For a time, we long remained under the effect of this soldier rebellion. I told my father about it and it could be said that it resurrected him.

He heard our story and said, "That's where Vereschagin's democracy leads."

He immediately telephoned Vasya Vereschagin who was upset and came over to ask about the riot in more detail. "I would like to see with my own eyes what happened. Will you be going there to bale hay again soon?"

"Tomorrow morning," I replied.

"Well, then I'll go with you and see for myself."

Next morning, Larson and I called for Vasya. On the way Larson gave him his account and impressions of the event. We went to the station together. The window was boarded up; only the small window had been replaced. They were waiting for some army official to inspect the damage and were not fixing anything until he came. The station agent was shuffling papers, trying to bring his files back to order.

Vasya walked around the station several times, and then stopped in deep thought. Finally, he said: "Yes, Peter, it's not just a matter of the station and that the soldiers wrecked it and wanted to burn it, but that this war-madness is driving people to a horrible state of insanity. This is only a symptom of that colossal historical delusion of people that war and bloodshed could ever do anybody any good. Even if the allies defeat the Germans, this won't result in real peace, but only another even more horrible bloodbath in the near future. It is well that I saw this picture; it told me a lot. You know, Peter,"—he always referred to me as though I was a fully grown man and an equal—"there are unenlightened fanatics among us Doukhobors. They cause all kinds of trouble; but these are enlightened fanatics. What an abomination!"

The station was later repaired and renamed Artois.

I think that Vasily Vasilyevich Vereschagin's return to Canada was partly due to this soldier onslaught. He realized that no outside label of democracy can save man from self-extinction, but that only inner consciousness and realization can lead people ahead. The Doukhobors, even though they often make mistakes, never lose sight of the future, and he resolved to go and be closer to his Doukhobors. Upon me, these incidents left an indelible impression and revived in me the thought of going to see the Doukhobors in Canada.

About this time, I was seized with an intense eagerness for reading. I spent whole nights over the work of Dostoevsky, Tolstoy, Gorky, Chekhov, Nadson, Jack London, Mayne Reid and others. Also, I began to take an interest in more serious literature, such as the writings of Henry George, James and Spinoza.

At that time a Doukhobor wave passed through our part of California and shook the little town of Chico to its foundation. The party of Sons of Freedom, Brother Vlasoff and the others, came back from the Hawaiian Islands. They marched on the town of Chico with preaching, and protested that they were not being given a place to bury their grandfather Leonoff. This made a strong impression on my father; he experienced a kind of elation, a feeling of enthusiasm and consolation from Vlasoff's march. The Vereschagin brothers— Vasily Vasilyevich had not yet left to Canada—did not fully approve of this parade, but made no comment. I was overcome by curiosity and went to see these Sons of Freedom for myself, but I did not stay with them long. True, a remarkable vitality and spiritual energy emanated from them, but at this time they did not deeply attract my interest. I was too much absorbed in my own world, my book-friends from whom I could not break away. I gradually assimilated the Vereschagin ideas, and Vlasoff's were entirely different, even contradictory, so my mind was divided, and my thought scattered.

Molokans of Southern California

In the spring of 1917 while working at a mill where alfalfa was being ground, I suffered a lung infection due to the dust, and this later resulted in a serious inflammation. I was forced to stop work and go south to recuperate. In Los Angeles, I met several others suffering from the same ailment. I became closely associated with Ivan Kozianchuk, a Bessarabian from Kishinev. He told me that he had come to know several Doukhobors. While working in a gold mine in British Columbia, he had contracted a lung ailment and found himself in a hospital in Vancouver. In this same hospital lay a patient named Alexei Vlasoff, a brother of Ivan and Vasia Vlasoff. Alexei Vlasoff was also quite an original character. We shall hear more about him later. As he lay in the hospital, feeling that his life was nearing an end, he was not worried about himself, but advised Kozianchuk to go to California to the Vlasoff brothers who were living there. On arriving in California, Kozianchuk was supported by the Vlasoffs, but being a conscientious man, he was worried that he was a burden upon them. He had entered America illegally so he could not appeal for help to any of the established charitable institutions, and was forced to seek assistance from private individuals. To this purpose he approached my father who gave him some money and promised to help him until he was well. And so, with the help of Doukhobors, he was able to get medical care at the Los Angeles hospital. Kozianchuk was already at the hospital when I was admitted. My father advised me to take him to my quarters and look after his needs, but I was not able to find a place immediately and while looking for lodgings, I stayed temporarily at Ivan Prokofievich Yurin's.

To be a guest of a Molokan is the greatest of privileges; they treat the Doukhobors as their own kin. Ivan Prokofievich was a sort of apostate, and looked upon life from a radical point of view, ignoring the Molokan customs. His wife was benevolent and good-natured and deeply religious. On this score they experienced friction.

At some distance from them was the Molokan home where the Klubnikin Molokans gathered several times a week with a great deal of shouting and commotion. Curiosity prompted me to go to the service and see for myself. When I got there, I saw bearded Molokans in an excited state: some of them jumping about as though they were not normal. This picture was strange, almost comical to me, but after attending several more services, I changed my opinion. I gradually saw their deep and sincere attitude toward prayer and toward religion in general. The Molokan rapture was touching, and their hospitality, fellowship and friendship could not be excelled.

Once Yurin's wife's parents, the Kechikoffs, came to visit them from Arizona. They invited others to meet them. A Molokan reception always has a sacramental aspect. It was intensely interesting to me to follow their communion. First, they prayed, then kissed each other, sat down at table and prayed again, ate and drank tea, and talked on a spiritual theme.

Philip Michailovich Shubin was present at this supper. I saw that he at once showed himself superior to the rest, a master of thought. How far-sighted he was and what insight he had, I could not evaluate. But often I recalled how skilfully he could arouse the interest of them all. I was strongly attracted to him that evening.

Afterwards, the old man, Mechikoff, told me: "Do you know, Peter, Philip Michailovich Shubin is one of our leaders, who brought us out of the Caucasus; he and another, Ivan Gursevich Samarin. Through them our God gave us His blessing and we landed in this Promised Land. They even lay in prison, in Tiflis."

Afterwards, Dedushka Mechikoff and I visited Philip Michailovich. He spoke with great respect of the Doukhobor movement in the Caucasus, and indicated some shortcomings of our present-day Doukhobors. "Some of your Doukhobors come to us in Los Angeles and cannot even so much as say a prayer over their daily bread; they have forgotten everything. This is a shame and spiritual retrogression."

I was biting my lips in shame for I, too, had forgotten the prayers that my grandmother taught me.

I attended such gatherings a few more times, and it was touching to witness their spiritual ecstasy. But I was amazed and repulsed by their gluttonous meat-eating; because of this, I left them and lived mostly by myself, at times mingling with various theosophical and vegetarian societies such as the Rosicrucian.

My father told me to be sure to call upon Panfilovich Kariakin. When my father was on his way to Colorado, he called at a Molokan settlement in the state of Utah, where they had been enticed by land agents. My father especially liked Kariakin. "Kariakin," he said, "is a remarkable man."

When I called, we almost at once began an argument about meat-eating. Aleksei Panfilovich at first tried to prove that the Bible permitted the use of meat and therefore there was no sin in eating it. I showed him Williams's *Ethics of Diet* which I always carried in my pocket and from which I never parted.

Aleksei Panfilovich looked at the excerpts from various philosophers and poets, who expressed their repulsion to meat-eating, and said, "Yes, I suppose our Molokan brotherhood will have to stop burying dead animals in our stomachs. But it will take a long time to re-educate them."

I was at Panfilovich's home at another time, when he had guests. On the table they had great platters heaped with meat. Panfilovich was obviously embarrassed. Turning to the guests he said, "Here's Peter, a Doukhobor, a strong vegetarian, and we have meat on the table."

One of the guests cited an example from the New Testament in which the Apostle Paul says, "Not that which goeth into the mouth defileth a man." "Yes," he said, "most important is what comes out of his mouth; that is what we should be careful about," he triumphantly concluded. I, of course, had no intention of going into a debate with him and made no further comment. When I left, I took Renan's book *The Apostle Paul*, which Aleksei Panfilovich advised me to read.

Aleksei Panfilovich was educated and a man of broad views. He had passed through college in Tiflis, where he had lived for some time.

Of all the Molokan families, I most often visited the Yurins, Ivan Prokofievich and Aleksei, the elder, whose parental name I have forgotten. The elder Aleksei was a remarkable old man, and a vegetarian. His face seemed to radiate a sort of invisible light, and I was very much drawn to him.

When I finally found lodgings for myself, I at once took Kozianchuk with me. He proved to be quite a skilful musician, a cornet player. He never parted with his expensive cornet, which he had brought with him from Russia. He told me that he had played in the Kishinevsky Orchestra. Word of his musical ability spread, and in the evenings other musicians began to gather in our lodgings and we used to have concerts. Nick Sokoloff, a balalaika player, Galeyuka, a guitarist, Alexander Vlasoff, a pianist, and Schepetneff, an accordionist, as well as several others, were frequent visitors. On one of the musical evenings, a prominent stage designer and technician, Puschin, from Hollywood, dropped in. Kozianchuk's playing appealed to him very much and he proposed that at the first opportunity he would find a place for him at the studio, as soon as he was well. But cornet playing interfered with Kozianchuk's health and he became worse instead of better. More than once, I advised him to stop playing, but his love for music overruled and he went on playing.

In this way we spent about three months. During the day we would stroll through the park in the sunlight. This was our main treatment. Sometimes we would visit the library, which was just across the street from where we stayed. It was in this library that I first became acquainted with many of the famous Russian journals. The *Russkoye Bogatstvo* (*Russian Wealth*), *Russkaya Mysl'* (*Russian Thought*), *Niva* (*The Field*), *Bulletani Literaturi I Zhisni* (*Bulletin on Literature and Life*) and many others.

About this time through the Red Cross, Kozianchuk received a letter from his brother in the old country, which gave him the final blow. The letter informed him of the death of his wife and son. Up to that time he had lived in the hope that they would be able to come to him, but at the outbreak of war the boundaries were closed and his plans cancelled. Upon receiving the bitter news, he broke down and wept irrepressibly and he read and reread the letter several times. His condition immediately became worse and he was soon forced to stay in bed.

A week later, we were visited by our benefactor, Ivan Prokofievich Yurin. He advised Kozianchuk to go to the Molokan settlement in Arizona as soon as he could. Yurin even helped to gather some money for the trip. Afterwards, I learned that Kozianchuk had died soon after he reached Arizona. He was buried by the Molokan brethren.

Arrest

My health improved quickly and I was soon able to leave Los Angeles. I found a companion, a robust Pole from Connecticut by the name of Kamensky, and he and I went south in search of work. But work was not easy to find and we roamed about the farms for some time until we accidently got into trouble. At one place we stopped a Mexican to ask him if he knew where it was possible to find work. He informed that due to a disagreement between the workers and the orchard owners about the low wages in that locality, several barns and other buildings had been razed. The blame for this was placed on the labour organization IWW [Industrial Workers of the World] and white strangers were regarded with suspicion.

We had no time to finish our conversation with the Mexican when along came a car, from which stepped two sheriffs. They showed us their badges and said to us, "We want you, get in the car."

We did not understand why we were being arrested, and tried to explain to them that we were looking for work. But they refused to pay attention to our explanation and told us that everything would be explained at the office.

We were brought to the town of Santa Ana and locked in jail. After some time, we were called for questioning in the sheriff's office. To our surprise we saw all our belongings there. Apparently, they had already searched our quarters. This, it seemed, was no laughing matter. We were suspected of serious crime. My friend, the Pole, undoubtedly seemed to them to be especially suspicious because of his businesslike manner. They could not believe that such an attractively dressed man was actually looking for work on a farm, and undoubtedly took him for a secret agitator.

The questioning began with the Pole. He was not in the least cowed but expressed in no uncertain terms his indignation over his arrest. He showed them his documents amongst which was a letter of introduction from the mayor of Bridgeport. He was freed and allowed to go. I was very much hurt when my friend left, without even so much as glancing at me. He could easily have freed me too with documents. But that was as far as our friendship went.

Then they began on me. I proved to them that I knew nothing of what was going on here and that I was actually looking for work. They no doubt knew that I was not guilty of any offence but still, they did not want to let me go free. This was a good chance for them to try to scare me into joining the army. They asked me for my registration, but I said to them that I did not have it, because I was younger than the registration age and besides, I was a Doukhobor and did not take part in war. They refused to believe my age, and tried to make me admit that I was older than I said and that I was just trying to evade the military responsibility. They took me back and locked me up in a jail cell. It was for the first time that the strength of my spirit in the struggle against militarism was tested. I sat and turned over in my mind every possibility: What if they should turn me over to the military authority? And no one would even know of my fate!

About eight o'clock in the evening, they took me out for questioning. I saw the head sheriff; with him was a young girl, apparently his daughter, and no one else. The sheriff began to question me; where I was from, who I was and why I was here, and so on. It taxed all my resources to convince him of my innocence, but he was not to be moved. This at last was more than I could stand. My soul surged within me, I cried like a baby, and through my tears I again and again repeated these words: "Do what you like with me, even kill me, but I'll never join the army."

These proceedings touched the young girl. She turned to the sheriff and said, "Father, let him go. He is telling the truth."

Upon this the sheriff immediately freed me. So ended my first struggle with militarism. I was beside myself with joy and in my thoughts thanked this girl hundreds and hundreds of times. The image of her charming face found a warm spot in my heart and will live in my memory forever.

This incident frightened me, and I resolved to give up wandering. I returned to Los Angeles where I met my former school friend, Thompson. He was driving to visit relatives in Tucson and invited me to go along with him for company.

Wandering

For the two weeks that we roamed, an inexplicable feeling of happiness filled my breast. It was April 1918. In Arizona, the beauty of the plains, deserts, cactuses, distant snow-covered mountains, tree-clothed lowlands and the singing of birds enraptured my soul. We also visited Mexico, staying for three days in the city of Magdalena. Here everything was cheaper than in the United States. It was warm and we slept beside the car, under the open sky. There was abundance everywhere. At first glance, the poverty of the people struck us; most of the Mexicans were in rags and barefooted. In spite of this, their faces radiated the joy of living and though poor, they sang and made merry. My friend was well acquainted with Mexican history and recommended that I read Prescott's *History of the Conquest of Mexico*. He said that the Catholic priests and the officials literally robbed the people here. He also told me that it was near this area that General Villa fought with Carranza during the Mexican Revolution.

Near the town of Magdalena, we chanced upon a spot where some Native Mexicans had pitched their camp. We were nauseated by their appearance; they had killed a cow and were cutting it up; dirty children were running around with pieces of barely scorched meat in their hands. Just to look upon them brought pain to the soul. These Native Mexicans were once a proud and, in their own way, a cultured race. Before the coming of Europeans, the Native Mexicans lived prosperously here; they had their own kingdoms, Yucatán, Peru and Chile. Traces of this culture are even now to be seen in the ruins of Mexico, Central and South America. Then the "civilized" Europeans began to crowd out the Mexicans and to destroy their lives. Now they are ruined and pushed to the very extremities of need.

This picture imprinted itself deeply on my memory. Afterwards whenever I heard plans and theories of setting up a life in accordance to nature somewhere in the tropics, I always recalled this picture of a crowd of people around a dead cow, infested by swarms of flies.

Afterwards, I saw another picture widely dissociated from the first: Native Mexicans in their holiday attire gathered around a huge church. I liked them for their simplicity. They gathered to share their grief and perhaps receive a little happiness. Their faces were radiant. As I looked at them, I thought, "You poor, deluded, exploited people."

We returned to Los Angeles. I worked a little here and there but soon went back to Yurin's. During this time, I met several other groups and individuals. I visited the Potemkins, Ustinoffs and Baronoffs. They told me that they had recently returned from British Columbia, where they lived among the Doukhobors and even tried to associate with the community in the Prekrasnoye (Shoreacres) district. With them lived the Pirozhko and Popoff families as well as others. They were all of non-Doukhobor origin and perhaps that explains why they could not live in the community. Their account of community life indicated that the people of the community were literally enslaved and exploited by various forms of injustice. Of Peter Vasilievich they spoke with horror. I cringed and felt very small indeed. It was embarrassing and provoking to have these outsiders criticizing my Doukhobor brotherhood, but I could not say a word on this matter, because I didn't know even the slightest thing about the life of the community.

I made the acquaintance of two students from the technical school: one was a Ukrainian from North Dakota who called himself Hamilton. He never told me his real name. He was a tall, robust and handsome man. His room was full of books, instruments, blueprints and sketches.

Once, after watching him leaf through his sketches, I asked him, "Hamilton, can it be that all this studying and torture is really necessary?"

He gave me a distracted look and said, "Yes, it is."

Once I found him in a troubled and irritated state. He could not grasp a geometric problem and was genuinely distressed. I said to him, "Leave this whole business or you'll lose your mind before you get to be a technician."

But he replied, "I'd advise you to take a technical course too."

"No, thanks," I said, "I am not interested in machines. Philosophy, that's different, that appeals to me."

"A philosopher," he rejoined, "but there's no future in philosophy. Who will give you money if you become a philosopher, even if you should solve some great riddle of wisdom? But for the technician there are many pathways open: invent, erect, build, perfect yourself. No matter where you turn there are new undeveloped possibilities: on the earth, under water and in the air, and about money—there certainly is no need to worry. Engineering is a big money business, and once you have money, you will have happiness and contentment."

I heard him out, but could not agree with him. There was another student with us, also a Ukrainian, whom they called Brown. He heard our conversation and said, "No, that's not right." Turning to me he said, "I see what you are interested in. Come along with me and I will show you something which will undoubtedly be to your taste. Today in our school there will be a lecture on the subject of 'War, its causes and prevention.'"

The lecture was interesting. The speaker was David Starr Jordan, a famous professor and afterwards the president of the Stanford University. How splendidly he presented his arguments on the causes and absurdity of war! Several students hooted at his anti-militaristic spirit. Afterwards I regretted that I did not take the opportunity to make his acquaintance that evening, to express my appreciation of his lecture and my sympathy with his views. Only when I read his two volumes entitled *The Days of a Man* did I realize that he was truly a highly gifted person.[45]

I sometimes visited the Russian Cultural Club. At first, they gathered at the home of Barisoff, a watchmaker, but later they acquired a suitable hall. In the evenings, Leschin from Hollywood often spoke. He was distinguished looking and resembled a professor; he was quiet, spoke well and lectured on various subjects. Often the loud-voiced house painter, Alexander Philipoff, also spoke. I used to visit this gathering and often wondered what was the reason for this display of skill and culture, right on First Street, where all around lived the Molokan brotherhood. Sometime afterwards, a Russian Cossack, who kept a store nearby, said to me: "This presentation is for the purpose of interesting the Molokan youth in Russian culture." But all the time I was there, I never once saw a Molokan there with the exception of Ivan Prokofievich Yurin and Vladimir Pavlovich Shanin.

At the end of May 1918, Ivan Prokofievich Yurin and I went to San Francisco. On the way we dropped in to see Kerman and visited several Molokan farmers. I remember being at Moïse Slivin's. They received us warmly and treated us most generously. Also, we called on the Mendrins. Then my fellow traveller, Ivan Prokofievich, engaged to work for Nikolai Ivanovich Bezieff. I was going to go home but I did not have enough money, so I telegraphed my parents to send me some. Nikolai Bezieff's father used to live in Oregon while we lived there and he often came to see us. In view of this, he now treated me as an old friend. He was a large man of a strict character. Added to this he had recently met with an unfortunate accident. A horse stepped on his foot and he was not able to work, but had to walk on crutches. While waiting for the money from my parents, I lived with them for some time, and rode around with them on horseback. One morning we went to the Mendrins'.

There I met a person hitherto unknown to me. Bezieff pointed me out to

---

45   David Starr Jordan (January 19, 1851–September 19, 1931) was the founding president of Stanford University, serving from 1891 to 1913, and author of *The Days of a Man* (Yonkers-on-Hudson, NY: World Book Co., 1922).

him saying, "Here's a Doukhobor of yours." This stranger was Vasya Pozdnia-koff, author of the pamphlet *Tales of the Doukhobor Vasya Pozdniakoff.* He looked at me and hurriedly greeted me. I already knew about him and his booklet, but I had never met him personally before. I scrutinized him carefully; his eyes were expressive; his nose straight, and his ears stuck out from his head. His black hair was streaked with grey. He seemed to me to be a man of uncommon depth. We talked at great length. I found that he was prejudiced against Peter Vasilievich, but had too little opportunity to interchange thoughts and ideas with him. Lat-er he sent me a notebook of his poems in which he expressed his feelings and thoughts on the Sons of Freedom, Peter Vasilievich and nature. Several of his compositions in memory of Leo Nikolaevich Tolstoy were also included. I often grieved and regretted that I lost this book.

This meeting was deeply imprinted on my memory. In parting, I ex-pressed the hope that I might call on him some other time and become more closely acquainted, but I was never to see him again. He died in 1921.

Meanwhile, my parents had again settled in Oregon, near Eugene, but they did not intend to stay permanently for brother Nikolai had returned to Canada and my parents talked of moving there so that we could all live together.

There was nothing for me to do at home. But again, I found a compan-ion, Trofim Vozni, and he convinced me to go with him to Seattle to a friend of his and work there for a time. His friend was a Ukrainian. Ivan Muchenko had once lived among the Doukhobors in Canada. In his features Muchenko was a duplicate of Stepniak Krawchenko. He was a shoemaker by trade, a vegetari-an, well-read, and even corresponded with Leo Nikolaevich Tolstoy but he was absent-minded and couldn't even keep track of his family. At times his conver-sation was interesting, particularly when he alluded to his past life. He always wore a cap decorated with a ribbon on which was inscribed in gold letters the words "I am Alpha and Omega, the beginning and the end."

Muchenko stayed in the home of some very religious Baptists, with whom lived several other Russian Baptist families. Trofim and I lodged in a hotel, and when in the evenings Muchenko returned from his work, we walked out to meet him and together went to his lodgings. Each time we walked in with him, we found everyone in the house on their knees engaged in passionate prayer; I had never seen anything like it before. The master of the house was a benevo-lent, kind-hearted man. It was said that he had lately come back from prison, where he served three months for protesting against war. I do not remember his name as we were not often there, and talked very little because they were almost always praying. I remember that there was one unusually tall man with a grown-up daughter who had recently returned from the Hawaiian Islands. The preacher of this group, a man of distinguished physique, was always in front of the others and, for the most part, on his knees. And how he called upon everyone to repent! His words showered like sparks of fire.

Trofim and I did not stay long in Seattle, but went on to Canada. Soon after we received a letter from Muchenko in which he informed us of an unpleasant circumstance in their Baptist congregation: their passionate preacher had run away with the wife of the master of the house, the one who had been in jail.

"Aha," thought I, "so while the one was in jail, the other was involved with his wife and all this fierceness and the passion of a preacher was nothing more than a shrewd pretense so that the husband would not suspect anything until they could find an opportune moment to run off together."

Pacifists during World War I

[Vera] Though Grandfather Pete was not able to attend university to study as he wished, voracious reading, an intense interest in people and their lifestyle choices and lectures in libraries, cultural clubs and free forums provided him with a higher education. Furthermore, acquaintance with resolute pacifists instilled in him a lifelong desire to do what he could to promote peace and justice in this world. Dr. Scott Nearing and Ammon Hennacy were two of his correspondents who, despite severe repercussions, spoke against war.

Dr. Scott Nearing (1883–1983) and his wife visited my grandparents' market garden farm in Thrums. My mother Elizabeth remembers the Nearings with fondness. A memory she shared with me was of her parents and Scott and Helen Nearing sitting on the porch of their farmhouse, munching sunflower seeds, laughing and talking, and after, true to their practice of organic gardening, they diligently collected a whole sack full of the shells and added them to the compost pile. I could almost hear their conversations on simplicity, vegetarianism and pacifism.

I had known Scott and Helen Nearing as the authors of *Living the Good Life: How to Live Sanely and Simply in a Troubled World*, the book that inspired many back-to-the-landers in the '70s, but I had not heard about his political involvement. On the shelves of my grandfather's library, I found Scott Nearing's book *The Making of a Radical: A Political Autobiography*, personally signed to Pete Maloff.

Nearing was born into a well-to-do family in Morris Run, Pennsylvania, where his grandfather was the superintendent of the coal mining and lumbering town. Scott Nearing had received a doctorate in economics from the University of Pennsylvania and beginning in 1906 taught at the prestigious Wharton School of Finance. I found it astonishing that his determination to promote financial fairness for all workers and speak against child labour practices got him dismissed from the university, though it gave me an indication of the attitude of private universities and business tycoons of the early 1900s.

I found this Ivy League professor and my grandfather, a largely self-educated Doukhobor, to have astonishingly similar philosophies of life. Tolstoy was a mentor to both Scott Nearing and Pete Maloff and I could understand their mutual joy at finding one another. Nearing wrote that Tolstoy spent fifty years in questioning, protesting and resisting government policy he saw as immoral. He sought peace for humankind through non-violent resistance to evil but insisted on speaking the truth and taking peaceful but decisive action. In this, Nearing and Maloff both followed Tolstoy's giant footsteps.

Ammon Hennacy (1893–1970) was imprisoned for two years for resisting conscription and was in solitary confinement for eight months for leading a hunger strike in jail. In a protest against militarism, he resolved not to support the war effort in any way and refused to pay income tax. For this reason, he worked as a day labourer receiving his wages in cash.

Hennacy had visited the Maloff farm, and my mother especially remembered his passion for peace. Mother often fasted for health reasons, but she was amazed to learn that Hennacy had fasted for forty days in protest against nuclear weapons and at another time against the death penalty.

Hennacy's dissent against funnelling tax dollars toward the military budget was an inspiration to Pete Maloff. In 1929 Grandfather organized a protest walk on Baker Street in Nelson against paying taxes for war. This march resulted in six months' hard labour for him and eight other organizers in the infamous Oakalla Prison. It was during this imprisonment that Pete Maloff's friend, Vladimir Ivanovich Meier, died under tragic circumstances. In the 1930s the Maloff family farm was expropriated for nonpayment of taxes. It was only when Great-grandfather William Hoodicoff pleaded with the new owner weekly to sell the land back to the Maloffs that they were able to buy it back, for the one hundred dollars in unpaid taxes.

My grandfather's reading habits motivated me to read extensively. I loved investigating the books in his library, upstairs in their home. He had a desk pushed against a northern attic window dormer from which he could see the forest and mountain where he loved to walk and think. Crammed bookshelves overflowing with books covered the walls and there was a dusty but pleasant smell of well-worn volumes.

In 1960, Pete Maloff was able to sell some of his collection of rare pamphlets and books to the University of British Columbia through acquisition librarian Robert Hamilton. This helped to fund an around-the-world trip to visit his many correspondents. He was met with open arms in twenty-seven countries including Germany, Russia, Egypt, Israel, Iran, Afghanistan, India, Sri Lanka and Japan. One writer whom he was unable to contact met him at the airport in Frankfurt. Grandfather was surprised to see him, but his friend said that he had dreamt a few nights previously that he must meet Pete Maloff at the airport and this was the second evening that he watched for flights from North America. He made many such connections with like-minded souls.

Recently, I met with a librarian at UBC to investigate the possibility of finding a list of books and pamphlets they bought from Grandfather. There was no such list, but I discovered a box of correspondence between Robert Hamilton, Pete Maloff and finally myself. The last letter, dated October 1971, was one I wrote to Mr. Hamilton conveying the sad news that my grandfather died on a bus trip to stay with his friend Dr. Bernard Jensen in California. He had planned to complete his memoir, particularly about his acquaintance with Doukhobor leader Peter P. Verigin, but it was not to be.

ON CHAPTER 11

THE SONS OF FREEDOM
OF BOZHYA DOLINA

[Vera] Bozhya Dolina is not to be found on a map of the Grand Forks area. Even long-time residents of Grand Forks were not able to give me the location of the settlement. It was John J. Verigin, the executive director of the Doukhobor organization Union of Spiritual Communities of Christ (USCC), who informed me about Bozhya Dolina. He said, "At the sharp turn of Highway 3, just before you cross the bridge into Grand Forks, take the Granby Road north following the Granby River." He said that his great-grandfather, Peter Vasilievich Verigin, provided this land for the most radical and stalwart Sons of Freedom Doukhobors. They wished to live entirely according to God's law, without exploiting the earth or using any inventions of civilization. Gospodnyi told them, if that is what you wish to do, then do not even cut down a live tree, but use ones already dead to build your homes. I found Pete Maloff's description and reaction to this unusual way of life fascinating and at times humorous.

CHAPTER 11

THE SONS OF FREEDOM OF BOZHYA DOLINA

My companion, Trofim Vozni, was planning to go to Saskatchewan, but first we decided to stop at Grand Forks and visit the family of Paul Skripnik. Skripnik was of Ukrainian ancestry, but through his convictions had joined the Sons of Freedom, a long time ago, and now he lived with them in their settlement Bozhya Dolina (God's Valley) not far from the town of Grand Forks.

We had no idea what awaited us in Bozhya Dolina and we did not intend to stay long. But when we arrived, a picture that was entirely new to us met our eyes. Though I had previously been acquainted with several Sons of Freedom, they were separate individuals, away from their nest. Here, however, was a settlement of about a hundred. My friends Grigoriy Vlasoff and Paul Drazdoff, who had left the United States some time before to avoid militarism, had settled here for the time being. I thought of staying two or three days and then going on to my brother's place in Castlegar. The Sons of Freedom received us cordially though we noticed at once that there appeared to be only women and children. We were told several men were arrested for not accepting National Registration and they were thrown into jail. Added to this was the fact that the Sons of Freedom had burned a harness belonging to Mitya Dubasoff, a Doukhobor who was not a Son of Freedom. In this connection some twenty-five men were arrested. We saw people living a simple primitive life, waging a fight to the death with a powerful enemy, the state. We besieged them with questions trying to grasp the aim of their effort, but their replies and explanations did not satisfy us. Some questions, like that of registration, we understood. This was a direct protest against war, but we could not see why the harness was burned. They argued that they were trying to set up a new form of life in Bozhya Dolina without using animal labour. Among them lived a man who did not share these views and kept horses. They repeatedly told him either to free his animals or go away, but he refused to do either.

"What else was there for us to do?" they asked.

We were preparing to leave, but they appealed to us to stay a little while longer, to help them until their men returned.

The Sons of Freedom of Bozhya Dolina lived a simple life without the use of animal labour and modern conveniences. They strove to free Mother Earth of exploitation, using only dead trees for their homes and firewood.

"Winter is coming and we have nothing prepared," they said. "Stay and help us and you will find out more about our life and our belief."

They prevailed upon us and we decided to stay.

They invited us to go with them to pick up some apples from a farmer who lived about ten miles south. At first, we saw nothing unusual in this, but how surprised we were when we saw that the Sons of Freedom, instead of hitching horses to the wagon, hitched themselves and we, being newcomers, were asked to help by pushing the wagon from behind.

Away we went. My friend and I walked along behind the wagon and laughed.

At first this was amusing and we were looked upon as a circus parade. All went well enough, but when we came into Grand Forks, our "horses" and especially old man Syoma Chernenkoff, turned in right through the main street of town. When spectators gathered, he jumped along in exact imitation of a trotting horse and neighed. His trotting was natural and effective, but at that particular time it appeared to me to be somewhat overbearingly naive. I found it hard to walk along with them. After all, I was a "civilized" man, just out of the States, and it embarrassed me to be a part of this primitive demonstration.

Arriving at our destination, we loaded the wagon with apples and pears and headed back. We were joined by two young women and a man who had gone ahead of us to pick the fruit. Again, we passed through town.

"Well," I thought, "at least I hope they don't stop anywhere." But the Sons of Freedom stopped in front of the drugstore in the very centre of Grand Forks. "It's a good thing," I thought, "that nobody knows us here, or we would have been given the horse-laugh!"

They soon finished their errand and were on the point of starting off again. Old Syoma started jumping, then suddenly he strained in the harness with a jerk and tossed his long hair about like a mane. On the street the spectators burst out laughing.

One young man shouted after us, "Crazy Douks!" This finished the matter for me. Then and there, I decided to get away from these people as soon as I possibly could.

All the way back I walked behind the wagon, pushing the load, with my head bent low so that no one would recognize me. Then they began to sing, and this singing cheered me up. The town stretched about two miles and as we walked the chorus of ten sounded like a symphony come to life. The tenor, so soft and yet so clear, sounded like a little bell. It seemed as if the singing was coming from an unseen distance and it whirled through my soul like an auger.

I had heard the world-famous Caruso; I had attended the concert of the great violinist Kreisler; I had seen Anna Pavlova in her "Swan Dance." In all these places the crowds heaved with emotion and applauded madly, but never in my life had anything affected me so deeply as the singing of these Sons of Freedom. The rest of the way back, I was under the spell of their singing, and I felt that these people represented something really great. But exactly what this greatness was, I could not understand.

On reaching home the "horses" unhitched themselves. I looked at the tired old man Syoma, and I saw him in an altogether different light than in the morning and I thought to myself, "He wasn't actually doing anything wrong by his trotting; it even seemed to suit him." On this day I had passed a crisis. Later trips caused me no embarrassment.

My friend Trofim and I stayed in the tent of Fenya Vlasoff, Vasiliy Vlasoff's wife. Many had not yet built their houses when the husbands were taken off to prison. Not far away was Alesha Vlasoff's tent. He had tuberculosis of the legs, and had just come from the Vancouver hospital. He was white as a sheet and his coal black hair contrasted so sharply that it made him look almost transparent. His hands were thin and delicate, artist's hands. As he lay in bed, he knitted fantastically beautiful articles from yarn. His intellect was keen and little by little as I became acquainted with him, he shared a great deal of interesting information with me.

Once he told me the story of this settlement: "Do you think that these people gathered here for the fun of it? No! Here life itself is unfolding its secrets. Well, then, to tell you a parable, there was, among the Doukhobors, a mighty sower. He made a plentiful sowing and the seeds sprouted and the plants began to appear. The sower was Peter Vasilievich Verigin. Read his seventeenth letter to Izumchenko in the compilation of his letters.[46] It will perhaps help you to understand where and why the Sons of Freedom originated. The aim of the Sons of Freedom is to bring their lives back to God's law of righteousness not in words alone. They recognize that God is the cause and the result of all life, not only on our planet but of all the universe. Man has violated this higher law of equilibrium, and that is why such a terrible life has resulted on this earth. The principle aim of these people is to free mother earth from the exploitation and the prostitution to which she is being subjected. The land is the mother-provider to all people equally, and no one should seize land for himself and lay title to it, or exact for it any kind of rent or taxes whatsoever. The Sons of Freedom are trying to do away with the chains and fetters with which man has burdened himself in his long journey on earth, and to establish a rational life, conforming to brotherhood, equality and love, as Christ once taught."

Such discourse confused me seriously. I could not understand all its implications and listened to Alesha as if in a dream. But my curiosity increased; more and more often I found an occasion to talk with him.

My friend and I became more and more attracted to these people. Here were several interesting families: the Chernenkoffs, Voikins, Dutoffs, Skripniks and others. Here too lived Petrunya Voikin who lately returned from prison in Saskatchewan, where with other Sons of Freedom he was jailed for burning the Otradnoe home. He was tall and sturdy, his long hair fell over his shoulders, and he looked like a giant. He had a peculiar twist in his speech and always gave the letter "g" a "y" sound in pronunciation. "Germany" he called "Yermany."

There was also the aged Savva Kolesnikoff, who for his convictions left his family and came to live here. Several old women, Aksinya Horkoff, Paranya Holuboff and a few others had done the same.

I was always planning to leave but circumstances held me. The Sons of Freedom were making what haste they could to build their homes before winter and my friend and I helped them. Because they could not use the labour of horses, all the work had to be done by human power. Logs were dragged for

---

46   Maloff, Section II, Part II, Chapter 3, in *Doukhobors: Their History, Life and Struggle*, ibid.

considerable distances and the Sons of Freedom could not be convinced that it was right to cut down live, green wood. They used only dry timber.

One morning three women said they had to go to the police station and asked me to go with them as interpreter. What could I do? I thought to myself: "You stayed to help, then go without a word. Here everyone does what he is able to do."

We went. The women were young, attractive and beautiful. I thought to myself: "The Sons of Freedom picked the best looking so that they could get the attention of the police."

On the way, the women explained their errand: Their husbands and fathers were working on the railroad, but when they were put into prison the railroad company refused to give the money they had earned to their families, saying that it would be paid to the men when they came out of jail. Their families were in extreme need and wanted the money at once. This was why we were going to town.

When we entered the Court House, we were met by two policemen with the words: "What now? Are you looking for trouble again?"

I replied that we came about a money affair.

They answered sarcastically: "What do you want money for? You used to burn it."

The question of the money was not yet settled when the police pounced on me: Who was I? Where from? They asked me to produce my registration card. I replied that I had only recently come from the States. At this point especially they jumped at me. "An agitator," they said. "We have more than enough of our own here."

The police gave me three days' time in which to register or be thrown into jail.

In spite of their aggressiveness, we came to a satisfactory agreement and the women received their money.

On the way back Groonya, the wife of Vasili Semyonovich Chernenkoff, said to me: "They [the police] are always like that; they think that someone or other is stirring us up, as though we are not able to think for ourselves."

Afterwards, when I became acquainted with this Vasili Chernenkoff, I found that he was one of the best of the self-taught Doukhobor orators. He spoke so eloquently that his words echoed in one's ears and were not easily forgotten.

I asked my fellow travellers when it was that they burned the money the police mentioned. "Oh, that was long ago while we were still in Saskatchewan, when we decided to live entirely according to God's law and not even make use of Caesar's dollar. The Sons of Freedom then burned not only money but even their trunks with clothing, and even the clothes they had on them. They were then taken to jail."

"In some cases, the Sons of Freedom go a little too far," concluded Aksinya Honcheroff. "They burned them, and then went out begging for them. Once you don't need the clothes, then stay naked!"

On the way, Tanya, Paul Skripnik's daughter, briefly mentioned that her eighteen-year-old brother Zot and the tall Ivan Voikin were the two tallest men among the Doukhobors. Voikin was over seven feet tall and had the build of a giant. Both of them were tortured to death in Moosomin jail by having hot broth poured down their throats through a hose.

When I asked Tanya why they were jailed, the women replied in unison: "They and other Sons of Freedom burned Petiushka's home in the Otradnoe village!"

"Why did they do that?" I asked.

"A home like that should never have been built in the first place. It was unnecessarily luxurious and Doukhobors shouldn't be getting into luxury or they will trample the Truth under their feet."

This reply confused the issues even more. When we returned to Bozhya Dolina, I went to talk to Alesha Vlasoff. I told him of my conversation with the women and asked him to explain why the Otradnoe home was razed.

He heard me out, thought a moment and began: "You want to know everything too quickly, young man. I advise you to go to the community and see for yourself how people live there, and then we shall talk about it; maybe after that it will be clearer to you."

His reply baffled me and, in a way, hurt me. Apparently, Alesha took me for a child and did not want to speak frankly with me. But I decided to take his advice and next morning my friend Trofim and I marched off to the Fruitvale district where the main community settlement was situated.

On the way Trofim suggested to me: "What do you think, Peter? When we come to the community, I will pose as a Doukhobor and you as a Russian. We will be able to find out more that way."

"You and your ideas!" said I. "But we will try it; maybe it will be better that way."

The members of the community received us suspiciously, but when they learned that one of us was a Russian, their attitude immediately changed. It seems that they distrusted the Doukhobor farmers. They complained that the Farmers and the Independent Doukhobors slandered them in the newspapers, falsely denouncing the community and their leader, saying that they had chosen a monarch in the person of Peter Vasilievich and were worshipping him.

The community was beginning to put up a brick factory and the work was in full swing. I, as a Russian, was taken everywhere by Grisha Zebroff, who showed and explained everything to me about the new enterprise. It was pleasant and cheering to watch the energetic efforts of the community members.

I began to question Zebroff about Doukhobors in general, and he told me frankly: "The Doukhobors are Christian communists. The Independents have already broken the main principle and are now trying to do away with all the rest. All they know how to do is to work against the community."

"Yes," I said, "and the Sons of Freedom? What do they represent?" Grisha thought for a moment, and then asked: "Where did you get to know about them?"

I told him that I happened in on them in Bozhya Dolina, had been there for several days, and was planning to stay a few more. "We know that they have had several incidents there lately: they burned the harnesses, they refused to register. They take their clothes off, and they do not recognize any man-made laws. To us this is hard to understand," I concluded.

Grisha thought awhile and then replied: "Among the Sons of Freedom there are some good people and their aim is good, but many of them are not true Sons of Freedom, but pretend to be. These spoil everything."

Grisha took us to dinner. All the workers sat behind a long table, singing psalms, and then all together, like soldiers they rose and prayed. They ate good vegetarian food. Afterwards they sang again, and then gave thanks.

"This," said Grisha, "is the usual order of every meal with us. Everyone must know their turn to say grace and this is our password toward a peaceful life."

I must admit that I came away from there depressed, as if we had just visited a military camp, where everything was under strict discipline; wherever you turned, there was law, you can't do this, and you can't do that. Everything must be just so or you are not a true member of the community.

When we returned, I went to Alesha Vlasoff and said to him: "Tell me, why is there such strict discipline in the community? That is in its own way a spiritual compulsion."

"Yes, you are right," said Alesha. "This is, of course, training. Were you ever in school?"

"Yes," I said.

"Tell me," he said, "could a school carry on without discipline?"

I answered: "That, of course, depends on the students. If the students would do their work conscientiously, discipline would not be needed."

"That's just the point," said Alesha. "If they would act conscientiously: The community is a school where Peter Vasilievich has gathered the Doukhobors so that they will learn a few things about life. Every man must have an ideal to strive to, but the Doukhobors living in Canada had begun to lose their ideal so discipline became necessary."

"This may be so," I said, "but it still does not answer the question why the Sons of Freedom burned the home in Otradnoe."

Alesha was not cheered by this, yet he was not exactly angered. He arose from his bed and with unusual exactness began: "How curious and full of questions you are. I will tell you a little that will perhaps help you to understand. You see, here is the point. Sometimes it happens that pupils can teach the teacher. The home in Otradnoe was built luxuriously and this was a contradiction not only to the contents of the seventeenth letter, of which I told you, but to all of Doukhobor philosophy. The Doukhobors consider Peter Vasilievich to be, as it were, an incarnation of the spirit of Christ, but Christ had not even a place to lay his head. But here, they built a veritable palace. Had the Doukhobors correctly understood their leader, they should have realized that Peter Vasilievich had no need of a luxurious house. He was not a king or the Pope in Rome. And so, when the Sons of Freedom burned down the Otradnoe home, by this action they gave a strong reminder to their teacher. No doubt, he did not expect this, but he took up this challenge heroically and, in his turn, nudged the Sons of Freedom. He told them: 'If you are the same idealists who wish to establish a more perfect way of life, without the use of the inventions of science and civilization, I give to you the district of Bozhya Dolina on condition that you build there a life to your own taste, but I warn you, not to dare to chop down a single living sapling, but use only dry and lifeless timber.' That is why the Sons of Freedom settled here, and why you see them carrying dry logs on their shoulders."

I saw much more here that was new and surprising, but it is impossible to remember everything. Almost every evening the Sons of Freedom used to gather together and sing till nearly midnight. On warm sunny days they would go to the river to bathe, and I was especially surprised that they all bathed together, men, women and children, and all were completely naked. For a long time, I could not get used to this, the sight of naked people used to be revolting to me. However, as I watched them, I never noticed the slightest intimation of impudence or sexual provocation and I was astonished how simply they did it. You could see that they were all used to nakedness and to them it made no difference whether a person was clothed or naked.

The three-day notice given to me by the police was expiring and I was preparing to leave Bozhya Dolina. The Sons of Freedom gathered and advised me to go as they did not want me to get into trouble because of them. I followed their advice and left.

However, I remained under the influence of that visit with them and followed the fate of settlers in Bozhya Dolina. Most of all, I was interested in Alesha Vlasoff. At times I received letters in which I was told of the events in their lives. In this way I found out that, after my departure, Alesha lived another nine months and died, but there was a story connected with his death. He directed that his body should not be buried in a grave, but thrown out into the bush for the wolves to dispose of. The Sons of Freedom accurately fulfilled his wishes, and because of this, his brother Vasya and several other men were summoned for trial and thrown into jail for a half-year term.

DOUKHOBOR SINGING

[Vera] Grandfather Pete was enchanted with the Sons of Freedom singing. If you haven't heard a Doukhobor choir sing, come to a Sunday morning prayer meeting, an evening choir practice or the annual spring long weekend festival that has been celebrated for over seventy-five years. An excellent online source is the Psalmody video on Ron Mahonin's website (DoukhoborMusic.ca/The Psalmist Project), as well as Neobaba Wisdom (neobabawisdom.com), where one can listen to and learn to sing Doukhobor psalms. We sing orally without musical accompaniment and in the past, it was emphasized that we learn the words by heart, so there is no spiritual divide between the words and the singing.

We sing our prayers in Russian, psalms that are a chant, low and with long drawn-out syllables; three or four words could be extended for over four to five minutes. One reason for this practice is sometimes thought to be so that non-Doukhobors wouldn't understand the words as the Russian Orthodox Church in the past mercilessly harassed Doukhobors, thus they hid their rituals. These psalms were formulated at the time of the breakaway from the Orthodox Church, so this may be true; however, some Doukhobor historians suggest that at the time of the gathering of Doukhobors in the Milky Waters area, talented singers created the unique melodies. However, listening to the psalms one can tell they most likely originated amidst suffering and persecution over centuries. They are the oldest form of mass singing among Doukhobors.

For me psalm singing is a prayer, a meditation, and as I join the flowing vibration of the psalm, I begin to feel peace in my soul. I first memorized the prayers by heart from my mother and from my great-uncle George Aseyev-Popoff. He was taught by his mother, Masha Aseyeva-Popoff, who had a great repository of psalms in her memory. These are a treasure of our heritage. A funeral starts with a prayer meeting and when the psalms were sung at my mother's funeral, I felt transported and reassured; birth, life and death are part of the natural cycle of life.

My mother loved singing and at home we sang hymns and the sad Russian songs of love, loss and exile. Hymn singing is divided into part singing and Mother sang the lead or soprano and I harmonized with her. Many hymns have been written by Doukhobor leaders and writers over the centuries, but some Orthodox hymns, hymns written by Tolstoyans, Molokans and other Russian writers, and even by English poets such as Alfred, Lord Tennyson, have been adapted and included in the Doukhobor repertoire. When I commented on this to a choir director, he said, "We incorporate everything good into our beliefs and songs."

A group that sings together daily as the Sons of Freedom of Bozhya Dolina did develops harmonies and overtones that flow effortlessly and harmoniously to touch one's being.

CHAPTER 12

THRUMS SETTLEMENT: INDEPENDENTS AND SONS OF FREEDOM

From Bozhya Dolina I went to Castlegar where my brother Nikolai worked at the sawmill. He invited me to get a job there but my parents wrote asking me to find them a place as they were preparing to come to Canada soon. After some inquiries, I found a home in Thrums.

While waiting for my parents, I temporarily settled in the home of a Son of Freedom, Ivan Terentiyevich Kinakin. He invited me to live with him until my parents arrived, for it was not cheerful for him, as his wife and son had gone to Hawaii with a party of Sons of Freedom. Only his daughter, Lousha, remained. Ivan Terentiyevich wanted to make a real Son of Freedom out of me. He was very displeased that I had formed a friendship with the daughter of an Independent Doukhobor and that Lukeria Vasilievna Hoodicoff was to become my wife.

Several times he said to me: "Why don't you get together with my daughter and live. There's no need for a wedding; do it just as the Sons of Freedom do."

He made such approaches and suggestions to his daughter also, and I noticed distress and embarrassment in her face; she would always run outside. I knew that in the evenings she used to go out with another young man, Ileusha Popoff, and was indifferent to me. When I explained to Vanya that it wasn't right to interfere with the natural attraction of young people toward each other, he angrily replied that it was.

"If you marry this Independent you will be lost! She will lead you into every kind of temptation and you will lose your Doukhobor faith, but if you will take my daughter, you will keep on the right track."

I could not accept his advice and married according to my choice in February of 1919. Later I found out that the Sons of Freedom in general were struggling against the accepted form of marriage and several of them exchanged wives.

Several years later, fate brought me again to Vanya Kinakin [Ivan Terentiyevich Kinakin], under very strange circumstances. To me he was a good-hearted man and in general, I liked him, but this time I was obliged to save him from a powerful jealousy, against which he had been struggling and which was driving him to an attempted suicide. When his wife returned from the Hawaiian Islands, she lived with him for a little while but soon left him and went to California with some other Sons of Freedom. According to the Sons of Freedom custom, exchanging partners with another Son of Freedom occasionally occurred by mutual consent. But for Vanya, separation from his wife was unbearable and several times he tried to drown himself before my very eyes.

I tried to help him and persuade him not to do it. "Pull yourself together, Vanya!" I said. "Don't do it! I will try to get your wife back."

I wrote several heart-touching letters to California and soon his wife returned to him.

Thrums is situated about four miles west of Brilliant, the main centre of the Doukhobor community. Independent Doukhobors settled in Thrums and among them lived some Sons of Freedom. I was especially impressed with the contradictions presented by the Doukhobors; the Independents on the one hand and the Sons of Freedom on the other.

The Independent group of Doukhobors in Thrums was represented by several strong personalities: Peter Ivanovich Abrosimoff, Savelie Fyodorovich Hoodicoff and others like them. It is said that Savelie Fyodorovich, when he was in the Tiflis prison in the Caucasus with other Doukhobors, led such a spirited debate against the Caucasus's priest Exzarf, who came to visit him, that the priest was brought to a state of helplessness and ran away.

The views of these people and their trials, their independence and freedom from any ties strongly attracted me. They used to say that Peter Vasilievich Verigin, with his anti-civilization ideas, was holding back the progress of Doukhobors. According to them, Doukhobors should not only have their own schools, but their own universities as well. Their close relationship to the outside world and the absence of fear of the leader seemed to me a significant achievement. Living among them, I found a congenial setting for my soul.

On the other hand, the society of the Sons of Freedom in Thrums also included several original characters. I will mention a few: Ivan I. Zarubin, Vasili I. Rezansoff, Nikolai Voikin, Anastasia Perepolkin (Zarubin), Alyosha and Masha Popoff (Aseyoff). Observing their way of life, it seemed to me that these people were striving for something higher, but still they were feeling their way in a fog. Some things were of very high standard. They lived communally and sustained themselves almost exclusively on raw vegetarian food. In general, they wielded great spiritual strength. But on the other hand, several of their extremes repelled me. For instance, on one occasion several of the Sons of Freedom came to visit us. I had recently acquired a valuable encyclopedia. Anastasia Zarubin, one of the most interesting characters among the Sons of Freedom, did not hesitate but seizing two volumes she threw them into the stove. Fortunately, there was not much fire in the stove, and I was able to rescue them before they were burned, though the covers were scorched. I gave her a hurt look, but said nothing.

She began to pour forth her advice. "Why do you gather other people's brains? Why don't you live with your own? Do you know that to print a book you need all kinds of factories and machinery and for the machinery you have to go down into a mine, and we do not want to exploit anyone."

I felt there was a little sense in her argument, but I could not at first agree with what she did. But she was not in the slightest placated and continued to scatter her "pearls."

"Not so long ago, I taught one bookworm an even better lesson than you. There was some kind of a doctor who came to visit us from Winnipeg. He had a great big Bible with leather covers printed with gold letters, and said he to us, even though we might be good people, we didn't know the word of God, and he read to us from his Bible every day. But I told him: 'Reading is well enough, but for your Bible you killed several men. Think how much labour is needed to print such a Bible! And beside this, you had to kill a calf to bind it with. But our Bible, our conscience, God put into our hearts. It is our guide.'

"Once he went for a walk while I was baking bread. I took his Bible and put it into the oven. He came back, looked for his Bible but could not find it. 'What's this?' said he. 'Where is my Bible?' And I told him: 'You yourself were reading the Bible where it says: If you do not heat the oven, you cannot bake your bread. I see your Bible was telling the truth, so I put it into the oven. Look what good bread your Bible baked.' How he gasped! And how he wept: 'You,' he said, 'have burned the word of God,' and for three days he sat there wailing. But I kept telling him: 'God wrote His words in our hearts, and we should pro-claim them with our tongues. The word of God can never be burned.' But he went away still very much hurt."

"Well then," I said to her, "I guess I'm also not a friend of yours. I like books, I like music, and that is all there is to it. This means, please leave me in peace."

She said to me: "No, we will not leave you, but will work to free you from these chains."

Once, the Sons of Freedom burned a whole suitcase of my books. There was a full set of Dostoevsky's writings and other valuable works. This upset me so much that I strictly informed them that although in some points I sympa-thized with them, such actions turned me absolutely away from them.

But they told me: "If you want to like us, do so, if not don't, but the truth will remain the truth. We are trying to get away from factories and machines, and books in most cases are being printed to give people entertainment and to lead them to licentiousness."

These arguments were not clear to me. There is a difference between one book and another. I tried to show them that truth can be arrived at through books also, and, as I saw it, there was no difference in what way man comes upon truth. The question was only this, that one path was more congenial to the temperament of one person than another to someone else, so every person should be given full freedom to seek it. But you want to force a man to accept your views. Well, tell me: Isn't that just what the Catholic Church did in the Middle Ages, or in general, what every church did and is trying to do?

Nikolai Voikin, a man of gigantic proportions and a sympathetic face, and Masha Aseyev-Popoff, an extraordinarily bright woman, as I afterwards learned, in one voice exclaimed: "Man is before everything, and you are trying to put a book before a man. That's the whole point!"

Again, I tried to prove to them my own conviction. I told them that when I was in Mexico, among the Native Mexicans who never saw any books, their life seemed to me to be lived to no purpose. That was all they knew.

Nikolasha Cheveldayoff, who looked gentle as a lamb, said to me: "There is a big difference between savages and spiritually enlightened people, and you are still a child to argue with us. We have spent the best years of our lives in Canadian prisons, and have left about a dozen of our brethren in graves behind prison bars, but all you know is books. Go on with your books, but we know the way without them."

Such repartee seemed to me much too heated, verging on fanaticism, and in time it irritated me. But no matter how much I argued, my reasons had no effect on them and they held to their previous convictions. I must admit, I was not especially concerned to convince them, but would have been more than satisfied if they had left me alone.

At that time my parents arrived in Thrums, and our life took its usual course, but encounters with the Sons of Freedom continued.

One day we saw a party of them coming toward us singing; they entered the house and asked: "Are you Sons of Freedom?"

"No," we answered, "but we sympathize with them in some respects."

The Sons of Freedom then without a word seized our cook stove and announced to us: "Raw fruits, vegetables, nuts, water and air, that's to be your food from now on."

Though I strongly advocated vegetarianism, such a harsh measure upset me, and I told them never to set foot in my house again.

They laughed and said: "This is only God trying his children so that they will be stronger in spirit."

From that time on, I hid my books. "So that is freedom," I thought. "Who is going to be attracted to that?" As a whole, the escapades of these Sons of Freedom pushed me further and further away from them and attracted me more and more to the Independents. There, no one forbade you to read books or listen to music. The Independents treated me with respect.

Love and Peace Building

[Vera] Pete Maloff married Lusha Hoodicoff from an Independent family in Thrums and they built their home next to the Hoodicoffs, creating an extended family neighbourhood. I treasure my memories of growing up where I was able to wander freely between my grandparents, aunts, uncles and cousins' homes next door and feel welcome everywhere. There is a sense of freedom, safety and trust in having so many people know and care for one.

The meeting of the Hoodicoffs and the Maloffs was the coming together of two families believing in education for their children and in the values of the Doukhobor faith, but like other Independent Doukhobors, working and developing friendships with many in the society of the time. I find a picture of the Hoodicoff family at their home in Thrums. Great-grandmother Masha and her three daughters, Mary, Polly and Lusha, and son Ivan stand behind their father, William, who is holding baby Bill. Lusha, the eldest of the five Hoodicoff children, is a classic beauty with light brown hair and a slim figure, and unlike the serious expressions of the others, has a slight smile. Pete was the second son of the Maloff family, tall, with dark hair and deep-set serious eyes. Being outgoing, Lusha had many friends and a neighbouring boy she went to school with was interested in her, but when Pete Maloff arrived in Thrums, they were immediately attracted to one other.

Grandmother Lusha told me that the moment she met handsome nineteen-year-old Pete, just returned from California, she knew that she was going to marry him. She was seventeen, not an unusual age to marry at the time, and unlike the Doukhobor custom of arranged marriages in Russia, Pete and Lusha chose each other.

They told their parents about their wishes and Masha and William Hood-icoff and Nikolai and Elizaveta Maloff met to discuss their *zapoy*, or engagement party, and marriage over a meal. Pete purchased land from Lusha's aunt Fenya, who was happy to pass on her share of the family property to her favourite niece. They planned a house that Great-grandfather Nikolai and Pete started to build.

Grandparents' marriage ceremony united them for fifty-two years of their lives. They had a traditional wedding. Masha Hoodicoff and Elizaveta

Maloff each baked a loaf of bread that they exchanged in a solemn ritual between families. Standing in front of parents, family, friends and neighbours, Pete and Lusha bowed to the ground for a blessing from the congregated who in turn said they would support and honour the marriage. They celebrated with my great-grandmother Masha's famous borsh, pirohi and a favourite rice and raisin dish, plow. Grandmother Lusha brought a hope chest, filled with a wool-filled blanket she quilted, to their new home.

The Doukhobor marriage rites were recognized by the British Columbia government in the late 1950s. My grandparents' marriage was not registered when they married in 1919, nor that of my parents in 1946. This did not make a difference in their eyes or to the community. The only time it mattered was when after my father passed, to receive his old-age pension, my mother asked friends to confirm their marriage.

Sons of Freedom and the Free Love Experiment

A friend of Pete Maloff's, Ivan Perepolkin, started a Sons of Freedom community in Thrums that about twenty people joined. They built several small houses around a bigger communal house where they gathered to share their meals, pray, sing and have meetings. They avoided using animal labour or products. Through discussions, the men and women decided to try a "free love" experiment where, with mutual consent, they could exchange partners.

Grandfather Pete approved of their vegan communal lifestyle, but disagreed with their free love experimentation. Pete believed man needed to develop ethics and moral control, not free love.

Pete told Ivan, "People have passions, wives, husbands, get jealous and angry. Free love will create worse results."

Vanya's retort was, "It's unjust to own a wife or husband. Relationships need to be free." Vanya eventually left his first wife, but stayed with his second wife until he was an old man.

Among community members, marriages could be dissolved if partners were unhappy, but the idea of partner exchange was not promoted.

Peace Building

Protests using arson have impacted the lives of all Doukhobors, Sons of Freedom and others, and the Maloff family was not spared. Besides the burning of my grandfather's books, there were serious attempts to intimidate my grandparents and other family members when they remonstrated against violent actions by the Sons of Freedom. Here is one such story.

Our cousin Filip Vanzhov was studying at a naturopathic school in Oregon and he was back for the holidays. Our extended family was health-minded and followed a vegetarian, organic diet, but, despite this, I was aware of health issues. Filip recognized that long-term trauma could have severe health repercussions and at his suggestion, my mother Elizabeth, cousin Elaine and I gathered to hear Luba share her story of a distressing incident that occurred when she was a teenager. Filip was interested in using an emotional release technique he had learned, so as Luba told her story resting on a bed, her eyes closed, we sat around her quietly witnessing.

Filip led us through a relaxing deep breathing exercise and when Luba felt ready, she began. Filip thought it was significant that Luba was not able to speak in English during this regression, but only in her first language, Russian.

Sometimes she spoke in a whisper, sometimes in a trembling voice.

"It is late at night, dark, fall … getting chilly. I am walking along the road … coming home from a friend's."

Filip encouraged her, "It's okay, Luba, you are safe now. What do you see?"

She continued. "I am close to our house, and … flames … at the corner. No lights…. Everyone asleep."

Luba shivered. We held hands and breathed a quiet prayer. Filip's hands hovered over Luba.

"I stumbled across the field … into the house … screaming, 'Fire! Fire!'"

Luba was a grandmother when she told this story, with grandchildren, but that day, she was that young girl again. We said a silent prayer, Filip carried out a reiki healing and gradually Luba's body stopped shaking and she slowly sat up.

"I don't know how I did it, but I dragged our heavy couch outside. It barely fit through the door and I definitely could not budge it before."

The fire was put out, but the fear and insecurity impacted Luba and the whole family for the rest of their lives. Needless to say, my family wasn't fond of bonfires.

The use of arson by the Sons of Freedom does not seem suitable for a peaceful people and to begin to understand I turn to Grandfather Pete Maloff's pamphlet, *A Report on the Doukhobors* (1950). Grandfather initially wrote these reports at the request of Colonel Mead, deputy commissioner of the RCMP. As I read my grandfather's statement of May 20, 1950, I am startled by his response, considering the effect arson had on the family. He involved many people in the contribution to and solution of this problem.

There is no doubt that the Sons of Freedom have caused quite a disturbance on the Canadian horizon, they have destroyed some valuable property. This they do not deny. But are they alone to blame?

This is a very delicate question. All I know, as everybody else knows, is that the Doukhobor muddle is the work of many hands, Doukhobor and non-Doukhobor.

Perhaps the many persecutions and abuses which the Sons of Freedom have suffered have embittered, disillusioned and discouraged them. Thus, being mistreated not only by the outside world, but even their own people who have fully trans- ferred all responsibilities and burdens on their shoulders. This tremendous bearing has aroused in them their ancestors' blood and they went into an unconscious rebellion against everything and everybody. At times I think they even themselves do not know what they are doing, but they only feel that they must do some sort of protest against general human blundering, falla- cies and follies.

Strange as it may seem, but of the Sons it may be said as Nehru has often said of India: "India contains all that is dis- gusting and all that is noble." The true Son of Freedom is there and the fanatic is there.

Why this is so, I cannot tell. I am even more astonished that a morally healthy, normal person should turn one night and become the hardest fanatic.

As to their guilt, they themselves have confessed in their misdeeds…. Their recent confessions and resolutions to ab- stain from violence is a step in the right direction. They must sincerely abide by these resolutions. They must prove to the world that they are capable of reforming themselves to loftier and nobler ideals.[47]

Maloff said that members of the Christian Community of Universal Brotherhood and the Independent Doukhobors need to be part of the solution.

First, they [Doukhobors] must cease the "cold war" existing amongst them and establish a more humane and respectful

---

47   Pete Maloff, pamphlet, *A Report on the Doukhobors* (1950).

relationship to each other. Second, they must either strive to follow the path of the forefathers and our great teachers or join all the good citizens of Canada and accept the full responsibility of citizenship. Those who choose to remain in the fold of sincere spirit-fighters must rededicate themselves to the fundamental articles of their faith of non-violence toward man and beast, acceptance of a life of mutual relationship, and common effort to rebuild their ideal.[48]

The Government of Canada, and especially of British Columbia, was included in Maloff's indictment.

The Government of Canada made a direct blunt encroachment upon the Doukhobor freedom by trying to force Doukhobors to accept allegiance to the British Crown and Land Registry Act.... Doukhobors continued to resist this encroachment and finally in 1907 the government confiscated the communal land and property valued at several million dollars. In these conflicts Doukhobors suffered tremendous losses, both of property and lives: the torture to death of several Doukhobors in Canadian prisons in 1903 and 1904 and again 1910 to 1916; the imprisonment of nearly one thousand persons including 365 children and babies in 1932 when about twenty [adults] died behind bars and four breast-fed babies died of negligence and malnutrition; the second confiscation of Doukhobor property in 1938 and the killing of Peter V. Verigin in 1924. Many Doukhobors feel that the government did not make sufficient effort to solve the mysterious killing of Peter Lordly Verigin. It continues to be a source of unrest among Doukhobors.

All these persecutions and oppressions upon the Doukhobors were presumably committed with the intention of assimilating the Doukhobors into the Canadian way of life.... It seems to me that this policy of assimilation, especially when done by violence, coercion and intimidation, is one of the chief causes of Doukhobor unrest.[49]

---

48   Maloff, ibid.
49   Maloff, ibid.

In 1953, when the Sons of Freedom continued using arson as a weapon in their protests, in an open letter Pete Maloff unequivocally said, "My last few words to the Sons of Freedom: Come to your senses and stop forever participating in this disgraceful business of arson and bombings. It should be clear to everyone by now that nothing good was achieved. A crime is a crime no matter with what intentions it is performed. The ends never justify the means."[50]

The peace that Pete Maloff envisioned, within the Doukhobor family, and with the government, took many years, and in some respects is still ongoing. Two research committees were formed to deal with this matter. The first was the Joint Doukhobor Research Committee, which conducted sixty-eight public symposiums from 1974 to 1982. The second of these committees, the Expanded Kootenay Committee on Intergroup Relations, met over a period of several years. This second group had the representation from groups of Doukhobors, government representatives, regional mayors and non-Doukhobor professionals. Many people shared their stories with the committees and my grandmother Lusha was invited to speak for Grandfather Pete, who by this time had passed. It took the commitment of many, among them Doukhobor leader John J. Verigin Sr., who originally envisioned this process, to carry through, reaching consensus to reconcile and live in peace.

It was this spirit of unconditional love and forgiveness that I first recognized in my grandfather's assessment of the "Doukhobor Problem."

In a search for more information, I spoke to a Doukhobor historian who was involved in the committees to develop peace among the Doukhobors and the British Columbia government. He didn't want me to use his name, but offered this quote: "The effort to fully understand some aspects of the Sons of Freedom story, is still ongoing, pursued by some dedicated historians." Seventy-five years earlier, in his final statement, Pete Maloff wrote: "Whole centuries are often needed to help men see the facts of the past in their proper perspective. The Sons of Freedom movement undoubtedly is of this character."[51]

---

50   Pete Maloff, Second Independent Report, May 15, 1953, p. 16.

51   Maloff, Part II, "Sons of Freedom" chapter, in *Doukhobors: Their History, Life and Struggle*, ibid.

Chapter 13

Money for Russia

In the spring of 1921, a committee was being organized to collect aid for the needy in Russia. I was appointed to serve as its secretary. At that time, Alexander Mamin from Los Angeles came to visit us in Thrums. In Los Angeles he was known by the name of Belousov. He was tireless in collecting aid for the starving Russian people. At first, he lived in Australia and married a girl of English origin, but at the time of the Russian Revolution he was deported to Russia. From there he was directed to the United States where he collected funds from the Molokans. Under his guidance the Molokans collected two shiploads of goods for the needy in Russia.

Mamin was a skilful agitator and could easily attract attention. He invited the Doukhobors back to the motherland. He stayed in the community for two days and there at a huge gathering Peter Vasilievich said to him: "The Doukhobors will, of course, return to Russia, but only when you do away with your guns and bayonets as the Doukhobors did in the Caucasus."

In Thrums, he also held a meeting, where he referred to Peter Vasilievich's reply to him. He said that Peter Vasilievich's thoughts were great, but how was it possible to adopt them when Russia was surrounded by enemies. "I, myself," said Mamin, "couldn't even kill a chicken, but I have killed a man. There was no other way."

The Thrums Sons of Freedom bitterly refuted these words. They said: "If we are going to set up a new world on blood, it will be just like the old."

Yearning for Russia

Mamin's invitation stirred me greatly and gave birth within me to the longing to go back to Russia. It seemed to me that only there was real life beginning. I was so inspired with the vast Russian spaces that I severely rebuked every repudiation of the new regime by the Doukhobors, including Peter Vasilievich.

Afterwards I was told by Peter Ivanovich Abrosimoff, with whom Mamin stayed several days, that Mamin was sent by the Soviet government to invite the Doukhobors to return to Russia. Abrosimoff told him that perhaps the Doukhobors would one day return, but only on condition that they would not be compelled to serve in the army.

Mamin had triumphantly announced to him: "We promise to give you, Doukhobors, exemption from military service forever, but only on condition that the Doukhobors give us their promise to (1) live in community, and (2) keep their moral purity as your community is doing here in Canada; that is, not to drink alcoholic beverages, not to smoke tobacco and not to eat meat. Doukhobors are to be an example for the Russian people."

This same summer we were visited by Raphael Koch and Frieda Moskovitz from New York. They were also gathering aid for the suffering in Russia. They were opposed to Mamin's proposal of migration to Russia. They were both strict vegetarians and, on this basis, we became very close friends.

Raphael and Frieda visited the community, but Peter Vasilievich for some reason did not entertain them and even spoke sharply to them, and they went away ill-pleased with him. This harsh attitude toward them added fuel to my opposition to Peter Vasilievich and I began to speak more sharply against him.

My attraction to the events taking place in Russia grew and who knows how it might have developed had it not been for an unexpected occurrence which gave me a severe blow and dampened my zeal.

At that time the Doukhobor community still bore a strong character of unity. Peter Vasilievich, like a huge giant, protected it from the attacks of various enemies that threatened its welfare. I built a home at my wife's parents' place and began to fortify myself with the ideas of V.V. Vereschagin, that a man should be his own leader, and that no one should interfere with the freedom of thought of another. I became so attracted by the Russian horizon and was so lost in this colossal movement that I had begun to take measures to get permission to go to the Soviet Union.

At that time, I was working at the sawmill in Castlegar. Once when work was over, I went to the station to catch the train home. At the station I met two men, one a Doukhobor who to this day I do not know. At that time, I knew very few people in those parts. The other was an outsider.

The Doukhobor turned to me and said: "Meet a Russian from Moscow!"

The stranger enthusiastically shook my hand, saying, "From Moscow, my friend, just recently, as you see. My name is Alexander Bakunin, a relative to the distinguished anarchist, Michael Bakunin."

Before me stood a tall figure, elegantly clad, handsome in appearance, and of middle age. He turned back his black coat and I saw the trade name of a Moscow tailor. While I was talking with him the Doukhobor disappeared and I was left alone with the stranger. He looked back as though afraid of being watched, and invited me into the washroom.

There he produced a passport from his pocket. "Look," he said, "examine it fearlessly."

The passport was signed Tchicherin. I, of course, was struck with surprise, and accepted him without reservation. He told me of his meeting with Okuntsov and with Vladimir Grigorievich Chertkov in Moscow, and he said that he talked with them about the Doukhobors. This interested me even more.

"Now, my friend," he said, turning to me, "I came to you, to the Doukhobors on an important mission. Could you take me to Peter Vasilievich?" I told him that he wasn't here; that he was in Saskatchewan. Again, he turned to me, saying, "But couldn't you gather together about six responsible old men?"

"I don't know," I said. "I am but little acquainted here myself."

The stranger was not discouraged and persisted. "Or maybe you can do all this for me yourself. I see you are a reliable man, so I'll tell you everything: there are four of us, two men and two women. We come from Vladivostok to Vancouver. We are carrying two bars of gold and secret letters to Martin's in New York, and we need three hundred dollars to get to New York. Couldn't you help us so that we wouldn't have to show ourselves too much, in view of our critical situation? For this service to me I will make you forever a full-fledged member of the Soviet Union."

This proposal enchanted me, and by the time we reached Thrums, I had it all planned out. I had a hundred dollars in my pouch and my wife had about a hundred and seventy-five dollars in her trunk. Twenty-five dollars I could borrow, and here was my Soviet Union.

My guest met my family. A few minutes later, my mother called me out and said, "Son, I want to warn you. This man whom you have brought with you is not good; he is a crook, have nothing to do with him."

I was hurt by this and told my mother in no uncertain terms that she did not understand. My guest and I lost no time. In spite of my wife's protests, I took out a hundred seventy-five dollars from the trunk and went with him along the railway track. When we got to the home of my friend, Ivan Terentiyevich Kinakin, my guest remained on the railway track on the pretense that he would be less noticed. When I asked Ivan Terentiyevich to lend me twenty-five dollars, he asked no questions, but gave me the money and away I went.

My guest was waiting for me on the track and when I came up, he said, "Please hurry, while there is no one around. Give me the money."

I counted out to him the three hundred dollars.

He hid the money and said solemnly, "I thank you in the name of the Russian people that you have acted so sensibly and saved me from undue danger. Believe me, my friend; I would never betray a working hand. As soon as I reach Martin's in New York, you will receive your money by wire."

In spite of his assurance and pledge, I began to feel uneasy in my heart. But he, attracted by my simplicity, did not leave me. He asked me to find him an automobile to take him to Nelson. We went to an English neighbour, who agreed to take him to Nelson for six dollars. The guest again turned to me: "Please take another six dollars upon yourself and I will send you back three hundred and six."

The stranger climbed into the automobile and away they went. I looked at the disappearing automobile and my last remaining hopes vanished. The closer to home, the more disenchanted I grew. With the departure of the stranger, his hypnotic influence passed and I became aware that I was the victim of a shrewd swindler. I began to think of the future: I had worked hard for a whole summer to earn that money, and now I had given away all that I had laid by for the winter, and had even run into debt. Could it be, I thought, that a man could so blatantly lie before a trusting human being? I couldn't believe it. But no matter how hard I tried to comfort myself, I felt in my soul that there was something wrong.

A week passed, then two and three. Not a word from, or of, my guest. It was as though the water had swallowed him up. My wife began to scold me: "Look what you have come to, you have started to give away money to every Tom, Dick and Harry you meet, but my life is bitter. I have nothing even to buy clothes with."

I paced up and down like a caged animal. The pain in my soul increased and after this incident I lost all faith in man. I thought, "If you can't trust a Russian, then who can you trust?" But no matter what I may have thought or done, it was too late.

When I was in Oregon in 1929, I incidentally mentioned this episode to Ivan Platonovich Potapoff and his wife, Anna Ivanovna.

They exchanged knowing smiles and then told me the following story: "This bird was here, at our place," said Ivan Platonovich.

Then his wife took up the narrative: "I see some kind of dandy coming up to our house with an important swagger.

"He came in and said, 'Good day, Mother.'

"'Good day,' I said, 'and who may you be?'

"He replied: 'I am a distinguished man, I have to see your men folks,' but kept staring at me. 'Do you have any money?' said he.

"I replied: 'What kind of money could we have? The children, you see, are crippled and it all goes for them.'

"'I understand your misfortune,' he said, 'but all the same, take me to your men. I want to talk with them of something else. Russia is great, a woman's mind cannot grasp it; it would be better for me to talk to the men about this.'

"I said to him: 'Very well, if you want to see them.' Our son Mishka took him to where the men were working near the river."

Here Ivan Platonovich took up the story: "I see an unfamiliar person coming toward us, who immediately struck us by his outer appearance.

"'Good day to you Russian people,' said the stranger. 'God speed your ploughing and grant you an abundant harvest.'

"'Thank you,' we said. 'May it so please God.'

"'I come to you, benevolent Russians,' he said, 'with an important matter and I trust that Russians will not forsake a Russian in distress. I am from far-away Mother Russia, and not alone, but I have in Corvallis fellow travellers, two women and another man. We were commissioned by the Soviet government to deliver gold and papers to New York, to the head office, and we are a little short of money to get this material there.'

"'That's interesting,' I said. 'I'll call my neighbour Dobrinin, to hear what you have to say,' and called to Vasil Semyonovich who was working not far off. Vasil Semyonovich thawed before such unexpected fortune, a man from Moscow.

"'My name, Reshetoff [meaning sieve]. You know, what you sift the sand through?'

"'A sifter through which fools are sifted,' thought I. Dobrinin reached for his purse, saying: 'Well, let's gather as much as we can under the circumstances.'

"I pulled him by the coattail and said: 'Wait, Vasil Semyonovich.' Then I said: 'Mr. Reshetoff, we will be glad to help you, only this is no Russian way to help. Let's first go home. You will then bring your friends, we will make some tea and drink together, and talk and then all in good order, we will gather the money and help you out.' Reshetoff immediately backed away from such a suggestion.

"'No, no, I can never show my friends here. We will be suspected and everything will be ruined.'

"Semyon Karaloff, a Doukhobor, who till this time was standing by silently, became irritated, and said: 'You Molokans are always afraid. Not even trusting a Russian!' He took out thirty-five dollars and gave them to Reshetoff.

"And that's how the matter ended," concluded Ivan Platonovich. "Reshetoff left us with Semyon Karaloff's thirty-five dollars. But it seems, Peter Nikolayevich, that this Reshetoff, this sieve, really sifted you. They can't fool me; I have learned how to recognize such crooks. A man can be told by his face whether he is telling the truth or only pretending to do so."

From their description of this Reshetoff, I was sure that this was that very same Tchicherin who took my three hundred and six dollars. I recalled this incident often enough. I was not sorry because of the money, but the pain he caused my soul was unforgivable.

ON CHAPTER 13

RUSSIAN CONNECTIONS

[Vera] Grandfather Pete Maloff loved all things Russian and followed as closely as he could the Russian struggle to develop a co-operative, communist way of life where all people, he believed, were allowed equal opportunity. However, once past his youthful zeal to join what he envisioned was an egalitarian society developing in Russia, he studied the situation more deeply and began to have doubts.

In his forties, Maloff wrote about the Doukhobor interest in Bolshevism, particularly among the Independents. He said the Doukhobor group called the Progressivists "revived the spirit of mutual aid, had sympathy and compassion for the suppressed working class and a hatred of the Fascist spirit. They took an active part in labour movements, joined Canadian labour unions and followed carefully the trend of events in the Soviet Union. Under their leadership, Doukhobors sent a considerable contribution of clothing and money during World War II to the Soviet Union."[52] But, he chastised the Progressivists for not fully understanding communist theory, saying that they imagined themselves Bolsheviks and repeated their slogans without knowing their true meaning.

My uncle Peter Maloff became very involved with the carpenter's union and was sent to Russia by the union to investigate unions there. I would have loved to have been part of the discussion with Grandfather and Uncle Peter when he returned, but the one comment I heard was that Uncle Peter became concerned that protection for workers from hazardous waste was non-existent at the time of his journey (1960s).

While supporting relief aid to Russia, Pete Maloff was not converted by communist rhetoric. First, as I knew Grandfather, he had strong spiritual leanings and believed in the principles of Christianity. An atheistic state would not appeal to him. Second, though information from Russia was censored, he must have been aware from his close association with Doukhobor leader Peter P. Verigin, who arrived in Canada in 1927, that Doukhobors in Russia were being persecuted in an anti-religious campaign. Historian Svetlana Inikova said that in the beginning of the 1920s, Doukhobors were viewed as "fellow travellers," but, by the end of the decade, the sectarians and kulaks were grouped together

---

52   Maloff, chapter on Independents, in *Doukhobors: Their History, Life, and Struggle.*

and seen as enemies of the state. Communism in Russia became harsh and repressive. Even possessing a book of Doukhobor psalms, *Zhivotnaia Kniga Dukhobortsev*, and reading it to others denied the owner voting privileges. Russian Doukhobors' brand of collectivization was based on their religious principles and this was not accepted.[53] Under the leadership of Peter P. Verigin, Canadian Doukhobors agreed to help the Soviet Doukhobors immigrate to Canada but they were denied by the Russian state.[54]

Other sources of information for Pete Maloff were the many exiles from the Soviet Union who had settled in the United States. He read the numerous Russian-language newspapers published in North America at the time and wrote to many of the leading expatriates. One such person was Professor Pitirim A. Sorokin (1889–1968), whose memoir, *A Long Journey*, I found in Grandfather's library, together with a photograph and dedication: "To Pete Maloff with high regards and best wishes of the author."

I was fascinated by Sorokin's memoir. He was born in a northern Russian village, surrounded by primeval forests, to a peasant mother who belonged to the Komi people. His Russian father and brothers led an arduous nomadic existence travelling the northern taiga searching for employment as craftsmen, painting and decorating churches, gilding and silvering icons, candelabras and other church objects. Despite their hardships, often being hungry, cold and homeless, growing up in this milieu, Sorokin said, was his "best school for mental and moral development; its lessons of direct experience were more effective and instructive than all lessons taught in formal schools."[55]

Through sheer hard work, determination and ingenuity, and, as Sorokin says, "with dame fortune smiling on him," he completed a doctorate and was appointed as professor at the University of Petrograd. During the revolution, he joined the Russian Provisional Government as secretary to Prime Minister Alexander Kerensky of the short-lived Russian Republic (July to November 1917). Then under Lenin's rule, Sorokin was imprisoned, ordered executed, then reprieved and exiled. In the United States of America, he established the Harvard Department of Sociology and in 1963 became president of the American

---

53   Svetlana A. Inikova, *History of the Doukhobors in V.D. Bonch-Bruevich's Archives (1886–1950s): An Annotated Bibliography*, ed. Koozma J. Tarasoff (Ottawa: Legas and Spirit Wrestlers, 1999), p. 106–7.

54   Minutes of the convention of the Named Doukhobors of Canada on March 30, 1930.

55   Pitirim A. Sorokin, *A Long Journey: The Autobiography of Pitirim A. Sorokin* (New Haven, CT: College and University Press, 1963), p. 28.

Sociological Association. Russia's loss was the United States of America's gain, much like the brain drain from many countries in the world to Canada now.

For me this quote from Sorokin resonates with my grandfather's beliefs: "Compulsory military draft is the worst form of coercive servitude imposed upon a free person by the Czarist regime, and military service is training in the art of mass-murder."[56] The "Czarist regime" could be replaced with the names of regimes throughout the world.

The Russian swindler, known as Alexander Bakunin, Reshetoff or Tchicherin, would have known of the connection of Vladimir Grigorievich Chertkov and the Doukhobors and used the information to ensnare Grandfather and possibly others who were wanting to help the Russian people. Grandparents Pete and Lusha led a simple life without much money and possessions, but they were always willing to help those in need. It was a harsh lesson in discrimination, trust and listening to the intuitive voice of the women in his life for Grandfather.

---

56   Sorokin, *A Long Journey: The Autobiography of Pitirim A. Sorokin*, ibid., p. 72.

Chapter 14

Nikolai and Elizaveta Join the CCUB

About the time I met this Tchicherin, drastic changes were taking place in our family. My parents were completely preoccupied by the community life. The Doukhobors' perseverance revived in their hearts something long forgotten, and they resolved to return into the community and took into it everything that we had earned together. Because of this we had a serious dispute with them. We, their children, thought that they should have shared everything with us, everything that we had earned together. Then they could have gone into the community if they liked. But they left my brother and me only five hundred dollars each, and gave six thousand to the community. I was at odds with them for a whole week and even tried to see where they had the money hidden. I turned everything upside down and looked in every nook and cranny, but I could not find it.

There was an enormous public gathering in the factory building in Brilliant at which I too was present. Suddenly to my utter surprise, my father walked out before the bread and salt, fell on his knees before the whole company and appealed to them, saying: "I am a traitor to the Doukhobors, and want to repent of my blundering before you all. Forgive me, brothers and sisters, for my sins. I am guilty."

I never thought my father capable of such humility and was almost stunned by his brave appearance. Peter Vasilievich stood there also. This hitherto unheard-of act of public repentance by my father touched the hearts of many, because most of the time the people were denouncing the community and its leader. Here was a man from among them who had dropped his antagonism and was repenting. To me there was something new in my father's act, and for the first time I saw in him something I had never seen before. After this incident many of my strongest convictions crumbled to dust. Here, too, for the first time I saw the greatness of Peter Vasilievich, when he, after my father's appearance, stepped to the platform and turned to the people with these words:

"What do you think, brothers and sisters? Can we accept such a repentant sinner as this man?"

The majority of the people cried "Yes," and Peter Vasilievich asked the choir to sing the hymn, "Yes, there is place; and God Himself invites you to His sacred roof, and guides you with His grace."

When the singing ceased, Peter Vasilievich turned to my father and said, "That was for you, Nikola."

Several times before this my parents had gone to Peter Vasilievich asking to be taken back into the community, but at first, he would not even see them, but after this public repentance he evidently relented. Shortly after this, my parents were in Brilliant where they accidentally met Peter Vasilievich. He called them to him and took them to his home.

There he told the housekeepers: "Feed this bearded one."

Turning to Father he asked him, "Do you also, Nikola, want to tempt us with your money? You know, the Kingdom of Heaven is not bought with money."

Father hastened to assure him that he intended nothing of the sort. He gave the fruit of his toil to the common good to repay as best he could for his betrayal and renunciation of the true way of life.

Then Peter Vasilievich said to him, "Well, then, Nikola, Christ carried his cross, and you take your own cross and carry it. You will not get away with Christ's cross this time."

At first Peter Vasilievich did not advise them to resettle somewhere else, but to go on living where they were in Thrums, as he said, to Christians the place made no difference. But to my parents this seemed unsuitable. They wanted to actually live in a community. Then Peter Vasilievich settled them in the Prekrasnoye district (Shoreacres). There they began to till the land without the use of animal toil, digging it all with garden spades.

Peter Vasilievich said to them: "This is a sacred matter, because all the animal creation awaits freedom from man and we especially must strive for perfection. You, Nikola, will be the first of the first amongst us."

Once when my father was in Brilliant on business, Peter Vasilievich received him in his office. Having finished the business, Peter Vasilievich indicated the office heads, saying, "And these, Nikola, are our business men. They understand very little about Doukhobor matters."

As a whole Peter Vasilievich was considerate and kind to my parents and often visited them in Prekrasnoye. Once he said to them, "I have seen one of your sons, but the other I do not know. Tell him to come to visit me sometimes. I would like to meet him."

He referred to me. When my parents told me about this, I refused outright. I considered myself a free-thinking man and such a meeting seemed to me like a servile obeisance before him; I was too proud for that.

Several days after this I did, however, meet with Peter Vasilievich. I was still working at the sawmill in Castlegar and every day I rode home on a bicycle. This time my bicycle broke down and I walked home along the railway track, through Brilliant. About half a mile out of Brilliant, I saw a huge man coming toward me. The nearer he came, the more excited I felt. When he was close by, I saw that it was Peter Vasilievich Verigin. I greeted him; he quietly replied, turned around and we went on together. This placed me in an embarrassing situation. I didn't even dare to glance at him. We walked on together not saying a word until we were past the station. Here I quickened my pace and without looking back, I left him behind.

This meeting with Peter Vasilievich left its mark upon me, and something sharp seemed to have pierced through my very heart. Even though we walked in complete silence, his silence seemed significant to me. Several more times in conversations, I denounced him, but before long a meeting with a complete stranger changed forever my attitude toward Peter Vasilievich.

Here I wish to note an incident which, I think, has a significance. Soon after my parents were accepted into the community, Peter Vasilievich asked my father to bring my mother to him. When both parents came before him, he asked her, "Why do you want to settle in the community? Have you no relatives among the nudists?"

"No Petiushka, I have not," she replied.

Peter Vasilievich seemed surprised. After talking for a little while, he again asked my mother, "Is it true that you have no relatives amongst the nudists?"

Mother again replied in the negative. Then he asked her twice more about this, but still she insisted that she had none.

What did this mean? Was it just curiosity on his part? Then why did he ask the same question over and over again? Or was he suggesting something to them?

I often thought about this and came to the conclusion that the Doukhobor community was then obviously coming to an end and that the next phase would undoubtedly see the Sons of Freedom in the leading role. In view of this, Peter Vasilievich was giving my parents an indication that they should not hold back in the community now, but should be taking one higher.

ON CHAPTER 15

LEADERSHIP OF
PETER VASILIEVICH VERIGIN,
SEARCHING FOR A COMMUNITY

[Vera] Over the years, my grandparents Pete and Lusha Maloff hosted many visitors at their market garden farm. Some came for a few days, then stayed for months, as did Olimpy Turvich. They welcomed them all, and several helped with the farm.

Olimpy was curious about the leadership of Peter Vasilievich Verigin and chastised my grandfather for not understanding the depth and meaning of his experiment, the Christian Community of Universal Brotherhood. As a young Independent Doukhobor, Grandfather Pete had questioned Verigin's leadership, believing that it curtailed individual freedom. However, after investigating his life, his vision and his relationship with the people in the community, he became an advocate. He was to write in detail about Verigin—Gospodnyi, Lordly, as Doukhobors called him.

During Gospodnyi's time, there were many people in the community who not only recognized Peter Vasilievich as their leader but practically deified him. It could be said that Gospodnyi promoted this by statements such as, "Our Heavenly Father predestined us to live in Canada. Christ's footsteps have been everywhere, but not yet in Canada. He was not here in the beginning of life. So, Christ had to come to Canada."[57]

This belief in an inspired leader with a connection to the Divine has been common to Doukhobors throughout their history. Pete Maloff wrote, "Their leaders played the pre-eminent part in all Doukhobor movements: they were the teachers, the inspirers, the comforters and the spokesmen for the Doukhobors, as in the beginning, so to this day. All the movements and all the history of the

---

57   Maloff, Part II, "Doukhobor Life in Canada," in *Doukhobors: Their History, Life and Struggle*, ibid. Chapter on Peter Verigin's Philosophy and Letters, Peter Vasilievich Verigin's speech delivered on December 19, 1911, at the Verigin station, Saskatchewan.

Doukhobors is closely intertwined with the life and history of their leaders."[58]

There were pragmatic community members who "realized that Gospodnyi was a man like themselves, but his spiritual and mental power placed him above the rest. Therefore, they listened attentively to his speeches, tried to understand their true meaning, and believed his prophecies. They did not consider community life to be ideal but they sincerely believed that by living in it and accepting all its ways they were carrying out the will of God."[59] They followed Peter Vasilievich Verigin's guidance because they believed he offered a true Christian way of life.

> Peter Vasilievich Verigin had a powerful effect on people. It was during prayer meetings that one especially felt his inspiration.
>
> Peter Vasilievich possessed a special charm, it might even be called charisma, which he knew how to use and transmit to people. He felt the power of inspiration, and his listeners came under the spell of his words, his gestures, his look, his voice, and the expression of his whole being. No words can describe what happened to this man and his audience at such moments. They were uplifted from the earth and transported into the world of the spirit. This was not a fanatical frenzy, but a peaceful and tender happiness. All faces, especially those of the children, radiated an angelic light. Adults and even children, after standing at the [prayer] meetings for several hours without rest, experienced no fatigue, but felt an unusual vital energy. This personal appeal of Peter Vasilievich was not a myth. Outsiders who happened to meet him also remarked upon their feeling of being near some wonderful presence not of this world.[60]

---

58   Maloff, Part I, Introduction to Part I, "Doukhobor Life in Russia," in *Doukhobors: Their History, Life and Struggle*, ibid.

59   Maloff, Part II, "Doukhobor Life in Canada," in *Doukhobors: Their History, Life and Struggle*, ibid. Chapter on P.V. Verigin's Philosophy and Letters.

60   Maloff, Part II, "Doukhobor Life in Canada," in *Doukhobors: Their History, Life and Struggle*, ibid. Chapter on Verigin's Philosophy and Letters.

Peter Vasilievich Verigin led the Christian Community of Universal Brotherhood, the longest-lasting commune in North America, from his arrival in Canada in 1902 until his death in 1924.

Searching for Community

Some members of the Sons of Freedom society restricted reading and instrumental music, believing that if man lived according to God's law, he would know all he needs to know without books and music. Grandfather declared that reading had been his window into a remarkable world and music was food for his soul. The Maloff family was to search for a community that provided a degree of freedom and allowed for intellectual curiosity and exploration. For a time, they joined a group of Doukhobor friends who created a co-operative in California where they attempted to manage their day-to-day lives by consensus. They welcomed a variety of visitors. Grandfather Pete's portrayal of this experiment and their discussions gives a picture of their openness and curiosity to investigate different ways of life.

CHAPTER 15

THE TURNING POINT

I came of age and was married. The fact of becoming a family man produced a more serious outlook on life and the desire for more attentive observation. Though for several years I yielded to wanderlust from time to time, I really considered the meaning of life, and tried to understand what was going on around me. My character deepened and became more mature. Meeting certain unusual personalities helped me to concentrate my attention on the many problems of existence.

Once we heard that a Russian man from New York had taken lodgings with Alyosha Popoff, who belonged to the Sons of Freedom. Grigoriy Vlasoff, Alyosha Chernov and I went to call on this man. When we entered the room, the stranger was lying on the bed. He did not even rise to meet us.

"Greetings to you, O Russian," said we.

He replied, "Greetings, Doukhobors."

We asked him to inform us on conditions, but he gave the answer, "I myself came here to find out if you, Doukhobors, have something good and interesting among you. I am a simple man, I know nothing. This wild hazel bush growing at the window knows more than I, and can tell you more than I can."

We left, getting nothing out of him. All he told us was that his name was Olimpy Turvich. We were dumbfounded by his answer and tried to guess what sort of human being this was that had appeared among us.

Later, the neighbours told us that this Russian took a bath every morning, ran around naked, waving his arms and jumping. He ate only bread, baked by himself. I was intrigued and went to visit him again. Then I invited him to visit us. He took lodgings with us and stayed for almost three months.

He proved to have had a classical education. He was thirty-seven years old, handsome and of strong build, wore a beard and spoke with a soft, well-modulated voice. A strict dietitian, he undertook from the very first day to teach us how to prepare food. "You," said he, "are vegetarians, but you do not know food values, that's why there are so many sickly people among you." He ground his wheat and corn by hand and baked a tasty bread. He was a follower of Muller's theory of physical culture.

At the beginning he asked us a great deal about life in the community. He was especially interested to hear about Peter Vasilievich Verigin. He never contradicted us, simply listened, as if taking note of everything we said.

After about two months, he began to tell us a little about himself. His parents were poor peasants from the Grodensk[61] government. Relatives helped him to get his education. He went to America, in hope of finding rivers of gold, but instead encountered unemployment and disillusionment. This confirmed his earlier theory that the world is governed by adventurers and egotists. His quest for a sensible and just life led him to the Doukhobors.

One day he declared that he was preparing to leave and would like to have a conversation with me. We went to the mountain and for a long time he spoke to me about my shortcomings.

"You," said he, "are by nature a good man. But to be a good man is not enough. One has to learn to penetrate to the very depth of things. One must not judge superficially, by the outward appearance, but look inward, to learn the elements, which compose things. I want to tell you that you have a wrong conception of the personality of Peter Vasilievich Verigin. You criticize him, but you do not really understand. I have not seen him and know only what you have told me. But I feel that he is different from what you described. I want to warn you seriously that if you will pay attention to my words—you will be happy, otherwise you are going to be unhappy. Beginning with this day you must stop all criticism of Peter Vasilievich. If you don't want to live in the community, no one is forcing you to do so, but do not condemn Peter Vasilievich. He is carrying on a great living experiment, which may in future be useful for humanity. I tell you, this man is the One about whom the Bible tells, who with one foot stands on the sea, with the other on dry land. With one hand he is ruling the material world, with the other the spiritual world. And I assure you that in the near future he will show you his wounds, and you shall know who he really is."

This was said in the summer of 1921. This admonition astonished me and caused a great change in my life.

Olimpy went from us to Grand Forks, where for a time he worked with Grisha Nazarov gathering potatoes for an Englishman. Olimpy longed to meet Peter Vasilievich. Finally, he went with Grisha to the community meeting.

When they appeared there, Peter Vasilievich noticed the stranger and asked several questions. Then he said, "Do you know that I have been to the end of the world?"

---

61   Region in northwest Belarus, bordering Latvia and Poland.

Olimpy answered, "I do not understand you, Peter Vasilievich."

Then Peter Vasilievich explained that he meant he had been where the eternal "taiga" grows. "In summer," he said, "one can fall through the growth, and in winter one may freeze to death." He continued, "Wherever you may be in the future, tell everyone that Peter Vasilievich has been to the end of the world."

Then he turned to the people and said, "Wonderful are God's deeds, there was darkness, but the light now shines."

Soon after this, Olimpy Turvich walked away toward the American border. Over twenty-five years have passed since then, but he disappeared, without leaving a trace.

Before his departure he gave me two manuscripts entitled *The Destruction of the World and the Kingdom of Christ*, and *To the Doukhobors about Physical Health*.

Learning from Books versus Learning from Nature

Once I broke my leg and was forced to stay in bed for a whole month. At that time, I had little communication with the Sons of Freedom because their attitude toward education did not satisfy me and sometimes even repelled me. But when hearing about my accident, they visited me. Vania Kinakin came quite often and we had long discussions. I noticed that he had changed since I first knew him. He made an effort to develop self-control and spiritual balance. His weakness and faint-heartedness had disappeared.

During his visits, seeing heaps of books, newspapers and magazines piled near my bed, he would chuckle and say, "You are still busy with your books? What for? Do you really need all this heavy load? One should live with ease always ready for a move. These are heavy. If you want to know, search the New Testament and read the Sermon on the Mount. There everything that a man needs to know is told. It is brief. You can learn it all by heart. But what wisdom is there."

Vania went on in the same way, on and on until I lost patience and said, "You, Sons of Freedom, have often burned my books, but I do not stop loving them, and shall not stop, because I know that the book is one of the most wonderful things that civilization has created for the benefit of men."

"If man would live according to God's law," answered Vania, "he would know all that he needs to know without books. Everything, not only the present, but also the past and the future. And, I repeat, without all this rubbish."

"Ah, Vania," I answered, "you have said many words, but for some reason your words do not come true. I remember how in 1917 the Sons of Freedom showed me a boy and tried to convince me that this boy was an example of the stuff which would produce the new Adam. 'He does not learn to read and does not go to government school; he learns the lessons of nature. Such children,' you said, 'are our hope.' Several years later I met the same boy as an adult. I looked him over and thought: 'The aim was lofty, but the great hope did not come true.' He preserved his childish simplicity and sincerity, but this did not protect him from the vices of civilization. He, like all the rest, learned to drink and smoke and many other things besides. We had so far removed ourselves from nature, that in order to return to it, we must use the good and beneficial aspects of science."

"Oh, Peter," continued Vania, "you are the only good guy among literate people, and I couldn't find another. All the readers of books, after reading them, turn into still greater scoundrels, thieves, crooks and exploiters."

Once the Sons of Freedom caught me at the moment when I started to play a Russian song "Korobushka" (the peddler's basket) on my harmonica. They simply gasped, "What a sin you are committing, Peter. Why do you play it?"

"What's bad about it?" I asked. "I am sorry that I did not learn to play a real accordion. Music has attracted me from childhood, but my father did not want to teach me how to play. And I see now that he did wrong; music is wonderful, such delight for the soul. The harmony of sound lifts men and awakens an idealistic feeling. You should think about it. I understand, though, why the Doukhobors in general detest music. It reminds them of war, saloons, dancing, dens of vice and the like. But there is another kind of music, and if you deal with it right, music can bring much good. It can even make sickly men healthier. Long, long ago Pythagoras played on the psaltery and Pan's pipe for the pupils of his school. And have you heard about the great composers, Beethoven, Tchaikovsky, Brahms, Wagner and others? They brought to earth sounds from Heaven, so that human souls could enjoy them … and how wonderful they are!"

"For centuries the Doukhobors existed without those Tchaikovskys of yours and we are going to go on without them for many centuries to come," said Vania Kinakin. "It's nonsense, useless luxury. But if you crave music, isn't it in your own throat? Develop and perfect your voice, and you'll have music."

"No matter what you say, I don't agree with you. I may be a sinner, but I love books and I love music. It would be a great loss to me not to know the history of humanity. True, this history is full of bloodshed, but there were moments of light, and it is good to know about them. Just think, Hesiod lived eight hundred years before Christ, but he composed a wonderful book, *Works and Days*, where he treated the same problems you treat now. And ancient Hindu wisdom? It also yearned for the lofty and ideal. In China and in Greece since ancient times there have been wise men. It would be a great mistake not to know about them and use the wisdom they attained."

"You may be angry, Peter," answered the Sons of Freedom, "but your sins are quite apparent. We know that you are a lively and alert man, and such men must get together. The Doukhobors for centuries have struggled with the wrongs of this world. You must wag your tongue less, get hitched to our common wagon and help to drag it. This is what you should do."

Once we had a very animated conversation on the subject of literacy, and I almost succeeded in convincing them, that literacy in certain cases not only does no harm, but could be useful. I said, "You exist in terrible ignorance, but you do not see it. You ought to study the different religious movements, this would shake up your religious fanaticism. I admit that you have much good and some real values in your teaching, but you have also much that is dark and negative. Often you take up someone else's idea—sometimes it is from the Bible or some other book—and then you imagine that no one else, except yourselves, know this idea. You don't know that the same ideas or others like them turned men's heads long ago. You don't realize how men have erred. And if you knew, maybe you would not go to extremes as easily. Listen to what happened among the Russian sects many years ago. In the seventeenth century a certain monk named Daniil began to 'proclaim the truth' to his people. It happened in the Tabloski district. Many men of different ranks left their homes, estates and cattle with their wives and children and went to live in the wilderness. 'To escape to the wilderness' was forbidden by the authorities and magistrate Peter Vasilyevich Sheremetyevo sent troops to arrest Daniil and all his followers. But the troops found only great piles of ashes. Daniil and his adherents had locked themselves in their huts, and with their own hands set fire to the huts and burned themselves to ashes.

"In Malevanschin, too, strange things have happened. Philipp Krivenko tried to ascend to Heaven. At another time and place a certain Yanko Manzapurro tried to do the same thing. But what came of it? Both fell down to the earth. One was found half alive, the other killed outright. One peasant, Nikitin of the Vladimirskiy government, burned down his house in which were his two little children whom he had previously killed with a knife. During the inquiry, he calmly declared that he had acted in accordance with the Bible, that he had sacrificed his children to God, following the example of Abraham, who was ready to sacrifice his son Isaac to God. Then in 1897, Fyodor Kovalev buried alive twenty-five members of his sect, believing that he was saving them from the snares of the Antichrist. He had a sister, sick with tuberculosis. She begged him to bury her too, but he refused, saying, 'You are going to die soon anyhow.' She, with tears in her eyes, reproached him, 'You do your best for strangers, but refuse to do good to your own sister.' Many other fanatical deeds took place among those Russian sectarians. It would be impossible to recount them all."

The Sons of Freedom were stupefied as they listened to these stories. For a long time, they remained speechless, not knowing what to say. Then Vania Kinakin said, "These men did wrong because they ate meat, and because the Truth did not reveal itself to them. If they had been vegetarians, they would not have done what they did. But on the subject of reading, well, maybe it would not be so bad to learn a little, not in government schools, but at home."

"That's better," I answered, "and nearer to the truth. I myself began to understand only because one literate woman lifted up for me the curtain that hid my thoughts." Here I read them a poem by Elena Petrovna Grot.[62] It is entitled "The Longing." "This woman did not know you, but how beautifully she expressed your thoughts."

A Doukhobor Co-operative in California

In the summer of the same year my friends Grigoriy Vlasoff and Fyodor Pepin visited me and tempted me to go to California again. He who has once visited those places forever longs for them.

We arrived in Yuba City, and because of our poverty spent our first night under a fig tree. In the morning the sun was so hot that it was impossible to remain under its burning rays. We got up, ate some figs and went to look for Vasia Vlasoff. Fortunately, we found him and he took us to see the native wealth of this region. We soon adjusted ourselves to the environment, and earned enough to bring our families to California.

In the autumn eight of us, five Vlasoffs, Fyodor Pepin, Ivan Planidin and I, rented a 150-acre farmland from Harry Hooper, the well-known baseball player of Chicago. We began work under communal conditions. There were many varieties of fruit on this farm, and we shipped from there twenty-two carloads of grapes, ten tons of raisins, six carloads of pomegranates, 250 tons of peaches, besides several tons of plums, nuts and other produce.

Our life on the farm, although busy, was exceedingly interesting. We worked hard, but during our hours of rest we discussed fantastic plans, dreamed

---

62   Wikipedia: Elena Grot was the founder and a member of San Francisco Literature and Arts Club in 1923. Her works and poetry were published in the *Russian Life* periodical of San Francisco.

of the ideal life and even planned to go to Mexico to realize it.

Here for the first time, I experienced life in community. To talk and to write about this life and about equal rights is quite different from experiencing it. Human nature, character, mind, desires and opinions form a complicated design. One man likes and wants one thing, another something quite different. We managed to adjust our lives and, in the end, our co-operative venture turned out to be satisfactory. It is true, we had much discussion, but the frankness and quest for justice bound several of us in lifelong friendship.

Visitors to Our Doukhobor Co-operative

A variety of people with different ideas and theories of life came to visit us. I remember especially one unusual guest who made a strong impression on us was Savva Andreev. Viewing our hustle and bustle, as we rode our tractors, trucks and horses in the dust and grime, he declared, "Your life is not at all a Doukhobor's life, but a constant, desperate struggle. There is no aiming toward the ideal in such a life."

One Sunday he promised to give us a lecture on "the meaning of human life." About twenty people came to hear him, including several Molokans. This is the substance of what he told us:

"Man is the most wonderful and complicated mechanism. It would be impossible to count all the strange and different parts of this machine. But what does man know about himself and his hidden inner power? I would say that man, notwithstanding all the machinery that he has invented, is ignorant regarding the problems of the spirit. But no matter how complicated the human soul is, it must be studied. All that is necessary is to desire to look into the mysteries of the soul, and the sublime picture of the meaning of human life will unfold itself before our eyes. But what I see here, my Doukhobor brothers and sisters, would not help a man to see this lofty picture. On the contrary, he would lose whatever vestige of inner light he may have possessed before."

Some of us were stung to the quick with these words and asked him, "But what should we do?"

Savva flatly affirmed that man should get rid of mechanization, and get into close contact with nature. According to his judgment, man should lead a simple, clean life, free from all that could encumber him. Savva's mind was alert and inquisitive. It could be said of him that he was a member of the "intelligentsia," without the attachments usually found in this class. His speech was logical, his argument convincing.

About himself he told us that he came from Volhynia.[63] During the First World War he was in Chicago. Unemployment, crisis and war forced him into the political struggle. He propagated peace, was arrested, questioned and told, "If you leave Chicago, we'll let you go free."

He left and began to lead a wandering life, but his conditions did not improve and after a time he felt desperate. He even contemplated suicide, but was saved from this by some hobos, who invited him to go with them to California. California did not satisfy him and he went on to Mexico. In Mexico he remained for a whole year. He said, "I liked it there. People there are pleasant, not a bit haughty."

He told us about his strange experience. "Once," said he, "I was walking over the mountains when a terrible storm caught me. I came upon an old abandoned mine, in which I took shelter from the storm. The wind carried rain into the mine entrance, so I decided to go farther in where the wind and rain would not reach me. I took a few steps forward in the darkness, and all of a sudden, I heard a voice, a real voice, shouting, 'Stop.' I was terrified. How could a human voice be heard in this empty, abandoned mine? I picked up a small stone and threw it ahead of me. It fell into a bottomless pit. All at once I understood; since then this understanding has become the foundation of my attitude toward life."

Savva Andreev spent three weeks with us, helping us with our work. He brought his belongings to our farm, a tent, a suitcase, some books, clothes and a few other things. One morning we heard shouts. Fenya and Vasia Vlasoff cried, "Fire, fire!" We jumped out of our beds and saw flames at the place of Savva's tent. We ran to it and beheld a strange sight. All Savva's possessions were tidily put together into one pile and were burning.

We asked Vasia Vlasoff, "Where is Savva?"

He replied, "Not here, he has disappeared."

We ran around the farm, but found no trace of him. We dug in the bonfire: one took out his watch, another the suitcase. I found a brush, singed by the flame.

Five years later I met Savva again in the mountains south of Los Angeles. He was with a friend, Kostia Rodin. When I saw him, I asked, "Why did you frighten us with that fire?"

Savva looked at me seriously and answered, "I had no intention of frightening you. I was protesting against your false belief, that you belonged to the Doukhobor sect, against your greed for those dead things—dollars. It was my things I burned, not yours. What was there to worry about?"

---

63 Volhynia is now a district in western Ukraine.

In 1927 Savva went home to Volhynia, where he had a large family. Since then, I have had no news from him.

Others also visited us. One who spent several evenings with us was so eloquent that we simply could not have enough of his conversation. We asked him if he was a vegetarian. He seemed embarrassed by the question. "I love animals so much," said he, "that if a cat should sleep on the skirt of my coat, I would prefer to cut it off rather than disturb the darling's nap. I am a nature lover. I know not only the animal world, but have studied the insects too. For many years I have observed the life of ants and have written several scientific treatises about them. These were printed in the magazine *Russkii Vyestnik (Russian Herald)*. Who, without loving ants, could spend weeks and months watching them, as I did?"

We were astonished at such attainment. This man knew how to make friends with ants!

One evening he admitted that he found himself in an embarrassing position. He and his family were suffering from extreme poverty. He was so convincing that we did not for a moment doubt his words.

Next day Grisha Vlasoff and I loaded our Ford with provisions and hurried to his house with our goodwill donation. When we arrived at our poor naturalist's abode, his wife met us with a look of displeasure.

She appeared to be a pert woman and answered our question, "Where is your husband?" with the explanation, "He is gone fishing. When he is free, he always goes to the river to fish. What do you want him for?"

Her unfriendly attitude embarrassed us. Here we were, we had brought something to help them out and did not expect to meet this kind of reception. Grisha and I exchanged glances but said nothing. We could not understand how this "strict vegetarian" could go fishing. We did not know what to do. Meanwhile the woman disappeared. From inside the house, we heard cries as if children were fighting. Grisha and I tried to decide what we should do. It would hardly look right to leave now without some explanation. Then we agreed to unload the provisions and leave our donation without asking ourselves if this had not proved to be a fool's errand. As we opened the door of our Ford, the yells in the house redoubled, and then we saw the woman run out with an iron poker in her hand chasing a boy of perhaps twelve. Finally, she threw the poker that fortunately missed the boy's head, but hit the fence with such a force that a few planks broke off and flew some distance. We realized that this was a bad business. If the poker had not missed the boy's head, it would certainly have killed him. We jumped into our Ford and escaped in a hurry. We drove for three miles without even a word.

Two more strange characters were on the periphery of the community. The first was Pavlusha Ponomarov, an old Son of Freedom, whose family had renounced him because of his convictions. He used to say that he intended to go to Russia to preach the complete liberation of man. He breathed sincere faith and genuine courage. I always envied his constant happiness and good disposition. In the course of the year not even once did I see him ruffled. Often, he hummed some Biblical song on the subject of the new life coming soon, and his soft voice penetrated deep into one's soul. He had blond hair and grey eyes. When he spoke to someone his eyes sparkled, he threw back his head and clicked his heels together, soldier-like.

Another was called Martesha. I do not know, and hardly anyone ever knew, his full name and his family. No one ever asked him who he really was. He was a Ukrainian by birth and lived in Canada generally near the Sons of Freedom. He spent long hours reading the Bible to which he gave his own peculiar explanations. For example, the word "Mesopotamia" he explained as having the meaning of meat-eating. The Russian word *miasopitanie*, which means meat-eating phonetically, resembles "Mesopotamia." It was ludicrous to hear him speak, but it would have been impossible to tell him the truth, so firm was his belief in the correctness of his own Biblical understanding.

Pavlusha and Martesha were inseparable friends and had the same outlook. They were both strict vegetarians, considering milk and eggs as unsuitable as meat. They never used to work on Sundays, saying, "Sunday is the day of rest for the body and the time for sending up the song of glory to the Heavenly Creator."

We had then a little girl named Lisa. At certain hours I would come home from the field to take her some food. One Sunday, when I came home as usual, I saw Pavlusha and Martesha walking naked in our yard. "What nonsense is this," said I. "Some American will see you, take a gun and shoot you."

"We are performing manoeuvres," they replied in their clumsy Russian. "When we go to Russia, we shall go to Trotsky himself and say, 'You removed Tsar Nikolai, but you didn't change his orders. You, too, believe in guns and bullets. You kill more men than the tsar.' That's why we shall go to Russia. And the naked body is our weapon. We shall need it there."

"What nonsense you are saying," I exclaimed. "Do you need to be naked to tell the truth? You could say all that you want to say without taking off your clothes."

"If we are clothed, no one would pay attention to us, but if we are naked, they will notice us," was their answer.

In 1923 Pavlusha and Martesha went with a group to Soviet Russia. I considered them to be underdeveloped mentally, but I was sorry to part with them because of their amiable natures. Many years later I tried to make inquiries regarding their fate. This was what I learned. No one knows whether or not they managed to see Trotsky, but soon after reaching Russia they were separated. Pavlusha went to the Don, to the local Doukhobors, where he continued his preaching. Once he disrobed, and was arrested and exiled to Siberia, where he died in 1933. Martesha left for Yenissei; he also continued to preach. He, too, was arrested and exiled to Tashkent, where in 1935 he died.

Planning a Doukhobor Commune in Russia

In the spring of 1923 two men, Anatoly Ivanovich Fomin and Ivan Pavlovich [Vania] Tolstov, came to us. The latter was a Molokan. They stirred us with their insistent persuasion, "To Russia, to Russia, let's go to Russia." This was their motto. "Let's organize a commune and begin a new life."

We talked this proposition over for two weeks, then we called a Doukhobor convention in Los Angeles. The meeting took place in the home of Daniil Sigal. A number of Doukhobors came: three Vlasoff brothers, Mitis Belousov with his Jewish girl, Nikolai Suchkov from Uruguay, Ivan Tolstov, the Molokan, Anatoly Ivanovich Fomin, Ivan Planidin and I.

Oh, what a meeting it proved to be. The whole week was spent in working out rules, but at last we succeeded in reaching general agreement. The main obstacle was money. When men began to bring up the question of their possessions and to declare their stipulations, one man explained that he had means and would not go if the newly organized society refused to register him as a Russian intellectual. Another insisted on some kind of tax, the same for all members, with permission to withhold the rest of one's possessions. It went on and on in this way, sometimes the situation was comical, sometimes sad, but the attitude of the men was always serious. Vasia Vlasoff declared in an excited voice, "You have a commune at the tip of your tongue, but in practice ... lies."

Ivan Pavlovich Tolstov was a bright man, sometimes sharp tongued, always stubborn, but able to reach a sudden, unexpected and definite decision. This trait was valuable. We would discuss a problem for hours without result, then Vania Tolstov would break in and with his help the problem was solved. In the end his help proved powerless. We returned to our homes without a decision, and our migration to Russia was not realized. In the early spring of 1924, I returned with my family to Thrums in Canada.

ON IMMIGRATION TO RUSSIA

[Vera] My mother always thought that one day Doukhobors would return to Russia, and she kept a suitcase under her bed in readiness. I could understand the yearning for one's motherland. Even though she and my grandparents were born in Canada, Russian was their beloved mother tongue; many of the hymns, psalms and songs they sang originated in Russia, and their faith was born from its soil.

I had been aware that a small group of Doukhobors had succeeded in re-emigrating to Russia after their settlement in Canada. I looked into Koozma Tarasoff's book *Plakun Trava: The Doukhobors* to find more information. He wrote that at the end of the civil war, 1923 to 1924, when many people in the country were starving, the USSR invited Molokans and Doukhobors to return, and were told that the state would provide fertile land in the southern USSR for them to settle and help the country regain agricultural productivity. About forty families made the trip.[64]

Russian historian Svetlana A. Inikova found confirmation that this venture ended in 1927 when all but four families went back to Canada.[65] She stated that this was because of mandatory military service, the lack of land that was promised, overcrowding, poor relationship with the local authorities and population, and a ban on prayer meetings. When the Canadian Doukhobors left, the remaining Doukhobors in the Salsk region were harshly and unfairly treated and the authorities even tried to break up the Doukhobor communes that were based on a religious communal life.[66]

When I look up the Salsk region on a map of Russia, I realize it is close to the Russian-Ukrainian border where we travelled in 1999 during the hundredth anniversary of the Doukhobors leaving Russia. We had chaperoned a youth choir led by Elaine and Alfred Podovinikoff and travelled to all the areas where Doukhobor villages were still in existence, including Ukraine. We were billeted in Doukhobor homes, prayed together, sang in their community halls and had heartfelt exchanges. It was amazing to hear psalms and hymns sung in Russia so similar to the ones we learned from our grandparents in Canada. Even our Rus-

---

64   Tarasoff, *Plakun Trava*, ibid., p. 261.

65   Inikova, *History of the Doukhobors in V.D. Bonch-Bruevich's Archives (1886–1950s)*, ibid., p. 86.

66   Inikova, *History of the Doukhobors in V.D. Bonch-Bruevich's Archives (1886–1950s)*, ibid., p. 108.

sian accents—southern Russian, we were told—were similar. The Doukhobor families there welcomed us hospitably. However, even then one could feel an underlying tension between the Russians and their Canadian cousins who had left. They had survived and fought in two world wars, the Russian-Afghanistan and Chechnian wars, from the latter of which many of their young men were still traumatized. In contrast, one could feel the health and vibrancy of our Canadian youth who were spared those wars and traumas.

CHAPTER 16

TO LIVE IN A COMMUNITY OR NOT?

Again, I worked in the sawmill at Castlegar. Several members of the community worked there, too, and their stories of community life disturbed my conscience.

We had rented our own house and were obliged to spend the winter with my father-in-law, Hoodicoff. They had an empty house, built on another lot. Larin Schukin, "a *Sibiriak*," had built it out of sturdy logs. During the winter of 1924 many members were leaving the community and there was a great demand for dwellings in the vicinity. One family that was leaving the community rented this log house where we were spending the winter on condition that they would move in as soon as we moved out in the spring. However, they did not wait for our departure, but started to transfer their furniture to the house. One day the new tenants asked us to give them some space for storage. We offered them an empty room, but they said this room would not be enough and insisted on occupying half of the kitchen. This really surprised me.

"What kind of community members are they?" we asked. "Where did they get so many belongings? In the community the accumulation of private possessions was strictly forbidden."

But this was not the end. In the course of two weeks these "members of the community" brought twenty-two cartloads of chests, bundles and all kinds of boxes. Even then their moving was not complete. "Well," I thought, looking at all those chests and boxes, "what sort of brotherhood and equality is this? What does it all mean? We have heard that Peter Vasilievich treats everyone in the community too strictly, that he is a real dictator and does not permit any private property, but keeps the people half starved and in dire poverty. And here we see all those boxes and chests. We lived on the farm almost all of our life, but in comparison with these members of the community we possess practically nothing."

We soon moved out of that house. All our belongings filled only one cart drawn by one horse. On our way out we met the new tenants bringing the twenty-third cart piled high.

Years after when they had left the rented house, every spring during ploughing objects made of iron and parts of machinery buried and apparently forgotten were ploughed up.

In the course of the same summer, something unprecedented, something I could not understand at all, took place. Almost all the government schoolhouses in the Doukhobor settlements were burned. The "Doukhobor problem" looked still more confused than I had believed it to be. I was beginning to think that I understood at least something about the Doukhobors but after this I realized that I understood nothing.

However, I went on observing and listening. The moral life of the community attracted me, but I thought that it lacked real initiative. For me, joining the community would mean denying myself the freedom of moving from place to place, a freedom I valued highly. I realized that my wandering life would create questions; the other members would ask why I should consider myself free to go from place to place instead of becoming a field worker, as all the other settlers were. For my nature, with its wanderlust, to stop wandering would be the equivalent of dying. I felt myself to be a real tramp, not fit to enter the common groove. I enjoyed a change of environment and could not imagine myself leading a life of routine, always working in the same place.

Sometimes Peter Vaslievich and the community appeared to me to be the realization of world brotherhood, the highest symbol, but at other times the community appeared to me to be a spiritual prison where one was obliged to obey orders and where even the shadow of freedom was absent. I corresponded with persons outside the community in the hope of finding others' opinions about the Doukhobors and their community. The persons I wrote to were: Andrei Karpovich Dubovoy, Vladimir Grigorievich Chertkov, and Anna Konstantinovna Chertkova, Pavel Ivanovich Biriukov, Nikolai Aleksandrovich Rubakin, Nikolai Scheuermann, Valentin Fedorovich Bulgakov, Professor Iliya Enchev and a few others. Some of them were persons known by Doukhobors. Their answers were contradictory, some were sympathetic, some were not.

The White Russian and the Bolshevik

In the summer of 1924 a Russian, Vladimir Ivanovich Meier, came to us from Germany, introduced by Nikolai Scheuermann. V.I. Meier had been a student in Moscow University. He was born in the Kursk Government.[67] His father, a German, took him to Germany to be educated there. Vladimir Ivanovich was a perfect specimen of human strength and beauty. He told us that he was used as a model by some Russian artist in Bulgaria. He was a man of

---

67   Wikipedia: Kursk region. A mixed Russian-Ukrainian region within the Russian Federation, northeast of Slobidska, Ukraine.

Russian poet Vladimir (Volodia) Ivanovich Meier sought justice and truth among the Doukhobors. He participated in Doukhobor protests against land taxes going toward the military, was arrested and was incarcerated with the Doukhobors at Oakalla Prison, where he died.

ardent temperament with a fondness for poetry. When he was not working, he often stayed in my home, and we became good friends.

After the Russian Revolution, Vladimir Ivanovich participated in the civil war, which he always mentioned with disgust. At the beginning he fought on the side of the Red Army, then he changed his opinions and went to the White Army of Lieutenant General Denikin.

He suffered deeply in his quest for justice and truth. He was generally in a condition of inner excitement; sometimes he accused the Bolsheviks of the destruction of Russia: "They are a bad lot," he used to say. "The scoundrels have devoured our great and beautiful Russia." Then he criticized the "Whites," himself included, for escaping from Russia. "We should have resisted there and undergone all trials, all bitterness. We should have been willing to meet death. We, the best children of Russia, are guilty of abandoning our mother."

At first, he was carried away by the Doukhobor ideas, but this did not last long. When he noticed in the community slackness and deviation from the original ideas, he was disappointed. "What kind of ideal is it," he wrote, "which cannot keep a man on his own feet?" His letters were filled with reproaches for the Doukhobors' shortcomings. "The movement," he said, "had not yet reached maturity, the community was 'lame in both legs,' the Doukhobor organization was sick and needed a Spiritual doctor." Often, he invited me to go to Bulgaria to join the theosophical brotherhood of Peter Deunov. "There I have seen more logical and more spiritually developed people. But what is going on here? Today one is a Doukhobor ready to die for his ideas; tomorrow the very same man is sitting in a saloon."

Our friendship was sometimes very close, but sometimes we drifted completely apart. It went on like this for several years. Once during a period when we had drifted apart, Vladimir Ivanovich met Pavlusha Skripnik, who exercised a strong influence over him. By chance they both spent the night with us. They measured each other and entered upon a hot dispute concerning the Soviet Union. At that time, I took "the middle way" believing that nothing definite could yet be said about the Russian experiment in communism. Time alone could give a definite evaluation. Vladimir Ivanovich had then turned back to the former opinion that Russia in the hands of the Bolsheviks was lost forever. Skripnik remained silent for a long time, he listened patiently, perhaps absent-mindedly, but Vladimir Ivanovich spoke with great vigour. I was careful not to become involved in the conversation. It was far more interesting for me to observe those two men of opposite types. I expected arguments from Skripnik because I knew that he was capable of uttering quite unexpected thoughts, powerful as a tidal wave.

"Don't get so excited, Volodia," began Skripnik at last. "There is no reason to lose our self-control. By birth I am not a Doukhobor, but in spirit I am. I came from the Kiev. My brother is a well-known Orthodox priest. I almost chose the same profession; indeed, I hardly know how I restrained myself from doing so. My conscience is now a Doukhobor conscience and I tell you frankly, as the Sons of Freedom do, that I recognize no government at all. If a dog should devour all the governments on the whole earth, there would be no loss, but real good would result. Well, Volodia, you always call the Bolsheviks names. You want the return of the White faction and you probably would like your tsar and all his ministers back to rule over Russia. You want to start a big revolt. But this is all that I can say, that story is over and finished. No one can believe that after so many trials and upheavals the Russian people would consent to return to the old regime. According to my opinion, the Russian people need what we all need, the pure truth of God.

Concerning the Bolsheviks, I can say that all Russians, you and I and all of us, stirred them up ourselves. No matter how angry we are now, they have sprouted from our sowing. Life is a flowing river, no one can stay or dike it, especially to suit his own whims, as they used to try to do in Russia and as men go on trying to do all over the world. Why could we ever have wanted those dukes and noblemen, Napoleons, judges, generals and especially archbishops with crosses, wearing vestments of gold. They were inventions of human minds, perhaps of a few insignificant but sly men, who built a dam across the living river. At last, this dam could not withstand the pressure, the river broke through and flooded Mother Russia not only with water, but with blood. I know, Volodia, that many innocent victims perished, but what could we do? I was in Russia during the uprising of 1903–1906, that is why I had to make my escape here to the Douk-hobors. I saw the riot of Potemkin. Other things also I saw. Yes, the revolutionists were cruel. I don't approve of their deeds. But the others, those whom you now praise, did they set the situation aright? Why should we talk about it? Could the falsehood that supported the ruling political and clerical power be so covered up that we could not see it? We all know what was going on in Russia. What oppression and persecution peaceful and good people had to suffer. They were imprisoned, exiled, forced to wander all over cold Siberia. In Russia there were millions of starving beggars and a handful of immensely wealthy men. Christ's Truth was non-existent there; this caused the rise of the Bolsheviks."

Volodia retorted, "You were not there, so you don't know the Bolsheviks. They built more prisons than the tsar himself."

"Well, they too shall fall. But the tangled skein from which the Bolsheviks emerged would, if it were unwound, show threads that go back further into Russian history. This is why I affirm that we all are guilty. I do not exclude myself. Revolution was an operation performed on our whole organism; any operation as extensive as this would be serious. If the intellectuals of Russia do not like this operation, they should have listened to the healthy, sensible voice, which sounded all over Russia in the clanking of the convicts' chains in Siberian taiga. Those messengers called the Russian people to bloodless recovery of their spiritual health. The Doukhobors, indeed all the sectarians, openly revealed their program to the Russian people, by the act of burning the arms. And Lev Tolstoy, didn't he represent the greatness of Russia? Did he not write to the Russian government and to the clergy asking, 'Why do you hang men? Stop it, you madmen, and if you won't stop, throw the same noose around my neck too. I cannot and do not want to live like this any longer!'

"Did he not, along with the Doukhobors and the others like them, try to raise beacons of salvation in the universal darkness of falsehood, militarism and vice. But the people would not listen to his appeal and we could not avoid the final catastrophe. But this is not the end. Darkness will continue to hang over the whole world, and condemn it, because we do not repent."

Skripnik's words fell like a heavy hammer on an anvil. I saw how they reached Volodia's very soul. His face was changing. After a long pause he said, "If a Doukhobor uttered those words, I would not believe him, but I believe you, Skripnik. A new era is opening for me now. I realize that life cannot be divided into parts. Life must be full and equal for everyone. Life must be created. We must all be its creators. We must create light and pure joy."

After a while Volodia brought me his poem "The USSR," which he wrote under the influence of Skripnik's words.

The Union of Soviet Socialist Republics

Could our Russia be destroyed and beaten?
Is forever locked to us her door?
No, it's open if you still desire to
Go and see your mother-land once more.

She is still the same dear country, Russia,
Still uniquely lovely in our eyes,
Did you hear the spinning-wheels of women?
Did you see on graves green grass arise?

Did you hear wolves howling in the forests,
As they howled a thousand years ago,
Did you see our beautiful young maidens,
Our soft meadows in the sunset's glow?

Old church yards, the graves, the wooden crosses,
Cries of geese, the fragrant, damp, spring night,
Medicines of wizard peasant women;
Did you know our Mother Russia's might?

Did you see the yellow ripening wheat fields
Stretching out to meet the fields of rye,
Breathe the air of unforgotten legends,
Ancient sagas that will never die?

Did you walk barefooted on the greensward
And caress a peasant's horse as friend?
Did you merge with all your heart, in nature,
Loving all with love that knows no end?

So by night beside the Volga River,
Even Red Moscow you may comprehend:
How its sons through strife and bitter trial
Russia's fame to foreign lands extend.

Let the world hear: "Live, love and show mercy!"
In her own blood laved herself, my land.
Like the phoenix she will rise from ashes,
Forgive all, forget and understand.

After reading this poem Volodia said, "Petia, these are my new thoughts. It was Skripnik who awakened them. He helped me to reach my final decision. I am determined to go with you to the end."

Volodia kept his word. He remained with us. His end was tragic: he gave his life for the Doukhobors' ideal.

Attacks on the Christian Community of Universal Brotherhood

The murder of Peter Vasilievich, which occurred in the autumn of the same year, caused a terrific shock, felt by all Doukhobors. Re-evaluation of values caused many Doukhobors to change their former opinions about their dead leader: those who branded Peter Vasilievich as a despot now began to speak of him in different terms. For me personally his death hastened a turning point in my opinions. I came to understand that Peter Vasilievich was the most impersonal of men, that he died without giving up the ideal of a Doukhobor, which he had so heroically represented through the course of his whole life. It was still too early to grasp fully the importance of this great man. In the blast that took his life died not only Peter Vasilievich Verigin, but also his beloved creation, the Christian Community of Universal Brotherhood. The enemies of this great social experiment managed not only to destroy its head, but they effaced from the earth its body, the community.

In the spring of 1925, the Grand Forks police with a band of about one hundred "patriots," lawless followers on horseback and on foot, rushed like a whirlwind on the community and began to seize possessions, earned by the hard labour of the Doukhobors. First, they took all that was stored in the warehouse and in the office of the Doukhobors' settlement in Grand Forks, then they went to the mill. The Doukhobor women with old men and children—the able-bodied men were almost all away engaged in outside jobs—gathered around the mill in which wheat and flour were stored to feed one thousand members of the community in Grand Forks. The women tried to prevent plunder of the storage room by the police, but they, armed with clubs, rudely pushed the women away, broke the locks and loaded several large trucks with wheat, flour, dry peas, agricultural implements and tools. The air rang with the cries of women and children, but the police used whips. One old man and one woman were beaten until they lost consciousness.

After plundering the mill the police declared, "If you won't send your children to English schools, we shall come again in one week's time and take away everything, except what's on your backs. If this won't make you comply, we shall kick you out of our country."

This assault of the police upon the Doukhobors disturbed many people. It proved without doubt that the Canadian government hated the Doukhobors and wanted to ruin the community. It also disturbed us, the Independent farmers in the vicinity of Thrums. Our sympathies went to our brothers, the members of the community. Without delay we gathered at a meeting and wrote a protest to the government. Vasily Pepin and Peter I. Abrosimoff were active in preparing the protest.

The next two years, 1925–26, were a hard and changeable period in the life of the community. I took to heart their disquiet. It was impossible to remain calm and indifferent, as I watched the gradual dying of so big and active a bee-hive. I had ample opportunity to become acquainted with the Doukhobors' life at this time. I continued to inform their friends in regard to their plight. Their sympathy encouraged me and I tried to establish still more connections. But my sincere interest in the Doukhobors' affairs was not always understood and accepted in the same cordial way in which it was offered. To many members of the community, I was just another Independent farmer, an outsider. They wanted to preserve their isolation, and participation in the affairs of the community did not appear to them to be any affair of mine.

This became apparent once when, during a meeting in the settlement Plodorodnoe, I came out in front and read several letters received by me from their friends. Those present thanked me in a very curt way. Some of the members did not even approve of that much recognition. They rudely declared that I never belonged to the community and had no right to concern myself with the community's affairs. This wounded my feelings. I had no personal aims, but was sympathetic and wanted to help them as much as I could. However, they misunderstood my motive.

Grigory Hadiken, who was working at that time in Brilliant either in the office or the factory, gave me a book in English by A. Evalenko entitled *The Message of the Doukhobors*. This small book surprised me very much. I asked if there were more of these books.

He said, "We have a great number upstairs in the factory."

Together we went upstairs and there in boxes, or simply loose in the dust on the floor, were scattered hundreds of them. I thought, "Should these books be abandoned here? Could it be that they were published with no other purpose than to remain unread and forgotten?" I took ten copies home and sent them to some of my friends. I visited Grisha several times and each time brought away some books and sent them out. Perhaps I took as many as two hundred. This put me in touch with people with whom I could never have dreamed of corresponding.

How Vladimir Ivanovich Miroliubov Came to Live with Us

There are men whom it would be impossible to pass by, without noticing them. Such was Vladimir Ivanovich Miroliubov. My meeting with him seemed predestined. In walking through a railway coach, I noticed a passenger with whom I felt an impulse to speak. He was a Russian, Vladimir (Volodia) Miroliubov, who had come to make the acquaintance of the Doukhobors. First, he lived in Prekrasnoye with my parents, then with my brother Nikolai in Castlegar; he spent several years in the village Krestova, and at last came to live with my family.

He was one of many whom the revolution cast out far from Mother Russia's boundaries. His bitter experience caused him to embark on an insistent quest for truth. Twenty years of self-education and spiritual ascent had made him a hermit, an idealist and a mystic.

In the autumn of 1926 with my wife and my two children I once more went to California, this time for my wife's health. More than two years in Canada had given me some understanding of the Doukhobors, and I left for the United States with certain fixed concepts regarding the Doukhobors.

ON CHAPTER 16

ON THE DEATHS OF
PETER VASILIEVICH VERIGIN
AND VLADIMIR MEIER

[Vera] Peter Vasilievich Verigin was assassinated October 29, 1924, in the bombing of a train in which he was travelling. The explosion, which also killed nine
others in the car, happened on the Kettle Valley Railway between Castlegar and
Grand Forks.

The death of Peter Vasilievich Verigin, Gospodnyi, Lordly, the Doukhobors called him, is etched into our collective memory. My mother Elizabeth,
four at the time, remembers the day. She had gone to visit her grandparents and
everyone there was sobbing and though she didn't completely understand why,
she cried too. Pete Maloff, then twenty-four, wrote, "It struck the Doukhobors
like a thunderbolt. All were terrified; some remained numb, unable to believe
what they heard; others wept."[68]

When I look at photos of the memorial, it is as if all 7,500 Doukhobors who
immigrated to Canada and their Canadian children were in the funeral procession, a mass of grieving people following the casket to the gravesite. Pete Maloff
was among them.

For five days Doukhobors mourned the death of their leader. All were
given an opportunity to view the deceased leader and pay him their homage.
Appointed singers took turns as a guard of honour, singing day and night. On
November 2, the whole neighbourhood rang with the sound of singing and
sobbing as great crowds followed the coffin in a procession to the gravesite.
Toward evening, as mournful psalms were sung, the coffin was lowered into a
grave hewn out of a cliff overlooking Brilliant.

We have gathered these last ninety-nine years to commemorate Peter
Vasilievich Verigin. We all knew Gospodnyi only through stories told by our
grandparents, but still about one hundred gathered to remember this giant of a
figure—both physically and historically.

---

68   Maloff, Part II, "Doukhobor Life in Canada," in *Doukhobors: Their History, Life and
Struggle*, ibid. Chapter on 1924, Petushka's last year and his assassination.

Peter Vasilievich Verigin was assassinated October 29, 1924, in the bombing of the train in which he was riding. His death was mourned by Doukhobors for five days and is still remembered yearly in a memorial prayer meeting.

It was a cold blustery day. A prayer meeting was held at the Brilliant Cultural Centre at the junction of the Kootenay and Columbia Rivers, below the Verigin Memorial Park where Gospodnyi is buried together with six members of his family. This tomb is surrounded by a rose garden that is lovingly maintained by volunteers and in the summer by students who explain the history of the Doukhobor leaders buried there to tourists. It was not always so peaceful. In 1931 the original marble edifice was blown up by a bomb, ostensibly by the Sons of Freedom sect who thought the structure was too ostentatious for a leader who spoke of simplicity.

Great-great-grandchildren John Verigin Jr., executive director of the Union of Spiritual Communities of Christ, and his brother Barry Verigin and sister Nina Decaire, bowing to the assembled, said a formal farewell to the prayer meeting. Those staying behind bowed and asked that they pass on our greetings to the *pokoyneekee*. While they attended the memorial park to say prayers and honour their great-great-grandfather and now their father Ivan Ivanovich Verigin, the service continued. We recited prayers, sang Russian psalms and hymns, some that Gospodnyi wrote, some dedicated to him. My favourite hymn is one he composed, and which resonates with the beauty and divine light of all creation.

Oh Lord, my everlasting light,
Forever I will sing your praise.
You have created me of dust,
And given me the soul of understanding.

Oh Lord, the beauty of your world
Makes me divinely exalted.
You have created me of dust,
And given me the soul of understanding.

The bright and sparkling stars of heaven
Call us for brotherhood of men,
You have created me of dust,
And given me the soul of understanding.

All nature in its ecstasy,
To you, Creator, sings of glory
You have created me of dust,
And given me the soul of understanding.[69]

Grandfather Pete Maloff's meetings with Gospodnyi and the shock of his death changed him fundamentally and he spent many successive years investigating his life, philosophy and beliefs and that of his creation the Christian Community of Universal Brotherhood.

The murder of Peter Vasilievich Verigin has not been solved. Rumours of who killed him and why continue to be rampant—from members of the Canadian government of the day who responded harshly to the Doukhobors after their leader died, to a historian suggesting that the Ku Klux Klan may have been involved in placing the bomb under Gospodnyi's seat. The police files are still sealed.

Vladimir Ivanovich Meier

Searching through the *Nelson Daily News* newspapers of September 1929, I find a reference to Vladimir Meier being charged with obstruction of a police officer together with the eight Doukhobor organizers of the march—including

---

69   *Vechnaya Pamyet: A Guide to Traditional Customs and Procedures at Doukhobor Funerals* (Castlegar, BC: USCC Kootenay Men's Group, 1995), p. 123.

Pete Maloff—against the use of land taxes for the military. Meier protested that he was there only as a sympathetic bystander, but Magistrate Cartmel replied, "You've been swimming around with this crowd for some time, so now you can sink with them for six months."[70] He sentenced them all to six months' hard labour.

A friend sent me the story of Meier's tragic ending in the *Prison Journal* (1992) titled "The International Prisoner: The Via Dolorosa of Vladimir Meier." According to Meier, he had been thrown into prison because he had been trying to mediate between the Sons of Freedom protestors and the provincial police. The Oakalla Prison, where they were incarcerated, was known as "a hard place to do time" with high numbers of suicides, beatings and isolation. Meier found the conditions of confinement cruel and his poetic soul was not able to bear the concrete oppression around him. Historians Tom McGauley and Jack McIntosh wrote about Vladimir's final days.

"One day at Oakalla, a small bird flew into his cell. He saw in this event an omen of his own desire for the release of death. Crawling out of his cell, scaling a guard tower, he shouted that he wished to be returned to Russia. To face death at the hands of the Bolsheviks, he argued, was better than to die 'from the smiling bullets of the English.' A few days later, on the second of January 1930, he died in the provincial psychiatric hospital. The authorities did not announce his death under the pretext that the surname of the insane man was unknown."[71]

---

70   *Nelson Daily News,* September 27, 1929.

71   Tom McGauley and Jack McIntosh, "The International Prisoner: The Via Dolorosa of Vladimir Meier," *Prison Journal,* November 9/10, 1992.

On Chapter 17

1926 California Inspirations

Travel to Oregon and California

[Vera] Lusha had been suffering from severe migraine headaches and she and Pete decided to consult Dr. Lowell in Los Angeles, who prescribed fasting cures. The treatment must have worked, for I remember Grandmother Lusha being well and active into her late eighties. (Many years later Pete Maloff and his good friend Dr. Jensen toured a Russian medical hospital in Moscow that specialized in fasting treatment.) It was the Maloffs' last carefree trip; beginning in 1929 Pete and Lusha were to spend years in jail, separated from each other and their children.

Pete wrote regarding the people he met and of the philosophical discussions they had. He said that unofficially he became a missionary introducing the Doukhobors' beliefs to people. Some asked about the Doukhobor striving for spiritual progress, others about Doukhobor marriages, relationships between men and women and the sex problem.

My mother Elizabeth had vivid memories, even in her nineties, about this trip when she was six. There was a faraway look in her eye as we sat down at her kitchen table with large cups of mint tea. As I listened to her, I marvelled at the many changes in the past century. The beginning of their journey was on the SS *Moyie*, now the oldest surviving sternwheeler, operating as a museum in Kaslo.

In the fall of 1926, Pete, Lusha, Elizabeth and Peter boarded the SS *Moyie* at the wharf in Nelson and waved goodbye to Grandfather Nikolai. At the end of Kootenay Lake, they transferred to an American steam train—destination Spokane. There they bought a Chevrolet with wooden spoke wheels and a top speed of forty miles per hour, but Elizabeth thought they were flying as they toured Oregon and California on that roadster. Elizabeth remembered staying with many Doukhobor and Molokan friends who welcomed them hospitably with warm beds and meals. The Maloffs provided the same hospitality in their home in Thrums.

Interestingly, Pete Maloff's first destination was San Quentin, the infamous California prison. But Mother said this was not unusual; when she went

On their last carefree trip, Pete and Lusha Maloff and their family visited with many Molokan and Doukhobor friends in Oregon and California who treated them hospitably. They reciprocated and often had people stay with them in British Columbia.

to Vancouver with her dad, they visited friends in jail there too. At a young age, Pete and Lusha's children were not spared the harshness of life.

Elizabeth remembered Los Angeles, where her mother fasted and she enviously watched children roller skating. She remembered the elaborate villa that the Tolstoy family lived in and Tolstoy's wife, Nadezhda, who wore a beautiful dress adorned with sparkling jewels. Many years later, Leo Tolstoy's great-grandson Vladimir Tolstoy visited Mother in Thrums to ask about their visit with Ilya and Nadezhda Tolstoy.

Vladimir Grigorievich Chertkov, who Pete and Ilya almost had a disagreement about, was the publisher of many of Tolstoy's books. Chertkov had been exiled to England where he established a publishing house and in 1900 issued the complete edition of Tolstoy's works.[72] Watching the movie *The Last Station* portraying Count Lev Tolstoy's last days reminded me of the discussion between Pete Maloff and Ilya Tolstoy. The movie reiterated Ilya's belief that Chertkov tried to divide Sophia Tolstoy and the Tolstoy children from Count Lev Tolstoy and take over the literary wealth of Lev Tolstoy.

---

72   Tolstoyans.wordpress.com/tolstoyans/Vladimir-chertkov.

The Maloff family with Dr. Zigmeister.

When Mother and I read about Walter Zigmeister in Grandfather's memoir, she smiled a broad smile and said, "He came to visit us here in Thrums. He was so tall, friendly and enthusiastic. He came with a couple of women friends and Dr. Jensen's family. We didn't have much room, but he told us, 'Don't worry, we'll sleep on the hay in the hay barn. It will be an adventure.' And they did."

Dr. Jensen, his wife Grace and baby son stayed with the Hoodicoff grandparents. That is how Pete Maloff and Dr. Jensen met and became lifelong friends. A photograph on the wall in Mother's kitchen documents the visit.

I was astounded about the many people who the Maloffs visited on this trip. Both Jiddu Krishnamurti and Hindu Swami Yogananda spread the practice of meditation to the West and wrote on philosophical and spiritual issues. Yogananda's famous book *Autobiography of a Yogi* sits on my bookshelf.

CHAPTER 17

1926 CALIFORNIA INSPIRATIONS

In the autumn of 1926, with my wife and my two children, I once more went to California, this time for my wife's health. More than two years in Canada had given me some understanding of the Doukhobors, and I left for the United States with certain fixed concepts regarding the Doukhobors.

On our way to San Francisco, we decided to visit San Quentin, the famous California prison. Imprisoned there was our old friend Ivan Pavlovich Tolstov. He and another friend were accused of some provocation against an influential insurance company. We were sorry to hear of his trouble and puzzled to understand how this idealistic man could have turned into an adventurer. Though I had been imprisoned for several hours in a small local jail, the sight of San Quentin stunned me. It looked like a giant.

They admitted us through several barred doors, and we found ourselves in a long hall, where at a table sat our friend Ivan Pavlovich. He was very happy to see us and we spent three hours with him. He told us something of this world behind bars. "Here," he said, "is a lot of everything both good and bad. Of course, it would have been better for me to have gone to Canada, when the Vlasoffs invited me. But it is all right with me. I am going to serve my sentence and may come out with more intelligence."

With these words he showed us to the yard where the prison guards were sitting at a table, and one of the convicts in a white apron was serving them tea.

"Look here," said Tolstov, "there are our guards drinking tea, and the man who serves them is Tom Mooney himself. His lot is really hard, they've imprisoned him for life, an innocent man. There are some more like him here."

We asked Ivan Pavlovich, "What is your occupation here?"

"I take care of the flowers and study painting. Maybe I shall turn into an artist," he answered with a bitter chuckle.

We went out into the yard. Passing the place where the guards were having their tea under a shady tree, I fixed my attention on Tom Mooney[73] whom I wanted to see more clearly. He was removing the dishes from the table. He

---

73   Wikipedia: Thomas Mooney, labour leader, militant, social reformer, socialist activist, charged with the 1916 Preparedness Day Bombing, released in 1939; died in 1942; pardoned in 1961.

looked at us perhaps wondering who the visitor was who looked so fixedly at him. I had heard about his misfortune in 1916 in San Francisco, when there was much publicity about him in the newspapers.

We stopped at the first entrance gates and sat down to let the children rest and to have a bite to eat.

I could not have imagined on that clear October day in 1926 that I, too, would be forced to spend several years behind high prison walls. I was shaken by what I saw. Back and forth moved the prisoners in their blue jackets from one building to another, one after another, chain-wise. Some of them were working, one whistled a well-known tune. The guards, standing on the prison towers armed with shotguns, gave this yard the appearance of a different world. It depressed me and strange thoughts crowded into my brain.

"Each of those prisoners," I thought, "has his own story, but no one seems interested in it; still they are men, like myself. They have their joys and grief; they cherish dreams of a better life. Here they suffer at the mercy of the whims of heartless guards. No one remembers them, no one cares for them. They are unwanted men.

"How many are in this prison? Thousands, and how many over the whole of America? And the whole world? But life goes on. It is bubbling all around, skyscrapers rise high. There are churches and parks. Respectable citizens, Christians, day and night, burn incense in their gilded temples. They sing hymns of praise to their God completely forgetting the unhappy millions who are buried alive in stone tombs called prisons. But why are they imprisoned? Are they the only guilty ones, or it may be all of us are guilty of making life such that it requires prisons, gallows and high walls?"

I approached the bay shore. The waves splashed gaily at the foot of the prison wall; the sun was reflected in the water, like greenish rays of light. The seagulls soared and whirled screaming over the prison buildings. I stood there perplexed, asking myself for what purpose were these high walls and iron bars erected here? Why these high towers with armed guards standing on them? Is it true that our civilized society could not exist without them?

But I found no answer to my question then.

A Doukhobor Missionary

This visit to California was at a fortunate time. We visited our friends and others with whom we had correspondence. We made new acquaintances. There were many encounters, exciting and inspiring. I could never have imagined it, but somehow it came about that I, entirely without any authority, turned out to be a kind of Doukhobor missionary. A few of these experiences laid the foundation for lifelong friendships, supported by our common interest in Doukhobors.

There was A.G. Wagner, the former well-known lawyer from Spokane, Washington. In 1900 he was carried away by the group of interesting rebels who were seeking the essence of spiritual existence. Wagner remained in the Ohio community with Walt Whitman, Bolton Hall, Clarence Darrow, Eugene Debs and Beilhart for five years. Wagner was a learned man, an academician in the field of morals. After leaving the community, he led the life of a hermit, but had correspondents all over the world. He gave freely in his letters the gifts of his broad mind. We spent three days with him, and he questioned us about the Doukhobors' life and in particular about the community. He invited his neighbours to meet us, and we drank tea together while we conversed on the burning problems of the day: how to live and what life is for.

The Sex Problem

Speaking about the sex problem, he maintained that the institution of marriage, as it now exists, causes one of the greatest confusions in human life.

I asked, "You are introducing different theories, but tell me what has one to do in actual practice? It is easy to say these things, and our Sons of Freedom tried to establish their life on the basis of free love, without having personal wives, and they ended by attacking one another with axes."

"Yes, this is a very important question," said Wagner. "The problem must be studied in all its particulars. Learned people must tell us how to use sex energy in the right way."

He spoke very highly of the Doukhobors, saying that "as a driving force the Doukhobor doctrine is unrivalled."

In Santa Barbara we visited Schauer, a German. The father of the family, a very interesting man, brought up his children in a healthy, alert and sympathetic spirit. He followed all idealistic trends, was a strict vegetarian and seeker for better ways of life. Two of his children had their own little dwellings high up in the oak trees. In the morning we could hear the whistling and the songs of the two brothers calling to each other.

Mr. Schauer took us to meet a well-known protestant missionary by the name of Greenfield. He lived close to the centre of Santa Barbara and his huge house and garden occupied a whole block. Many trees, which he had collected from all over the world, grew in his garden.

Our host, barefoot and shirtless, met us in his garden. Schauer introduced us, "Doukhobors from Canada."

Greenfield rushed to us, as if we were coming from another world, and said, "I love the Doukhobors. Their heroism is unsurpassed."

He led us into the house, where his wife met us very pleasantly. They asked us about the condition of the Doukhobor community and about the death of Peter Vasilievich. I told all that I knew.

Our host disappeared for a moment and returned with a small book which he gave me with the words, "Take this little book as a keepsake from a man who respects the Doukhobors' movement very highly. I too have had an experience, resembling the experience of your people, though on a smaller scale."

Greenfield's book was entitled *The Ethics of Killing*. He inscribed it with these words: "Several hundred copies of this book were burned by the government of the United States of America. Two were hidden where they could not be found by the federal officials. The author of this book was twice put in prison for nothing except promoting the circulation of this book. He paid a 5,390 dollar fine, was denied the right to vote, and even now, November 21, 1926, he still cannot participate in municipal or other elections, but he pays big taxes just the same."

Mr. Greenfield surprised us and made a great impression. His house was several storeys high, all sparkling with silver and marble, but he, as we heard from his own lips, had the Doukhobors' movement on his mind. He died soon after our visit.

In the same town we visited a Mr. Littlefield, who for many years tried to create a community. He had experience in this field and a few communities that he established existed for several years.

We found him working in his print shop. He met us pleasantly and showed us his works. Then his wife invited us for dinner.

His first question was, "What makes your community continue so long? All other communities exist for five or six years and then disintegrate, but yours goes on and on."

During our conversation he noticed that I had a habit of gesturing with my hands when I was talking.

He said, "Tell me, do all Russians have this habit? I have noticed it before. Once I met Maxim Gorky and his friend Andreeva in Boston. I noticed that when Gorky spoke, not a muscle of his body remained motionless, his arms and legs helped him to express his thoughts."

After their cordial hospitality and conversation on different subjects, we said goodbye and went on our way.

With the help of A.G. Wagner, I established a connection with William Lloyd and Dr. Leroy Henry. These two unusual men lived on a hill near Roscoe, some thirty miles distant from Los Angeles. They called it "The Mountain of Freedom." When we reached their homes, Lloyd was absent, but we dropped in to see Dr. Henry.

He was a typical retired American doctor with an unusual sense of humour. He had his own printing shop, where he printed the books of the Beilhart community and published a satirical magazine filled with bright sarcasms on the subject of our present civilization.

He was well acquainted with the history of the Doukhobors' movement from Aylmer Maud's book. He told us his hopes: he and Lloyd wanted to establish a community with the aim of initiating a struggle to liberate land from private ownership. He knew about the first "march" of the Doukhobors in Saskatchewan in 1902 and planned to carry on his struggle along the same lines.

On the subject of women, Dr. Henry was of the same opinion as A.G. Wagner. He told us something of the history of the Beilhart community. There were a few men in the community whose nature was "too loving." In this community free love was practised and marriage was non-existent. Several of the men proved to be indefatigable and never left the women alone, so the community decided to exile them as an undesirable element.

"So, such was the practice of free love," I said.

Dr. Henry laughed and answered, "Yes, this problem is not at all easy. But the way the law of marriage exists in the world now is also impossible. People are suffering and that is that."

"But this would not solve the problem," I insisted. "What about the children? Who will take care of them?"

"If man becomes a really moral being," Dr. Henry said, "all problems will be solved."

"This confirms my opinion. Man, before everything else, needs to be moral. Man needs ethics, not free love. But how can men be turned into moral beings?"

"Man must be born free," he said.

"Well, but where is this freedom? You have so much brain power, but Wagner sucks his pipe all the time and has no strength to free himself even from this insignificant habit. And according to the Doukhobors' understanding smoking, drinking and meat-eating are an oath to the devil."

"You may be right. I will not argue," concluded Dr. Henry.

Meanwhile I found out that William Lloyd had returned home, so we went to see him. He met us pleasantly, took us to see his dwelling: one bedroom, kitchen and a third room, his study. In this study he had his huge library and a fireplace, made by his own hands. On the mantelpiece were all kinds of souvenirs. Of special interest were some articles he brought from Tahiti, where he had once spent a year. In one corner there was a room with good acoustics where he had several hundred gramophone records of the best composers and musicians. He played some selections from his collection of Russian music.

William Lloyd was an excellent writer, scientist, poet, a personal friend of Walt Whitman, of Dr. Beck, and of the author of *Cosmic Consciousness*, Edward Carpenter. He was also on friendly terms with English physiologist and psychologist Dr. Havelock Ellis.

Lloyd's appearance was majestic. His forehead was prominent and, as someone told me, Lloyd's head was the image of beauty and strength. He read us from his works and gave me an article about the beauty of religion that he had dedicated to the youth of the Doukhobors. "Maybe some day I shall go to visit the Doukhobors. I share your strivings for spiritual progress."

It was apparent that the problem of women and marriage was popular in this locality. No wonder, then, that Lloyd's first question to us was, "Tell me, what are the relations between men and women in the Doukhobor community? Can it be that you Doukhobors are still entangled with the state-church deception—marriage?"

We answered that the majority of Doukhobors accept marriage, although without church rites. The Sons of Freedom, however, pay more attention to this problem, and although they have experimented in this field, so far, they have not managed to solve it satisfactorily.

Lloyd replied in surprise, "But why don't all Doukhobors"—he said "Doukhoboria," meaning the whole sect—"study this problem? Woman, as mother of the race, is the centre of life, but man has enslaved her and exploited her for his egoistic whims. The sex problem is the most important social problem. Its solution would at the same time disentangle if not all, at least many human complications."

We had an animated discussion. I tried to prove that at present free love without moral control leads to still worse results. I told him about the accident I had in my childhood with the forty bulls and one cow, and expressed the opinion that something like this could take place among human beings. I began to feel annoyed because our conversation kept returning monotonously to this subject.

I asked emphatically, "Do you agree among yourselves, A.G. Wagner, Dr. Henry and the rest of you? The main problem of your life seems to consist of man's relation to woman. Yet you remain bachelors for over twenty years. You are lonely, without women. The thought of them haunts you day and night. You invent all kinds of nonsense to decide their fate without even once asking their opinion. You are just like our Sons of Freedom. But to tell the truth, Mr. Lloyd, what right have we men to decide what to do? Our Sons of Freedom almost force their women to take turns sleeping with them. Mr. Lloyd, after all, isn't this terrible nonsense?"

Lloyd thought for a while, then said, "Of course, there must be no compulsion. If a woman wants to sleep with a particular man, she may do so. Otherwise, she may refuse. This is exactly the point at which man is guilty. For thousands of years, he enslaved women so that woman, the mother, lost her true way of life. This caused, and continues to cause, much madness. Everything is in the hands of the women. If she, the Woman-Mother, would only wake up to the realization of her mission, as God's most perfect creation, I am certain she has the power to lead humanity to the natural, healthy life."

But when I cornered him with the straight question, "How can this be?" he began to retreat from his words and said, "We should call for the help of science such specialists as Dr. Havelock Ellis and a Swedish Dr. Westbrook. They have studied this matter and they could tell us how and by what considerations we should be guided in this supreme problem."

Los Angeles: Philosophers, Pacifists, Molokans

In Los Angeles we took lodgings in the Jewish sector. My wife was treated by Dr. Phillip Lowell. During my free hours I took a few trips in the vicinity.

A certain Molokan, Yasha Yurin, visited us occasionally. He was a saintly, unsophisticated person. When he came a kind of spiritual warmth enveloped our souls. Yasha was so inoffensive, so well-wishing toward everyone that I wondered why there are so few Yashas in this world of ours.

Nathan Eagan is also worth mentioning. His soul was burning with an intense longing for universal brotherly life. He truly reflected the quest for creative life in complete freedom and perfect beauty. I found him at his plough in the suburbs of Hollywood and I noticed at once the contrast with Hollywood's moving picture stars, whom we also saw in their resplendent palaces. Nathan Eagan, in his simple surroundings, probably found more joy in life than they did.

Here I also met Mikhail Petrovich Pivovarov. This remarkable man had great aspirations. He gave a lively narrative of his trials. He and his brothers migrated from Russia and by a mistake reached the republic of Panama, where they suffered from heat and unemployment. Later in Arizona, he was with a Molokan brotherhood. They burned their arms in Phoenix and became vegetarians. This impressed me very much and I understood that truth has no limits and may be revealed anywhere. Some of Pivovarov's thoughts were so sharp and witty that I remembered them.

"I greet you, Doukhobors," he said, "the old, the middle-aged, the young. All of you are dear to my heart. You are children of great fathers, God's chosen men. Truly the Doukhobors were blessed from Zion by God's Spirit and Word. That's why they went out so bravely on the battlefield of life against the universal power and the Beast of Militarism, and became witnesses of freedom. They did not bow before human power and endured cruel persecutions, Asiatic settlements, disciplinary battalions and Siberian exile. The Doukhobors truly preserved purity of spirit, and now all of us and you, too, can exclaim together: Great and wonderful are your deeds, Oh Lord, our Creator and our Master. Great and wonderful deeds have you completed through your prophet under the leadership of Peter Vasilievich Verigin. Let everlasting memory be his and of all those who participated in the great "march," and have now left our world for eternity. May their remains grow flowers and the Doukhobors' banner of freedom reign over all nations, and let their descendants have bliss under its shade for ever and ever. The Doukhobors are heirs of the eternal life and of the spirit of resurrection. Only through the Doukhobors could our Molokans' brotherhood grow the seed of Truth, and reject military service. Here we found ourselves in America, saved from the terrible Armageddon."

Many years later I looked over Pivovarov's literary work, a kind of confession about his aspirations, accomplishments, downfalls and disappointments. I was stunned and shaken by his confessions. What incomparable vigour of mind and heart, how the brothers around him neglected his wonderful gift! They did not even try to publish the story of his broad vision for the Molokan sect. The following passage is taken from the last part of his confession:

"The Molokan brotherhood," he said, "has its own history, which is hardly shorter than the long history of the Doukhobors. Their settling in Los Angeles was not an accident but the result of a century-long quest of a 'promised land,' of a new and better life. Their path, not once but many, many times, led them through hard toil and sharp thorns. They suffered many wounds; many victims fell by the way."

Only after I had lived for a while in Los Angeles and saw many religious sects and groups did I learn to pay the Molokans their due, acknowledging them to be a truly valuable and alert people.

I visited meetings of the Theosophists, the Zoroastrians and several vegetarian societies and, though I found a few valuable ideas, as a whole these groups were marked by spiritual shallowness. What good is it, I thought, that they do not eat meat, when their inner self is sound asleep? The Molokans possess the most precious trait: inner warmth of heart. They make you feel this warmth, which fills you with unspeakable gladness. All they lack is the vegetarian habit.

If they would reject meat-eating, they would be real spiritual zealots. So much for Pivovarov's confession.

On my travels I found a certain difference between the Molokans of Los Angeles and those of San Francisco. In Los Angeles the brotherhood of "Jumpers" had more spiritual courage, more quest for God. In San Francisco there is religious apathy.

Fanny Bixby Spencer, an unforgettable purveyor of eternal values, lived not far from Los Angeles. I exchanged letters with her on the subject of Evalenko's book, *The Message of the Doukhobors*, which I had sent her. She wrote me that she was astonished by its contents and wondered why it was so little known.

Her home was a farm near Costa Mesa, where she maintained a small orphanage. She had no children of her own, perhaps because she protested so ardently against the injustice of man toward woman in contemporary life and against the way children are educated. When I visited her, I found in her orphanage one Molokan girl, a Filipino boy and several white orphans. She told me that she was convinced that human nature everywhere is the same: good and evil are inherent in all human beings without reference to race or nation.

In Mrs. Spencer I found one of the most broad-minded women who daringly fought for the cause of women's lofty concept of justice.

"I am for complete freedom of the human being," she said. "I am absolutely against the fact that woman-the-mother in the course of thousands of years has been in the eyes of men just a slave, a toy at best, a child-bearing apparatus: bear and bear children, then die before your time, worn out and overworked. The chains she has to wear humiliated not only herself, but all humanity, which could not rise to its natural height. This is my definite opinion, on this matter. I repeat: Woman must free herself from her bondage."

She read some of her writings, among them a poem "I Am Woman the Soul."

She asked about the Doukhobors. She had read literature on this subject and had just finished the biography of Lev Tolstoy, written by P.I. Biriukov. She was a confirmed anti-militarist and socialist. As a keepsake she gave me her book entitled *The Repudiation of War*. In it she mentioned the struggle of the Molokans against militarism during the First World War.

"This is the kind of men we need," she said.

She gave me a letter from a Molokan imprisoned for two years from 1917 to 1918 in Fort Leavenworth for refusing to go into the army. It was unsigned, and she asked me to find the name of the author. I tried to do this, but without success. Years later I discovered that it was written by Ivan Vasilyevich Sisoev, a real martyr.

In the beginning of 1917, Vladimir Ivanovich Nemirovich-Danchenko of the Moscow art theatre arrived in Hollywood for a visit. Daniil Sigal invited me to attend his lecture in the newly opened city library. The subject was "Art." The audience was made up of three or four hundred people, Russians of the upper class and Americans. Nemirovich spoke to the point, without haste, each sentence harmonious, as if produced by some musical instrument. Among other things he said:

"You have no art in America. All your attempt at art consists of a male pursuing a female, or vice versa. To add action, they shoot one another. That's all."

After the lecture I met Ilya Lvovich Tolstoy, with whom I had corresponded for several years. He patted my hand and gave a strict order, "Tomorrow with the whole family and without fail, come to see us!"

Sunday morning, we went to Crescent Drive in Hollywood. Their home was a palace in the Spanish style. Ilya Lvovich stood in the yard with a cigarette. He was the very image of his great father. He greeted us with these words: "I would like to live with the Doukhobors for the rest of my life. I have one sin, this cigarette. I don't want to hide it from Doukhobors. But I don't eat meat and I don't drink."

He explained to us that he was staying in Hollywood to help stage the movie based on his father's book *Resurrection.*

We had a long conversation, then his wife, Nadezhda Klementievna, appeared at eleven o'clock, after a bath, wearing a luxurious dress and looking like a real princess. The telephone began to ring. Important Hollywood personages were inviting the Tolstoys for tea.

We spoke of the past and present. Ilya Lvovich was interested in the Doukhobors. "I did not understand," he said, "why my father paid so much attention to your people, but after my stay in Hollywood the curtain rose for me and I understood that the Doukhobors represent all that is healthy and vital in our Russian people, but here in Hollywood things are topsy-turvy. For my father, Doukhobors were the symbol of a spiritual wealth, of that power which alone is able to lay a permanent foundation for the future. He used to say that the Doukhobors were blessed with the natural ability not only to see the truth, but to live according to the truth."

We almost had a disagreement, when we discussed the teachings of Tolstoy and its interpretation by Tolstoy's followers. Ilya Lvovich insisted that Vladimir Grigorievich Chertkov was one of the basest men among those who had surrounded his father during the last days of his life. I refused to accept this assertion and maintained the opposite opinion, asserting that Chertkov was one of the most interesting followers of Lev Tolstoy. His son denied it. I then expressed the opinion that he and the other children of Tolstoy would naturally share the family's belief that the right to manage their father's literary wealth should belong to them and not to Chertkov.

During my next visit to Ilya Lvovich, he brought three copies of the magazine *Rossia* published in Moscow in 1923 and read me a few passages from his father's writings.

"Read what Lev Nikolaevich wrote about the Doukhobors," he said.

I took the magazine, read what he told me to read and was amazed at his powerful thoughts. Then I remarked, "Those lines are wonderful. But see, it was Chertkov once more who collected and edited those thoughts of your father. And you don't approve of Chertkov."

"When Chertkov did something good, he did it in order to hide something bad," said Ilya Lvovich.

"Better stop here," I said.

He laughed and added, "Well, let it be as you wish."

Our acquaintance with the Tolstoy family turned into a close friendship. We saw them for the last time on our way home. They told us a few facts about the private life of Hollywood.

"If my father could see what we have seen here, without doubt he would call this place the second Sodom and would curse it for its vices. We shall not stay here long; we shall soon leave. We shall come to live with you Doukhobors. Remember that. My father wanted this, but he did not realize his wish. At least I shall be able to die with you."

We went to look for Savva Andreev and Kostia Rodin. People told us they were expected in Ontario, about fifty miles south of Los Angeles. On our way we saw a man walking by the road and stopped to give him a lift, saying, "Maybe this is Kostia?" And so it was the self-assured, joyful optimist himself.

He had managed to visit the Doukhobor community but was disappointed. He said, "They don't have what I expected them to have." He called on us in Thrums, but we had already left.

We stayed for the night in the farmhouse of a Jew, Ilya Durnov. There we found Savva Andreev and another guest.

In the morning our children ran out in the yard to play with our host's children. Soon a man came in leading the children with him. He was a young man with a beard. He said, "I saw your little girl and knew at once that she was a stranger here, so I came to ask who you are and where you came from."

Introducing himself, he said, "I am Walter Zigmeister, son of a well-known surgeon from Brooklyn. I just finished my doctor's degree at Columbia University."

When we told him we were Doukhobors, he was delighted.

"I have read about the Doukhobors," he said, "and I believe that my ancestors were Doukhobors. Maybe that's why I am so attracted to them myself. I am organizing a local community. Maybe you would give us an example of how to conduct this experiment. I am not the only initiator here. I have a friend, an American named Ezra Taylor."

Zigmeister introduced his friend, a man of about sixty, but still so full of energy that he seemed to be made of steel springs, lively, active and joyful.

Their idea about organizing a community impressed us. We had already heard that the Doukhobor community was now slowly disintegrating; former members did not want to remain in it. But here, in this place were men eager to organize. I myself refused to become a member, explaining that I never lived in a community for a long period of time, had no real experience in the organization, so I could hardly be of use in helping them. Then they asked me to help by lending my car to drive them to visit possible future members. To this I consented, found suitable lodgings for my family and we three, Zigmeister, Taylor and I, began calling on neighbourhood people. We spent several months covering great distances and established connections with many idealists who took an interest in our "Noah's Ark," which was gathering people for the new life.

We visited the famous theosophist Annie Besant and her pupil Krishnamurti. It was our intention to see Krishnamurti, but we discovered that to do so we had to report to Dr. Annie Besant. She was a wise, matriarchal and careful woman. She made inquiries, found out why and for what we wanted to see Krishnamurti, then she gave permission. Krishnamurti gave us his approval and encouragement for our enterprise. We also visited many others, the Hindu Swami Yogananda and scores of other scientists and plain men, all seeking the true ways of life.

Then a general convention was called. It took place in Los Angeles on Washington Hill where some loving hands had made miniature models of different churches, temples, homes for the poor, synagogues and mosques. About forty people attended our meeting. Each had his own dreams and opinions. Reports were made about existing communities. Especially interesting was the speech of one young woman representing the publishing house Rowney, known for its humanitarian books.

Zigmeister fervently insisted that I should join the community. He had a tender, thoughtful heart, but was ignorant and tactless in practical things. I doubted the success of his efforts.

CHAPTER 18

ANARCHISTS, AGNOSTICS, PACIFISTS, RUSSIA INTELLIGENTSIA, DOUKHOBORS AND MOLOKANS

Those three months and the acquaintance with the variety of people suggested to me that before entering any community I ought to return to Canada and investigate the details of our own Doukhobor life. This was confirmed by my acquaintance with Peter Cassidy, who often passed our lodging place. His long hair fell to his shoulders, he never wore a hat and always walked barefoot. He was one of the most peculiar Americans I ever met.

I invited him to visit us and from then on, we became such good friends that he seldom missed a day without dropping in to see us. He knew the brothers Vlasoff and was acquainted with the ideas and history of the Doukhobors. He even called himself a Doukhobor. He was a real child of nature, ate only fruits and nuts, picked up free from the markets that were throwing them out. All he needed for a home was his small tent. He had the soft and flexible nature of a child, which drew him, where he saw a chance, to find friendly human accord. His soul overflowed with love of humanity. He was a free unattached and happy man.

Each Sunday Cassidy went to the park with his guitar. There he sang songs and spoke on spiritual and moral themes. Several times he was taken to court, because of what he said in condemnation of war. He never had any money and hated it, often quoting a poem, "Money the Evil."

When I told him that Zigmeister and the others were inviting me to join their community, Cassidy listened with attention and then said seriously, "Don't deceive yourself, my friend. Go to your own people; they have more experience in this matter."

On Saturday nights we visited free forums where we listened to reports on international subjects and labour problems. A Scot named Thomas Bell, an anarchist, tall, straight and lean, was often present. He had beautiful thick hair and beard and deep-blue piercing eyes. He never missed an opportunity to criticize the speakers. He knew the value of words and maintained that the critic played an important part in human life, giving a jolt to move people ahead. He had known Peter Kropotkin personally and in Edinburgh had bought a coat for Kropotkin from the socialistic circle, of which he was a member.

"Kropotkin had a talent," said Bell. "He knew how to awaken an idealistic response and the sympathy of his listeners. He was the kind of man we need here. The intellectual part of his speech was usually very clear. He was the first who suggested to me to study the history of the sects, especially of the Doukhobors who in his judgment represented one of the highest attainments of the co-operative movement."

Bell spoke on different subjects, often concluding his addresses with the famous words of William Morris, the well-known English revolutionary, whom Bell also knew personally. "Truly, my friends, brotherhood is Heaven and absence of brotherhood is hell; brotherhood is life, the absence of brotherhood is death; all that you do on this earth, do for the sake of brotherhood."

Speaking privately about Kropotkin, Thomas Bell said, "So you know that the Doukhobors moved to Canada on the advice of Kropotkin? In 1897, P.A. Kropotkin made a trip to Canada and after his return to England, he met Aylmer Maud and Prince Khilkov with the delegates from the Doukhobors. He expressed his opinion that the Canadian prairies would be the most suitable region."

Lectures in the Los Angeles Library

On Sunday evenings, Cassidy and I attended the lectures of the Society of Agnostics in Walker's Auditorium. The lecturers were of the highest intellectual attainment: scientists, philosophers, doctors. On one occasion the philosopher Ferdinand Wolf delivered a wonderful lecture on Christ. I remember particularly the witty Manley Hale, a profound student of religious thought and ancient philosophy. His lectures always attracted a great number of listeners and were delivered with animation.

Usually after such lectures Cassidy would step forward and declare, "All your knowledge is worthless. If you want real wisdom leave the cities and go out to till the soil. Live nearer to nature." He stood out in sharp contrast to the educated lecturers, but they treated his simplicity with sympathy.

Lectures were also delivered in the vegetarian dining room. Arnold Erretto, author of the book *Hunger as the Factor of Health*, asserted that sickness is mainly due to overeating. If people would eat less and go without food more often, they would never suffer from the gastric disorders that torture them now. The personality of this lecturer was brilliant in a way, but he passed to the other side of life under very strange circumstances and was soon forgotten.

208 — THEY CALLED HIM A RADICAL

We also heard George Drews, an advocate of the raw vegetarian diet. At the first lecture he asserted that he understood all the secrets of the right diet, which would cure sickness and give eternal youth to healthy people. These secrets he promised to reveal during his next three lectures, if each listener would pay him fifty dollars. Hearing this my friend Cassidy could not restrain himself but shouted, "That's quackery. I don't want to know your secret if it is so expensive!"

Bruno Petzold was an interesting man, a German by birth and a seeker for a new and better life. He lived for a time in Brazil and other South American countries.[74] He asked us a number of times, "Would the Doukhobor brothers accept me into their community as a member, if I would come to them?"

We listened to the brothers Rolas who had just arrived from Germany. They told the story of the German revolution of 1923, when Hitler made his first and still insignificant appearance. How ardently they spoke in describing the danger which was darkening Germany's horizon. What a terrible evil was Prussian militarism. This they predicted would grow to monstrous proportions.

What seems so strange now is the fact that in 1926 such warnings were taken by the public in a very light mood. They were even met with laughter. Such a serious man as Thomas Bell made fun of the brothers Rolas: "Your fears have no foundation," he repeated. "Hitler is no more than a soap bubble. He will inflate himself and burst."

In the same environment I met Otto Carque, a well-known hygienist-vegetarian,[75] who wrote on the subject of nutrition. When I told him that various diseases appeared among Doukhobors, though they are in the main strict vegetarians, he answered that this should not be so; perhaps the Doukhobors did not combine their food properly. He agreed to come to Canada to investigate the Doukhobors' diet and find their mistakes, but he was soon after killed by an automobile.

At the beginning of our acquaintance, Carque invited me to his home. There we met Carl Robinson, whose experience interested me. In 1927, America had sent several ships with American troops to China to protect the Rockefellers' wealth. Many Americans protested this act, among them Carl Robinson.

---

74   Wikipedia: Bruno Petzold (1873–1949) was born at Breslaw, Silesia, which at that time was part of the German Empire. He attended Leipzig University and Berlin University. For several years he was the correspondent in Paris for the *Berliner Tageblatt* and other German newspapers.

75   Wikipedia: Carque advocated a fruitarian as well as a vegetarian diet, exercise and fresh air. He introduced the term "natural food."

He delivered a fiery speech in a city park, was arrested, tried and sentenced to three months in prison. This did not cool his indignation. He decided to continue his protest by means of a hunger strike, ready to starve to death if necessary. Carque bailed him out of prison and took him to his home. When we first met him, he was just out of prison, and looked as if skin and bones were all that was left of him.

In the beginning of the summer of 1927, we decided to leave Los Angeles to earn a little money and then gradually go farther north. Cassidy came to us full of tears, begging to be taken with us. His silky golden hair and his childish blue eyes always reminded me of Nikolai Nikolaevich Ge, a famous Russian artist. His pleadings still burn my heart. I am sincerely sorry that we did not take him along. Each time I remember him, I feel guilty that I did not care enough for the purity and sincerity of his soul. Two years after our departure he died in an old men's home.

We stopped for a time in Yuba City to work and from there went on to Shafter and visited Nikolai Ivanovich and Daria Fyodorovna Rilkova. Nikolai Ivanovich was a "Siberian," who served time in the disciplinary battalion and had been beaten with rods. His wife was a Molokan.

N.I. Rilkov proved to be both pleasant and intelligent. He did not approve of idle chatter. His words were well thought over before they were uttered. I spent several delightful hours in his company.

Not far from him lived Alexei Panfilovich Kariakin with his family and Nikolai Lukyanovich Sisoev, the old man whom I knew from San Francisco. We also visited them. Alexei Panfilovich expressed progressive ideas, advocating in particular better contact between the Doukhobors and the Molokans. He asked us if I read in the newspaper *Russkoe Slovo, The Russian Word*, his sketches about Peter Vasilievich Verigin's visit with the Molokans in 1923. He wanted my opinion about them.

I replied, "Yes, I read your sketches and liked them very much. As I read them, I could have thought that you were a Doukhobor." He laughed.

We found Nikolai Lukyanovich in the fields, cultivating his potato patch. His huge figure and great beard could be seen from afar. He followed his cultivator with long steps, but his horse had a sickly and starved look. We came up to him and asked, "Why is your helper so skinny? Don't you feed him enough?"

"No, it is not the feed," said Nikolai Lukyanovich. "The worms choke my poor bay friend. I think of calling a veterinarian for him."

I liked Nikolai Lukyanovich very much. He was a Molokan but did not belong to the Brotherhood of Jumpers. He embodied the ideal of lofty spiritual living. I think that he missed the accomplishments and sacrifices of the active struggle and that his quiet life was a burden to him.

In Yuba City we took the same ranch that we had rented earlier. Our house was comfortable and with us was Anatoly Ivanovich Fomin and his son Anatoly. Anatoly belonged to the Russian "intelligentsia." A graduate of the University of St. Petersburg in astronomy, and later from a technical school, he had carried on a trade in machinery and technical instruments. Before the revolution he was a wealthy and important man. In 1916 he came with his family to America for the purpose of making purchases for his business. The revolution caused him to remain in America. Then he conceived the idea of ignoring the conventionalities of life, and free from the armchair of a wealthy and powerful master, he descended to the simplicity of a child of nature. He went so far as to go completely naked in his free time, remaining however inside his house. This naïveté became him. His nakedness did not bother us, although we considered it unnecessary. He would sit at his typewriter naked, writing letters to his friends, and considered this quite natural though for us it was strange, even comical. His eyes always had a look as if he were seeing something far away. All his reasoning was philosophical.

After my wife and children went to bed, Anatoly and I liked to sit in the yard till late at night and chat by the light of a bonfire. He had travelled widely and could give impressions of his wanderings with beauty and refined observation. His business had taken him all over Russia, Siberia and Turkestan, a land which he said was like California. In 1904, he had spent a night with the Doukhobors in Slavyanka, on his way to a copper mine.

"They made no impression on me then," he admitted. "They seemed nothing more than sad drunkards, all of them."

He told me about his life in the Hawaiian Islands and on the island of Samoa in 1918. He went there to buy copra and cane for his factory and stayed for six months.

"Savages," he called the people. "We are accustomed to regard this word as a humiliating epithet, but in fact morally these savages are much above the people who live here in America. If I do not go to Canada to the Doukhobors, I shall go to Samoa to these wonderful savages."

We expected his wife, Anastasia Dimitrievna, to come to us for a visit. I had met her before, but Lusha, my wife, had not. In preparation for her coming we spent two whole days washing, cleaning and scrubbing. Anatoly himself flew around, as if he had grown wings preparing for the visitor. When Anastasia Dimitrievna entered the home, she did not even greet us. She looked our simple dwelling over, saw that we had neither bathtub nor electricity and declared, "Only swine can live in such a house."

Anatoly tried to calm her, "Natochka, darling, why are you saying that? See we all live here and we enjoy life."

But she did not want to listen. For a whole week she cried and, in her vexation, repeated all kinds of sharp words.

"Anatoly Ivanovich, you are an educated man, an astronomer, an engineer. Why then do you make a monkey of yourself? Only monkeys climb trees."

Anatoly and I had climbed up a tree to fasten the branches with wire.

During her whole stay, Anatoly did not associate intimately with her at all but treated her like a small child. He would make up her bed every night, kiss her good night and put her to sleep. Then he would take his own cot and go out to sleep under a tree.

This chaste treatment of his wife surprised us, but at the same time touched me deeply. It did not seem natural, but I realized that his approach to the sex problem was sincere and serious. I read widely on this subject and had many discussions with my friends, but it all remained for me in the realm of words. Anatoly on the contrary said little, but practised real chastity.

Anatoly Ivanovich tried to persuade his wife to accept our simple life. He explained to her the new ideas about the necessity for men to return to nature, to live in almost primitive conditions. Anastasia Dimitrievna categorically refused to understand. Sometimes she became hysterical.

Once she addressed me with despair in her voice. "Peter Nikolayevich, when we lived in Russia, I called him to accept simple and unconventional ways of life, but he refused. Now I refuse. Anatoly once bought a forty-room house in Vyborg, Finland, and a summer palace. I did not like it, but he repeated, 'This is my wish.' We arrived in New York, and he used to pay a thousand dollars a month for our apartment in the Hotel Vanderbilt. I tried to dissuade him, but again he said, 'This is my business.' For four years we lived in the Hawaiian Islands and he bought three Cadillacs, worth five thousand dollars each. I told him that this was unnecessary, and again he answered, 'This is my business.'"

Eventually, she left without accepting our ways of life. But I really enjoyed living and conversing with Anatoly Ivanovich. In spite of his learning, he was gifted with a simple heart and possessed real spiritual insight.

I asked him once what caused him to change his life so drastically. This is what he told me: "In my life I have experienced two terrible shocks. They caused me to change my life. The first was during the Russian Revolution of 1905. I stood on the steps of the main post office building in St. Petersburg. A crowd of people was pushing in the direction of the Winter Palace. All of a sudden, a shot sounded, and a man fell at my feet, killed by that shot. Why did it happen? This remained one of the great questions of my life.

"My second shock was the death of my little daughter in the Hawaiian Islands. This caused me to change my whole life and to unwind the ball of wrong living that I had wound around my neck. I realized that my little girl's death was the last warning sent me by the Voice of Life. Now I want to repent and to redeem my sins against my Creator. This is my aim."

In Yuba City I met Mark Andreevich at the home of Grigoriy Efimovich Vlasoff. He lived there among Molokans as a Russian-language teacher. I had heard about him several years before when I read his appeal to people in the *Russian Voice*. Since then, I had wanted to meet him. I believe that his appeal has not lost its meaning.

Mark Andreevich said,

> It is stifling to live in our contemporary society with its hypocrisy and greed for profit, with its flattery and cold indifference toward the greatness and divine beauty of nature. Contemporary civilization with its artificial beauty does not satisfy me. Men should rise above the everyday cares that engulf us in darkness, and choke the impulses of free thought. Living as the crowd lives, man loses the meaning of life and lowers himself to the condition of a beast.
>
> Human life must be filled with unceasing aspiration for self-perfection, because everything in nature strives for perfection. Man should aspire to reach the height by developing physical beauty of the human form, strong and powerful muscles and nerves, clear eyes that sparkle with nobility and greatness, a mind able to penetrate the hidden secrets of nature, a memory able to retain even the slightest details, a strong and unbending will that can overcome obstacles in the way of attaining the desired aim.
>
> No one doubts that by certain exercises man can develop physical strength, but many persons do not know that it is possible to develop the memory and the will, to ennoble the character and even to change the outline of the face. One has only to possess a true desire and will.[76]

Mark Andreevich was a frail being. He appeared to be made of crystal lace. But his soul was all aflame, sending out rays of light and warmth. He

---

76   Maloff, *Doukhobors: Their History, Life and Struggle,* ibid.

affirmed that the main thing in life is to try not to extinguish even the smallest life-giving thought and the warmth of inner intuition. "The trouble with man," he often said, "is that he does not use and does not try to develop his spiritual possibilities, which are the true foundation of all the beauty of life. What would greatness be for, if it were hostile, proud and self-admiring? We need a greatness that is noble, merciful and rhythmic. Then beauty will permeate everything and be present everywhere."

At about this time we received word that the Doukhobors' new leader, Peter Petrovich Verigin-Chistiakov, would soon arrive in Canada from Russia. I wanted to return at once to Canada, so without delay we packed our belongings and left for British Columbia.

Anatoly Ivanovich decided to go with us, but to our regret he did not receive a permit to enter Canada so he had to return from the border to his former residence while we, without incident, arrived in Thrums.

RETURN TO CANADA

[Vera] The Maloff family returned to British Columbia in 1927 and Grandfather Pete looked for employment. The highway through Thrums was being built and the supervisor liked Pete, saw that he was a good worker and wanted to hire him. However, he told Pete, "They say that you are a radical and if I hire you, I'll lose my job." Grandfather was disappointed but decided that growing good food was an honourable way to make a living, and the Maloffs started a market garden on the banks of the Kootenay River. Farming supported the Maloff family throughout their lives. There are numerous pictures of Lusha and Pete working together, planting, weeding and harvesting, selling at markets; they look happy and content. One photo I love shows Grandfather driving a McCormick Farmall tractor and Grandmother balancing on the narrow metal seat of the hay rake.

In the 1920s employers wouldn't hire Pete Maloff because they believed he was a radical. Pete and Lusha decided that growing good food was an honourable way to make a living and they grew a market garden on the banks of the Kootenay River in Thrums.

Pete Maloff leading a protest in Nelson against land taxes going to the military, 1929.

Grandfather Pete formed a close relationship with newly arrived Doukhobor leader Peter Petrovich Verigin-Chistiakov. Chistiakov sent him with a choir to visit the Molokans in the western United States and Doukhobors in Saskatchewan. They prayed, talked and sang together, strengthening their pacifist connections. With Verigin's support and Sons of Freedom involvement, Pete helped to organize peace walks in Blaine Lake, Saskatchewan, and Nelson, British Columbia. They were protesting against land taxes going to the military budget.

The 1929 Nelson peace march resulted in a six-month detention in Oakalla provincial jail for the nine "ringleaders" and subsequently 104 of their supporters. In a further escalation, that fall and winter, 321 adults and 216 children were interned in an abandoned logging camp, Porto Rico, in the mountains south of Nelson. In 1932, 546 men and women were jailed for a three-year term on Piers Island, a prison built specifically for the Doukhobors. Over 300 of their children, mostly under fourteen years of age, were taken from their parents and sent to government institutions, orphanages and foster homes. The actions by the government were responses to the peaceful protests that my family participated in, and the pretext to the arrest of so many particularly in 1932 was that some Doukhobors involved protested naked. Again, in the 1940s, Pete's refusal to register in the National Registration led to further arrests.

My mother Elizabeth recalled how Grandmother Lusha always supported Grandfather Pete's participation, even though when he was arrested it meant

In the 1960s Pete Maloff spoke at the International Peace Garden on the border of Manitoba and North Dakota and in anti-war protests in Suffield, Alberta, against the use of chemical and biological weapons. Photo Koozma Tarasoff, author of *Plakun Trava: The Doukhobors*.

she was left raising the family, often for years. She utilized their meagre resources to provide a home and sustenance through her incredible ability to make something out of very little. She home-schooled her children, teaching them arithmetic, and Russian and English reading and writing. Lusha raised her family as vegetarians, and in the early years they did not use any animal products. She sewed leather-less *laptee* shoes for all the family. Pete, Lusha and the family survived the difficult years through their firm belief they were doing the right thing to make the world a better place.

It is true that Pete's drive to make a difference in this world dominated their lives and often Lusha and the family bore the brunt of his pursuit toward this goal. In their youth, the Maloff children, Elizabeth, Peter, Luba, John, Nadya and Walter, often missed their father's guidance. Although they continued to be his supporters and cheerleaders, they must have wondered what his protests achieved.

The accomplishments of pacifists are often not realized for years, but I believe in the power of the cumulative effect of even a small group of people. This statement by Margaret Mead (1901–1978), a distinguished professor of sociology and anthropology and a contemporary of Pete Maloff, gives me hope:

"Never doubt that a small group of thoughtful committed citizens can change the world: indeed, it's the only thing that ever has."

Pete Maloff planned to write a second book about the 1927 arrival of Doukhobor leader Peter Petrovich Verigin in Canada and events to 1948. Perhaps some stories are not meant to be told, as Grandfather passed away before he was able to do so. To give readers a glimpse of Maloff's life during those turbulent years, I include an excerpt from his *A Report on the Doukhobors* (1950) to Col. F.J. Mead, deputy commissioner of the RCMP (p. 3–5):

> My first contact with the Doukhobors was back in 1928, when the Doukhobor community staged a spiritual revival and displayed a unique example of idealistic aspirations worthy of high consideration. This religious revival attracted my whole being and I sympathized with all three movements in the community, and in particular with the Sons of Freedom who represented at that time the strength of spiritual and moral power. Their unceasing struggle against war and causes of war attracted my whole attention; and to find such a movement among my own people was certainly a joy, since I was already acquainted with many similar movements—Ghandhi and his followers, Tolstoy and his adherents, Fellowship of Reconciliation of New York, Quaker Brotherhood of Philadelphia and so on.
>
> My ten years of close contact with the Doukhobors from 1928 to 1938 have faced me with some bitter experiences and revealed to me some unusual glimpses into their strange faith. For the last seven to eight years, I have led more or less a secluded life, and for the last four years I have entirely severed my connections with the Doukhobors, Sons of Freedom and, as much as possible, with all society. I did this for certain reasons. In my dealings with human nature, Doukhobors and the civilized society as a whole, I have suffered two big surprises, disappointments and terrific stunning blows.

My Number 1 Disappointment

> Practically speaking, during the past twenty years, I have not left any stone unturned, nor any attic unsearched, either here in Canada, in the USA or in Europe, in my quest for Doukhobor history, the reason for their struggle, and the persecution

they endured. And what did I find? My whole study reveals that Doukhobors have made a tremendous contribution to genuine religious life and thought. Their original point of view faithfully follows the teachings of the great master of the ages—the Galilean—who revealed the truth to mankind, that for a genuine Christian there are no nationalities, classes, parties, sects, cults, denominations, etc. For him there is only one superb, universal Almighty Creator inherent throughout the whole life forces. Consequently, to the Christian, there is no such thing as sectarian Doukhobors, Independents, Sons of Freedom, Britishers, Canadians, Americans, Jews, Arabs, Russians, Germans … Conservatives, Liberals, Democrats, Socialists, Communists and so on and on. To him, there is only humanity in terms of a world brotherhood.

This early Christian conception was the foundation of the Doukhobor movement. And what do I find today? … I find that this sense of brotherhood, far from embracing every race and creed, no longer bridges the splits that have appeared in the Doukhobor movement.

My Number 2 Disappointment

I was never a great believer in either theory or dogma, even the Doukhobor sort. The faith by which I live did not come to me ready-made, but gradually religion came to me more and more, through the growth of the human soul; the cultivation of the first shoots of the ideals of others and one's own ideals; the understanding of the ideals of others, and even the understanding of the ways of animals. In this way, by degrees, I reached the point where war, and any sort of killing, was absolutely repulsive. It followed, therefore, that I did not feel myself bound in any way to society that had declared war on another group of human beings. It was not long after the outbreak of the Second World War that the reality of my convictions was to be ruthlessly tested.

Yet, I would like to note that despite my earlier experiences with British law, I still maintained a certain degree of respect for the British traditions of justice. But something happened that gave me a severe shock.

Pete Maloff broke his arm while he was in house arrest in a remote cabin in Blewett in the 1940s and it was several days before anyone found him. After three years he returned home, but was not allowed visitors outside the family.

I was imprisoned in Nelson on three different occasions for violating the National Registration Act [1940–1946]. During my last confinement there, I was confronted with an ultimatum, that unless I registered, I should be transferred to the Essondale Insane Asylum for the duration of the war and perhaps for the rest of my days. The only cause for this threat was my alleged stubborn resistance to registration on conscientious objection to war, which according to the representatives of this democratic, civilized society, was an influence on others to follow my example.

I had a serious fight on my hands to keep myself out of the bughouse, and if it had not been for the help of my family and a few friends here and there, I may not have been here today.

Pete was rescued from beatings and the threat of confinement in a mental institution thanks to several people speaking out for him. A prison guard, fearing for Pete's life, sent a message to Lusha that Pete was being beaten and threatened by Warden Macdonald. Lusha contacted Reverend John Haynes Holmes of the American Civil Liberties Union whom Pete had corresponded with. Holmes immediately sent a telegram to Macdonald stating that the ACLU would defend Pete's right to freedom of speech. The beatings stopped, but Elizabeth and Lusha continued to make many trips to Nelson to beg Warden Macdonald to release Pete Maloff from prison. Eventually, an alternative of house arrest in a remote mountain cabin in Blewett was agreed upon. My aunt Luba, at thirteen years old, was allowed to bring him supplies and stay with him for a period of time. On her first visit there she had to row across the Kootenay River in a leaky rowboat though she had never rowed a boat before. This is an excerpt from the "Exile in Blewett" chapter in my book, *Our Backs Warmed by the Sun: Memories of a Doukhobor Life* (Caitlin Press, 2020):

Papa was in Blewett for three years. I especially remember the winter of 1942 when I thought he might die. It had been snowing for days, and it was a couple of weeks before I was able to get a ride to Blewett. Dyadya Ivan drove me to Blewett Road above Fortynine Creek, but the side road was blocked with snow. "Don't worry, Dyadya," I said as I pulled on my mittens and tied my woollen kerchief tightly under my chin. "It's only a mile or so. I'll walk from here."

I tied my packages onto our wooden sled and trudged off, pulling it through the knee-high snow. At the bottom of the hill where the log bridge crossed the creek, I stopped for a breather. The usually noisy creek was now a series of frozen waterfalls that draped over boulders and moss and I heard only a tinkle of water. The driveway leading into the trees on the left of the bridge was the last sign of a home—John Horcoff's—before the wild forest began. I had been there to fetch water when the creek had frozen and to visit Florence, John's sister. John was in his forties and had separated from his wife, so Florence, twenty-four and still single, came to help her brother cook, mend his clothes and knit his socks. I decided to let them know I was back.

The dogs John kept for chasing coyotes barked as I approached the house, and John came out, pulling a wool cap over his short brown hair. "Luba, *vsyo kharasho?* Everything fine with you?"

"Oh yes," I answered. "Back to stay with Papa."

"Come and warm up before you head up the mountain," John said. "Florence is here."

"I'd like to make it to the cabin before it gets dark, but I'll visit soon."

"Say hello to your Papa. Hope he's well. There's a flu going around," John told me.

I crossed the bridge and tramped up the road on the other side of the creek until I came to the trail on the left—Bird Road, they call it now, but back then it was just a rough path that was used by prospectors. Tall fir and cedar trees, giant snow sentinels, leaned in on either side. As I walked, I imagined the welcome Papa and Sport would give me: warm hugs, conversation, sharing the soup I had brought from home.

I turned up the path to the cabin. No smoke from the chimney. No footprints in the snow, either, but I heard barking. I pushed the last few feet through the snow and shoved the door open.

Sport dashed toward me and jumped up and down, doing a frantic welcome dance. I petted the furry head. "Sport, I'm glad to see you, too. Where's Papa?"

The sour smell of sickness and the thin figure under the tangled quilts on the bed told me all was not well. Papa was scrunched up into a ball and, though every blanket that was available was on top of him, I could see he was shivering. Hurriedly, I threw off my coat and boots and knelt by his side. His forehead, when I felt it, was burning, but his hands were cold.

Papa opened his eyes, grimaced, swallowed and said, "Masha, it's you."

Masha? Masha Hoodicoff was Grandmother! "Papa, it's me, Luba," I answered him. "I've just come back. I've brought fresh barley soup that Mama made, and Leeza baked bread just like Babushka used to make."

But Papa was looking past me and mumbling something I couldn't understand. I busied myself: I lit the stove, put the soup on to warm and kept up a banter, more to ease my worry than to talk to Papa. He had closed his eyes.

"Good news, Papa. Warden Macdonald said that you may come home for a few days. No visitors, but we'll be so happy to have you home."

In 1971, Pete and Lusha Maloff were on their way to visit their good friend Dr. Bernard Jensen at his health ranch in California where Pete planned to write Volume II of his book on the Doukhobors. Sadly, at the age of seventy-one, he passed away on the journey there.

I close with a summary of Pete Maloff's last years. When he was free to travel abroad, in the 1960s, he visited his many correspondents in Europe, Asia, India and Russia and made a pilgrimage to war memorials in Hiroshima and Auschwitz. He was asked to give speeches at peace rallies: at the International Peace Garden on the border of Manitoba and North Dakota, against the testing of chemical and biological weapons at Suffield in Alberta, and to Rotary Clubs. He counselled many American war resisters who landed at the Maloff farm doorstep. All the while he continued to support his family through a bedding plant and market gardening enterprise.

In October of 1971, my grandparents, Pete and Lusha Maloff, were travelling by bus from their home in Thrums, British Columbia, to the hills of Escondido, California, to stay at the health ranch of their good friend Dr. Bernard Jensen. Pete had written to UBC librarian Robert Hamilton: "I hope to break the tyranny of the greenhouse business that is so demanding. I want to start writing about my time with the Doukhobor leader, Chistiakov."[77] In the serenity of the retreat, Grandfather Pete Maloff was to start Volume II.

On day two of the journey, on October 22, 1971, at age seventy-one, my grandfather suffered a heart attack and passed away on the bus with his wife, Lusha, by his side. His untimely death was a shock to his family, friends and community. Many mourned his passing at a three-day Doukhobor funeral in the Tarrys Community Hall.

When Pete passed away Lusha mourned, "I never wanted to be a widow." Lusha lived another twenty-five years in their home in Thrums, a matriarch of a large extended family. Lusha spoke for Pete Maloff at the Expanded Kootenay Committee on Intergroup Relations. A member of the committee remarked that her presentation there was impressive.

Pete Maloff's closing statement to the Rotary Club in Trail is as pertinent today as it was in 1968. "Do we think to overcome this worldwide crisis by using the same old outworn methods: bigger armies, navies, air force, hydrogen bombs, poison gases and all our other confused values? I myself doubt it. I stand for creative intelligence which is distinctly distilled in the unchanging truth of that one cosmic law: 'Thou Shalt Not Kill.'"

---

77   Letter found in the UBC special collections dated 1971.

BIBLIOGRAPHY

Bartolf, Christian, and Dominique Miething. "'Flame of Truth': The Global Significance of Doukhobor Pacifism." *Russian Journal of Church History* 4(4) (December 2023): 6–27, DOI:10.15829/2686-973X-2023-142.

Day, Dorothy. *The Long Loneliness: The Autobiography of the Legendary Catholic Social Activist.* New York: Harper and Row Publishers, 1952.

Donskov, Andrew, ed. *Sergej Tolstoy and the Doukhobors: A Journey to Canada.* Ottawa: Slavic Research Group at the University of Ottawa, 1998.

Donskov, Andrew, ed. *The Doukhobor Centenary in Canada.* Ottawa: Co-published by the Institute of Canadian Studies, University of Ottawa, 1999.

Evalenko, Alexander M. *The Message of the Doukhobors.* New York: International Library Pub. Co., 1913. https://open.library.ubc.ca/collections/chung/chungpub/items/1.0056054.

George, Henry. *Progress and Poverty.* San Francisco: W.M. Hinton & Co. 1879.

Inikova, Svetlana A. *Doukhobor Incantations through the Centuries.* Ottawa: Legas Publishing, 1999.

Inikova, Svetlana A. *History of the Doukhobors in V.D. Bonch-Bruevich's Archives (1886–1950s).* Ottawa: Legas Publishing, 1999.

Jordan, David Starr. *The Days of a Man.* Yonkers-on-Hudson, NY: World Book Co., 1922. https://archive.org/details/daysofmanbeingme01jord.

Klibanov, A.I. *History of Religious Sectarianism in Russia (1860s–1917).* Oxford: Pergamon Press, 1982.

Maloff, Peter N. *A Report of the Doukhobors* (1950) to Col. F.J. Mead, deputy commissioner of the RCMP.

Maloff, Peter N. *Doukhobors: Their History, Life and Struggle.* Thrums, BC: self-published, 1948. Unpublished manuscript, translated by Peter N. Maloff.

Maloff, Peter N. *In Quest of a Solution (Three Reports on Doukhobor Problem).* 2nd ed. Trail, BC: Hall Printing Ltd., 1957.

Maloff, Vera. *Our Backs Warmed by the Sun: Memories of a Doukhobor Life.* Qualicum Beach, BC: Caitlin Press, 2020.

McGauley, Tom, and Jack McIntosh. "*The International Prisoner* The Via Dolorosa of Vladimir Meier." *Prison Journal,* November 9/10, 1992.

Mealing, Rev. F.M., Ph.D. Prefatory notes to commentary on Pete Maloff's *Doukhobors: Their History, Life and Struggle.* Castlegar, BC: Selkirk College, 1973, 1974.

Nearing, Helen and Scott. *Living the Good Life: How to Live Sanely and Simply in a Troubled World.* New York: Schocken Books, 1970.

Nearing, Scott. *The Making of a Radical: A Political Autobiography.* New York: Harper & Row, 1972.

Sherbak, Anton Petrovich. *The Kingdom of Russian Peasant Doukhobors* or *Tsarstvo Russkih Mushikov.*

Skolrood, Harold A. *Piers Island: A Brief History of the Island and Its People, 1886–1993.* Lethbridge, AB: H.A. Skolrood,1995.

Sorokin, Pitirim A. *A Long Journey: The Autobiography of Pitirim A. Sorokin.* New Haven, Connecticut: College and University Press, 1963.

Spencer, Fanny Bixby. *The Repudiation of War.* Costa Mesa, CA: H.F. Schick, 1922.

Sulerzhitsky, Leopold Antonovitch. *To America with the Doukhobors.* Regina, SK: Canadian Plains Research Center, 1982.

Summarized Report, Joint Doukhobor Research Committee: Symposium Meetings 1974–1982. Edited and translated by Eli A. Popoff. Castlegar, BC, 1997.

Tarasoff, Koozma J. *Plakun Trava: The Doukhobors.* Grand Forks, BC: Mir Publication Society, 1982.

Tolstoy, Leo. *Resurrection.* New York: New American Library, 1961.

Vechnaya Pamyet: A Guide to Traditional Customs and Procedures at Doukhobor Funerals. Castlegar, BC: USCC Kootenay Men's Group, 1995.

INDEX

ABOUT THE AUTHORS

Peter "Pete" Maloff was born in Saskatchewan in 1900, the year after the Doukhobors immigrated to Canada. He spent the first years of his life in the Doukhobor community of Khristianovka. He lived through the eras of World War I and World War II, dedicating himself to pacifism and the promotion of peace. He was jailed for his activism, forced into isolation from his family for many years. During his time under house arrest, he wrote his memoirs of the first thirty years of his life. Upon his release from house arrest in 1943, he continued to write and to speak to audiences about peace and equality. In the 1940s, he authored his comprehensive book, *Doukhobors: Their History, Life and Struggle*. In the 1950s, he edited the literary journal *Rassvet: The Voice of Free Thinkers*. His work led to recognition from Mahatma Gandhi, Ilya Lvovich Tolstoy and J. William Lloyd, with whom he corresponded. He lived alongside his family until his passing in 1971.

Vera Maloff was born into a Doukhobor family in the Kootenay valley of British Columbia. The values of vegetarianism, peace, and sustainable living, Doukhobor traditions and customs—Sunday prayers, Russian psalm and hymn singing, cooking groups for weddings and funerals, and participating in peace rallies—were an inherent part of her family life. She raised her four children in this Doukhobor community while teaching for the local school districts. After retiring from a career in teaching, Vera began to record family stories passed down from generations. Her essays have been published in the Doukhobor magazine *Iskra*, in the *West Kootenay Journal* and in *The New Orphic Review*. Her first book, *Our Backs Warmed by the Sun: Memories of a Doukhobor Life*, was described by the *Vancouver Sun* as "a wonderful contribution to our understanding of Canada's past." Vera lives with her partner, Steve Denisoff, in the community of Shoreacres on the Slocan River.

Parting Words

I appeal especially to the Doukhobor youth, and with them I include the youth of other spiritual wrestlers, the Molokans, Quakers, Mennonites, Tolstoyans, Gandhians and all other anti-materialistic groups and brotherhoods:

Yes, you young men and women, take into your hands the gold that your predecessors have earned, and in this gold you will find salvation from the dark shadow of militarism that is clouding mankind. Strengthen in yourself all that may be shaky: pick up that which has fallen from your hands, put aside everything that hinders your advancement. It is your responsibility to establish the future world to which we have always been called by the better and wiser teachers of mankind. And your platform will be strengthened and you will become through the ages the invincible embodiment of truth. Build it up so that it will last forever, and let the mighty banner "Thou shall not kill" be the guiding principle of your everyday life.

—P.N. Maloff, March 20, 1948
   from Pete Maloff, *Doukhobors: Their History, Life and Struggle*